Scarecrow Professional Intelligence Education
Series Editor: Jan Goldman

1. *Communicating with Intelligence: Writing and Briefing in the Intelligence and National Security Communities* by James S. Major. 2008.

Mike—Thanks!

Jim Major

COMMUNICATING WITH INTELLIGENCE

Writing and Briefing in the Intelligence and National Security Communities

James S. Major

Professional Intelligence Education Series, No. 1

The Scarecrow Press, Inc.
Lanham, Maryland • Toronto • Plymouth, UK
2008

SCARECROW PRESS, INC.

Published in the United States of America
by Scarecrow Press, Inc.
A wholly owned subsidiary of
The Rowman & Littlefield Publishing Group, Inc.
4501 Forbes Boulevard, Suite 200, Lanham, Maryland 20706
www.scarecrowpress.com

Estover Road
Plymouth PL6 7PY
United Kingdom

Copyright © 2008 by James S. Major

All rights reserved. No part of this publication may be reproduced,
stored in a retrieval system, or transmitted in any form or by any
means, electronic, mechanical, photocopying, recording, or otherwise,
without the prior permission of the publisher.

British Library Cataloguing in Publication Information Available

Library of Congress Cataloging-in-Publication Data
Major, James S.
  Communicating with intelligence : writing and briefing in the intelligence
and national security communities / James Sidney Major.
      p. cm. — (Professional intelligence education series ; no. 1)
  Includes bibliographical references and indexes.
  ISBN-13: 978-0-8108-6119-0 (pbk. : alk. paper)
  ISBN-10: 0-8108-6119-4 (pbk. : alk. paper)
  1. Communications, Military. 2. Military intelligence–Authorship. 3.
Composition (Language arts) 4. Oral communication. 5. Briefing, Military.
I. Title.
UA940.M35 2008
808'.066355–dc22   2007048685

∞™ The paper used in this publication meets the minimum requirements of
American National Standard for Information Sciences—Permanence of
Paper for Printed Library Materials, ANSI/NISO Z39.48-1992.
Manufactured in the United States of America.

For Joan,

who always had faith that I could do it.

Contents

PART 1:
WRITING WITH INTELLIGENCE
1

Foreword

By Herbert E. Meyer

When a new president is elected he—or she—enters office with a foreign policy agenda. In other words, as an incoming president looks at the world beyond our country's borders, there are certain things the president wants to happen, and certain things the president wants *not* to happen. If the "good" things are going to happen, then the new administration can devote its energies to other matters—education, health care, energy, or the environment. But if the future is going to unfold in a "bad" way, then the president will want to act. More precisely, the president will want to change the future before it happens.

So the most important question an incoming president can ask is "What is the future going to be?"

It is the role of intelligence to provide this answer. And this is why the work of our country's intelligence officers is so crucial—and so interesting.

To succeed as an intelligence officer you must do two things. First, you have to be right—you have to project the future accurately. Second, you must deliver your projections to the president, and to his national security team, clearly enough so they can grasp what lies before them—and soon enough so they have sufficient time to act. Simply put, an effective intelligence officer must combine the talents of judgment and communication.

While a great deal has been written about the issue of judgment—some of it by me—less has been written for intelligence professionals about the issue of communication. That's too bad, because the two talents are equally important. Even a brilliant projection of the future is worthless if it isn't delivered to policy makers so clearly, and so concisely, that even the dimmest among them cannot fail to grasp it.

Read this book. And after you've read it, read it again—slowly—and take as much time as you need to work through all its exercises. By doing so you will vastly improve your communication skills, and thus increase your chances of success in the complex business of intelligence.

Before you begin, allow me to make one point about writing that Jim Major makes throughout his book: When you set out to write an intelligence report, or estimate, or the text of a briefing, actually writing it is the last thing you do, not the first. Think for a moment about what happens when you set out to cook dinner for yourself or your family. You don't just turn on the stove or rev up the grill. First, you must decide what it is you're going to cook. Then you make a list of the ingredients you're going to need. Then you check the fridge and the pantry to see which of these ingredients you have on hand. And if you're missing some ingredients, you make a list of these missing ingredients and then run out to the supermarket to buy them. Then—and only then—do you actually begin cooking.

It's the same with writing. You've got to get organized before you start. You must decide what it is you're going to write—a report, an estimate, or some other intelligence product—and you've got to be sure you have the necessary facts on hand. Most important of all, *you've got to know what it is you want to say.* In other words, you've got to do all of your thinking before you start to write. Indeed, the most common mistake among intelligence professionals—among professionals of all kinds, in fact—is that they start to write too soon, on the theory that their thoughts will somehow organize themselves while their fingers strike keys on a keyboard. That's a bit like believing that a recipe for tonight's dinner will somehow emerge if you just start throwing ingredients into the pot. Unless you're a genius—and you're not—this won't work.

You've got to do all your thinking—*all* your thinking—before you start writing. Of course you can make some changes as you go, for instance, by deleting points that don't pan out and by inserting ideas and points that suddenly pop into your head as you work— in the same way that an experienced cook will sometimes make a last-minute decision to leave out or add an ingredient that isn't in the recipe. But if you haven't thought through the issue clearly and completely and reached your conclusions before you start writing, you're going to find yourself in trouble. In fact, when you're in the middle of writing something and you suddenly find yourself "stuck"—this is often called "writer's block"—it's an indicator that you started writing too soon, before you had your facts organized and before you'd reached your conclusions. When this happens, just stop writing. Then take the time to figure out what's missing— facts or conclusions—before you start again.

Remember, in the intelligence business you get paid to be right. So take all the time you need to figure out what the future is likely to be. And with your copy of *Communicating with Intelligence* on the desk, you're ready to begin the equally vital process of communicating your judgments to the policy makers you serve.

As I said earlier, this is crucial and interesting work. Our country's survival depends on your success, so when you're sweating bullets in your office at midnight struggling to communicate effectively with the president or members of his national security team, don't forget that the best wishes and the prayers of all Americans are with you.

Herbert E. Meyer served during the Reagan administration as special assistant to the Director of Central Intelligence and vice chairman of the National Intelligence Council. He is author of *Real-World Intelligence* and coauthor, with his wife Jill, of *How to Write*. He is also author of "How to Analyze Information: A Step-by-Step Guide to Life's Most Vital Skill," which is available online at www.howtoanalyzeinformation.com.

Preface

In the summer of 2007 I had an epiphany. Even though I had served in the profession of intelligence for almost 40 years, I learned that those in the profession today, and those aspiring to it, face more challenges than ever before. That realization came when I printed a copy of this book to edit. For some inexplicable reason a vertical line printed down the center of each page. Knowing that I couldn't submit it to my publisher that way, I sought help from friends who knew their way around a computer and from my technologically savvy son. With no solution forthcoming, I found myself calling the computer software company.

In minutes I was talking with a pleasant young man whose place of business was on the Indian subcontinent. He calmly and professionally spent several minutes talking me through a series of "click this" and "unclick that" commands. When nothing worked, he asked me to e-mail him the chapter I was working on. I did so, expecting that he would say he'd call me back in a day or two; but in seconds he announced, "I have it," and began some new trials. Less than a minute later, the problem was fixed.

In those few minutes on the telephone I realized how instantaneous today's communications are. Information flows faster than ever, and improvements are made every day. Keeping up with the technology is tough, but even tougher is ensuring that one can stay ahead of the information flow. In the profession of intelligence, information is our life's blood. And today's intelligence professional must be cognizant of high-tech means of collection, yet remain sensitive to the analytical methods of turning that information into intelligence and providing it in a timely manner to waiting consumers who depend upon it. Our primary means of communicating that intelligence are through written products and oral briefings.

Writing and briefing are fundamental to the intelligence profession. The ability to communicate clearly, concisely, and coherently is basic to all intelligence disciplines, even the most technical. Writers and briefers in the intelligence and national security communities have a different audience for their products, but the basic principles remain the same. Intelligence writing and intelligence briefings still have a beginning, a middle, and an end; and the stages of creating an intelligence product, like any other product, include prewriting, writing (or drafting), and rewriting (or revision). Those principles are being taught at many colleges and universities with intelligence studies or national security studies curricula.

This book is aimed primarily at faculty members and students pursuing studies in intelligence, national security, homeland security, or homeland defense. It is designed to provide essential information regarding the preparation of written products or intelligence briefings that will satisfy the intended consumers. But it also has considerable value for working intelligence professionals who simply wish to hone their "rusty" writing or briefing skills.

The book is divided into two parts: Part I, "Writing with Intelligence," contains material on reading intelligence publications and on the basics of writing in the intelligence profession. Every chapter ends with exercises, many of which can be done in the classroom to facilitate group activity. Part II, "Briefing with Intelligence," deals with the fundamental principles of an intelligence briefing and includes information on gaining—or regaining—self-confidence behind the podium. Five appendixes carry additional information for quick reference.

If you use this book independently, without the benefit of classroom instruction or peer group activity, try the exercises on your own before you go to the answer section. Like the "Real World" out there in the community of intelligence professionals, we are seldom lucky enough to have *The* answer; more often we must settle for *An* answer. Therefore, you will find that many of the exercises have a suggested answer rather than a hard and fast one. That is realistic in much of the writing we do.

You will notice that each chapter begins with a summary, encapsulating the most important points made in that portion of the book. By comparing my summaries with the main body of the discussion, you should get a better idea of how a summary is written in an "intelligence format." *That is one of the main ideas you need to take with you from this book.*

I have written this text in an informal style, using the first and second persons, contractions, and rhetorical questions that would be inappropriate for formal papers. Considering my potential readers, I chose to write in a style that might be more palatable. You nonetheless should learn the appropriate style for whatever demands will be placed on you—from the formal research paper or college thesis to the concise staff summary sheet or background paper later in your career. Whatever the demands, I hope that this book can help you in some way communicate intelligence to your intended audience.

We can exercise our most sophisticated intelligence collection systems, gather rooms full of data, and analyze those data until we reach sound conclusions; but unless we effectively communicate the results of our research, we've wasted our time. I have prepared this book with the belief that anyone who sincerely desires to improve his or her communication skills can do so. It requires some work but so does anything else worth achieving. I hope that *Communicating with Intelligence* will provide at least a blueprint for improving your writing and briefing skills.

James S. Major
Arlington, Virginia
Fall 2007

Acknowledgments

Like all works of this nature, it is never a solo effort. Much of the material in the exercises was contributed earlier by Dr. Jean Filetti, and I remain indebted to her for helping me put together so much material years ago. My friend and colleague Dr. Jan Goldman guided me patiently through the minefields of publication. Cecile Rogers gave me the benefit of a disinterested observer's sanity check, greatly improving the utility of the work. From his telephonic post in India, Rajkumar Panjal talked me through the clicks and unclicks that prevented a vertical line down the center of the printed pages.

The patient staff at Scarecrow Press helped me immensely in putting the work together in a sensible way. For that, I thank Corinne Burton, Naomi Burns, and Andrew Yoder. Liz Ruppert provided some crucial help in final manuscript preparation; and my son Clay Major, on the phone from Tekamah, Nebraska, walked me through some technical problems that eased the pain considerably.

Finally, I offer my deepest thanks and appreciation to the person who has been my inspiration for the last 15 years: my wife, Joan. She offers constructive criticism when and where it is needed most, and has never failed to be right on the mark with her comments. She gives me every reason to believe in myself and the work I am doing. I love that work, and it comes second only to her.

Introduction

It is with pleasure that with this book Scarecrow Press initiates its series on professional intelligence education. Today, in the post–September 11, 2001, era, we have seen rapid growth in the number of intelligence training and educational programs in this country and abroad. Colleges and universities, as well as high schools, are developing programs and courses in homeland security, intelligence analysis, and law enforcement in support of national security.

However, becoming a professional in any field of intelligence work requires communication. Collectors of information—whether it is human intelligence, signals intelligence, or imagery intelligence—rely on their ability to capture and transform information into intelligence for the analysts. It is the analysts who rely on their ability to communicate effectively, to translate ideas and actions into "finished" intelligence products for the commander or policy maker. Effective communication is the raison d'être of the intelligence community. Briefings and reports are the lifeblood of what is produced in the intelligence community.

This book is an important cornerstone for any program seeking to develop courses related to intelligence. Based on almost 40 years of experience, the author offers insight into what has worked (and not worked) in the past and provides a blueprint for how intelligence should be provided by the professional if it is to be effective. I especially like the exercises provided in this book, which allow for practical experience in the subject matter of each writing chapter.

Jim Major is extremely qualified to discuss intelligence communication. I have known him for more than a decade and witnessed how he helped both midcareer and senior-level intelligence analysts become better intelligence professionals. Without a doubt his techniques improved their communication skills. Mr. Major was the director of the writing center at the federal government's only accredited postsecondary school for intelligence education; and throughout his earlier career in the military, his passion for writing never waned.

This book should help both novice and seasoned intelligence analysts transform facts into useable information, information into analysis, and analysis into a solid assessment. It is assessments that drive actionable intelligence for operations and policy.

Although this book is intended for individuals studying for careers in intelligence, or to improve the skills of those already in the profession, many similar professions can benefit from this series. Intelligence work has traces of anthropology, sociology, journalism, and library science, to name just a few. Investigative work, whether you are writing a research paper or a story to be published in the local newspaper, relies on the fundamentals of conducting intelligence work and writing well.

I hope you will continue to follow the growth of this series, since it is our intention to educate the public in how intelligence work is conducted *and should be conducted* in this important and vital profession.

Jan Goldman, EdD
Series Editor

I
WRITING WITH INTELLIGENCE

1

Reading Intelligence Publications

Summary

There are techniques for reading intelligence publications. To communicate intelligence successfully in writing, you must understand the products of the intelligence community. *Read* intelligence before you try to write it.

- Intelligence products have three general forms: basic, current, and estimative intelligence. Each form might then describe, explain, predict, or evaluate.
- Although there is no single "national intelligence format" for all products, we can usually identify a distinct beginning, middle, and end. The beginning summarizes the major judgments of the publication and includes other components such as the title page, contents, and preface. The middle is the meat of the discussion, providing the body of information, analysis, and judgments. The end is a conclusion or summary, with a forecast, outlook, or implications of the topic for the future.
- Evaluating finished intelligence is a process of carefully reading a product and examining the author's success in meeting the reader's expectations. We scrutinize all

aspects of the form and format for adherence to basic writing principles and the tenets of intelligence analysis.
- Intelligence professionals should recognize whether sources are generic, primary, secondary, or other. A reader should be able to distinguish between known information and analytical supposition.
- Annexes or appendixes can be used for details, charts, analytical methods, or lengthy expositions.

Through careful reading and evaluation of other people's writing, you can improve your own writing. Reading intelligence publications is an important first step toward writing with intelligence.

Read to Write

> Read, read, read. Read everything—trash, classics, good and bad, and see how they do it. Just like a carpenter who works as an apprentice and studies the master. Read! You'll absorb it. Then write. If it is good, you'll find out. If it's not, throw it out the window.
>
> —William Faulkner

It might surprise you that the opening chapter in a book about writing deals not with the techniques of writing but with products themselves. First I will discuss some ways that intelligence is formatted for publication—the closest thing to a "national intelligence format," although there is no such thing. Then I'll try to convince you that reading intelligence publications can help your writing in the long run. In later chapters I'll show you some really bad examples of writing and suggest how you can avoid the same mistakes. So my goal in this chapter is to show you how intelligence is written by others; then I'll move along to your own writing.

It is unlikely that you would try to be a novelist without ever having read a novel. So don't try to write intelligence products without an in-depth look at how they are put together. Some of the exercises in this chapter call for you to assess the form or content of an intelligence publication. That product need not be classified. In fact, greater emphasis is being placed today on "open-source" information—material that is readily available to the general public. Much information is being widely distributed, including unclassified or declassified national intelligence estimates. Those kinds of materials are accessible in media archives and on the Internet.

Who Needs It—and Why?

Policy makers, decision makers, and military commanders all rely upon intelligence professionals to provide them with the best possible information, either in written or oral form. That is a constant challenge for members of the intelligence community; but it can be done by adhering to the principles put forth here.

Potential readers of intelligence usually turn to a product for a specific reason: perhaps it deals with their area of expertise or interest; maybe they heard about it from a colleague; or perhaps the boss said, "Read this and tell me about it." Whatever the reason, a reader seldom pays attention to the *shape* of a publication—its form, format, and style. It's usually the *substance* the reader is after. Yet some hardworking intelligence analyst spent hours (days? months?) molding that product into a shape acceptable for a publication with that agency or command's logo on the cover. So let's give that analyst the benefit of our undivided attention for a few minutes as we focus on how that product achieved its final shape.

The Forms: Basic, Current, and Estimative

There are more varieties of national intelligence products than there are pages in this book. I will not—and cannot—begin to cover them adequately in this modest endeavor. But I will, and can, introduce you to some of the more important forms and formats of national intelligence. The general principles I address are applicable to almost any substantive intelligence publication.

I intentionally address only *substantive* intelligence publications—that is, finished intelligence products dealing with a military or paramilitary force, terrorism, a foreign nation, or some other aspect of foreign military intelligence such as biographic, scientific and technical, or transportation and telecommunications intelligence. Specifically excluded from consideration are administrative and management-type publications.

Not all intelligence theorists will agree that the three forms I've listed as the section heading are correct, or even that they're all-inclusive. But they're a start, and they help us sort out in our own minds the types of intelligence product we're interested in reading or writing. The "forms" of national or strategic intelligence refer to a product's configuration—an "external" characterization. We can further categorize those forms by their approach to the topic: descriptive, explanatory, predictive, or evaluative.

Descriptive intelligence relies upon nouns and adjectives, relating information in sensory terms. *Explanatory* writing attempts only to make something plain or understandable. This book, like many other college textbooks, is largely explanatory. *Predictive* intelligence is future oriented, relying heavily on analytical judgments for an outlook or for future implications. On the other hand, when you get into *evaluation*, you're trying to determine the worth of something by appraising or studying it. A value judgment is attached to evaluative intelligence that usually is not present in explanatory intelligence.

It is helpful to look at each of the three forms (basic, current, and estimative) in terms of its relative focus and the time period with which it would be associated. To help guide you through this process, I'll use a fictitious fighter aircraft, newly discovered by intelligence analysts, dubbed the SU-44/Fizzle.

Basic Intelligence: The Fundamentals

Basic intelligence is the bedrock of many intelligence community publications. It encompasses probably the widest variety of published "encyclopedic" products. Basic intelligence concentrates mainly on descriptions, with a secondary focus on explanation and evaluation. Using the example of our SU-44/Fizzle, basic intelligence might describe its physical characteristics one by one, then explain its performance as a fighter aircraft. The Fizzle might also be evaluated as superior to its predecessors in terms of combat radius and payload. Basic intelligence deals largely with past events, bringing them up to the present time.

Current Intelligence: The Here and *Now*

By its very nature, current intelligence is dynamic and highly perishable. For that reason, it is concise, to the point, and transmitted electronically. Dissemination of current intelligence is instantaneous. The continuing proliferation of computer systems offers special challenges to writers of intelligence products. It can be intimidating to consider that something you have just finished writing can be read minutes later by thousands of people around the world. Follow-on "hard copies" of many current intelligence products are disseminated widely.

As you might expect, a great deal of information about terrorism is in the current intelligence realm. Terrorist organization, training, location, capabilities, and potential targets are all of immediate interest to those charged with homeland security and national defense.

The primary focus of current intelligence must be to explain events as they unfold, interpreting their meaning for an impatient audience. Secondarily, current intelligence tries to describe events and to predict their possible outcomes, usually by means of an analyst's comment. Suppose that a Defense Intelligence Agency analyst noted a squadron of SU-44/Fizzle fighters newly deployed to an airfield near Pakistan. That fact might have immediate impact on a situation of interest to a large segment of the intelligence community. It would be reported electronically, with an analyst's comment regarding the significance of the event in terms of forecasting future Fizzle fighter flights. (Sorry about that.)

Estimative Intelligence: The Future

Estimative intelligence is forward looking. It relies on the best available current and basic intelligence on foreign forces and nations to forecast a condition that might be expected to exist months or even years hence. Because it deals with events or subjects that have not yet happened, its concentration must necessarily be predictive. In forecasting future occurrences, estimators try also to explain what the events will mean and to assess their significance.

The analyst trying to estimate the importance of the SU-44/Fizzle aircraft might start with a forecast of Fizzle production over the next five or ten years. From that baseline, guided by known production rates and basing of other aircraft, the analyst might predict a possible deployment pattern for the aircraft years hence. Finally, the analyst would try to assess the implications of those deployments in terms of U.S. strategic interests. Estimates are often used by planners, policy makers, force developers, and decision makers to design and modernize future forces and equipment, or to project U.S. foreign policy needs in the future.

Content: Looking at the Format

I've discussed some ways of looking at the external configuration of an intelligence publication in terms of its form. Now let's dig deeper into that publication and see if we can determine anything about its *internal* shape—its content.

Wouldn't it be nice if there were one specific format for all strategic intelligence products? But there isn't. And there might never be such a thing because it is largely the consumer who dictates the ultimate shape of a product, and diverse consumers will never agree on a single format, even with the advent of the singular Director of National Intelligence. There is, though, a readily discernible pattern to almost all substantive intelligence products: a clearly definable beginning, middle, and end.

I'm not trying to insult your intelligence with this blinding flash of the obvious. The fact is, many readers of an intelligence product waste a lot of time skimming aimlessly through its pages, when they could turn quickly to the part of that document most useful to them. In the following paragraphs, I will describe the organization of a typical intelligence product. The next time you read one, compare it to this format. You'll probably find a distinct beginning, middle, and end.

The Beginning: Bottom Line Up Front

British author Anthony Burgess said, "I start at the beginning, go on to the end, then stop." That makes it sound easy. The beginning of an intelligence product, however, is not just a starting place. Most often it is a *summary* of the key points made in that document. It may be called "Key Judgments" (especially in analytical products such as a national intelligence estimate), or it might be termed "Summary," "Executive Summary," or "Introduction." Whatever its title, that section's purpose is the same: to summarize for the executive reader or casual "browser" the major judgments contained in the pages of that publication. Remember, you're not reading an Agatha Christie novel. Intelligence leads with its strongest punch. We don't "save" anything to surprise our readers at the end.

Often you will find a "Preface," "Scope Note," or some other introductory material preceding the summary portion. These pages are not usually substantive in nature; they serve only to provide additional administrative information to the reader concerning the organization of the product or the identification of the author(s), staff members, or others who have helped with the publication.

Remember two important points about the summary: Although it is up front in the publication, it is written last; and it stands alone. The major issues will emerge from the text of the product as it is written; therefore, the author should always write the main body first, then reread it and extract the main points afterward. As I wrote earlier, most readers will go no farther in the document than the summary or key judgments. So it must stand alone, representing all the major points that are made in the product, with none left out.

The Middle: Details, Details

If you've seen an intelligence publication and read its beginning section, you've done what the majority of readers do. Few consumers of intelligence products do more than read the key judgments or executive summary. And what a pity, because it is this middle section—the "meat" of the product—that has cost the analyst the most time. Here are the results of the research the analyst performed to arrive at those key judgments. Here are the compiled data of that analyst's exhaustive efforts. The middle portion of a publication is the longest part of the document by far. Lengths vary, of course, but 80 to 90 percent of the document's total length devoted to the middle section would not be uncommon.

Most publications try to avoid lengthy, complicated charts, figures, or tables in the text. Instead, the producer will confine those data to an annex or appendix at the rear of the document. I'll discuss those later.

The End: Wrapping It Up

After you've waded through the body of the product and absorbed all the information the author presented, you come to a concluding section. This part is before any annexes or appendixes. Most often, this section will contain a brief summary or conclusions drawn from the research, and then it will project the subject into the near-term or long-term future. It's like a "mini-estimate" of that publication's main theme. Like the other parts of a document, you'll find no common title for this section. Headings range from "Outlook" to "Conclusion(s)," from "Prospects" to "Summary." Many analytical publications call this section "Implications for the United States." These final words of the author are the ones that will remain in the reader's mind. While the concluding section should not merely rehash the summary or key judgments, it should at least reinforce the main points made in the document.

After the End: The Add-Ons

It may seem paradoxical that anything would follow "the end." But many intelligence producers reserve annexes or appendixes for complex figures, tables, charts, or other backup analytical material that might otherwise clutter the main body of the document. Increasingly, authors are including bibliographies in appendixes. Whenever these add-ons are used, they should be referenced clearly in the main body of the publication.

Evaluating Finished Intelligence

Intelligence professionals are often asked to read and critically evaluate finished intelligence products. This section will assist you in looking at an intelligence document in the future, especially if the boss or your professor drops one on your desk and says, "Read this and tell me about it!"

Getting Started

Treat the product at first like you would a magazine you've just picked up on the newsstand. Study the cover and firmly implant in your mind the document's title. Turn to the contents, if any, and scan the publication's general layout. Then thumb through the entire document, cover to cover, to get a feel for its format and graphics. If something catches your eye, pause; but not for long. Make a mental note of the items that tended to interest you. Were they maps? Photographs? Charts? Noting these "attention grabbers" may help you in your own future writing. Before you begin to read the publication, note the number of pages in each major subdivision: the front section, main body, conclusion, and annexes or appendixes. Then sit back, relax, and read each section thoroughly.

Front Section: The Bottom Line and More

Earlier I discussed a "generic format" for an intelligence document. I told you how most documents will have a distinct beginning, middle, and end. The front section of a publication introduces you to the subject, tells you a little about its producers, and contains some portion that will stand alone as a summary of the entire document for its busy readers. In general, this front section should not exceed about 10 percent of the basic publication's length. (Don't count annexes or appendixes in this equation.) You'll often find a title page that repeats the document's title and some security or other administrative data. Often, the author's name and organization will be shown.

Because of its brevity relative to the rest of the publication, and the fact that this portion is for executive readers and browsers, the front section must get directly to the point and not waste words or space. Somewhere in these first few pages, there should be—stated or implied—a clear indication of the *purpose* of the publication. Why was it written? Maybe there was a requirement from "on high." That usually is purpose enough for most of us to write. But often there will be some implied purpose that relates the document to the interests of U.S. national security. It may be readily discernible in a publication about Iraq, Iran, or North Korea, but often the reader must assume that there is some important reason for this product's existence. In some documents, a purpose statement is the lead sentence in the preface.

If the publication has a contents page, note its placement in the front section. Is it before or after the key judgments or executive summary? There may be no hard and fast rule for its placement, but it is worthwhile to note the difference it makes when it is placed before the summary: the reader must thumb through another page or so—the contents—to reach the summary. That may ultimately prove to be an advantage if busy readers stumble upon something that attracts their interest. Maybe they'll read more. But for executives with limited time, it will more likely distract.

Main Body: The Heart of It All

Here we are in the middle of the publication already. Remember that this section, too, may have different names. The main body is the "meat" of the product—the body of the author's analytical work. Look for a number of things in this part of the document, including the author's use of sources, judgments and any supporting evidence for those judgments, and assumptions that the author may have made.

Nail Down the Source

Intelligence professionals are constantly asked for evidence to support their judgment calls. That evidence may be readily available from specific sources, or they might have to rely on citing "generic" sources, depending upon the classification of the product. *Generic* sources include such statements as "satellite imagery," "special intelligence," "a reliable source," or "press reports." Note that I refer here to a wide-ranging type of source, without being too specific about where the information came from. Generic sources enable us to hold down the classification of our documents by preventing the compromise of sensitive intelligence sources or methods. But, as you can see by those generic sources cited above, they don't tell the reader much.

There are degrees of specificity, even in specific sources. You should be aware of primary, secondary, tertiary, and quaternary sources. The *primary* source is the raw, basic data or information. For example, if a defense attaché sees a new variant of the SU-44/Fizzle aircraft, that firsthand look is a primary source of information. One step removed from the primary source is the *secondary* source. When the attaché writes his observations in an Intelligence Information Report (IIR) to you, that report becomes your secondary source. It is not the basic observation itself, but it is the closest thing you have to that source.

If you then write a study entitled "New Fizzle in the Inventory" based on the attaché's report, that study would be a *tertiary* source. It is now a third step removed from the original attaché report.

Assume that your study generated considerable interest in the intelligence community and formed the basis for a defense intelligence estimate (DIE) called "The Future of Fizzle." That estimate, one more step removed from the original (primary) source, is a *quaternary* (fourth-level) source.

Read the following excerpt from a fictitious newspaper article in the *Springfield Gazette*, written in a journalistic style similar to much intelligence writing. As you read, ask yourself about the sources: Where did this information come from? What was the primary source for that information?

> Panaraguan helicopters flew scores of sorties into eastern Nicador last week in violation of a United Nations ban, the Security Council was told today [February 27, 2008]. At least 42 helicopters flying too low for radar detection were spotted by United Nations observers on the ground on Tuesday through Friday north of the rebel stronghold of Agua Pura, according to a representative of the United Nations Secretary General. The representative, Undersecretary General Hans Zimmermann, said that one large contingent flew in a military formation.

The *primary* source for that statement is impossible to determine from information given in the article. The "United Nations observers" are the ones who reportedly saw the helicopters. But how many layers of reporting intervened before you read about it? As a minimum, you know that three people participated in the report: "Observers" means at least two; and the undersecretary general reported to the Security Council. You can be reasonably certain that there were more than two observers, since the sightings occurred over a four-day period (Tuesday through Friday). Those observers probably reported the incidents through their chain of command, each report adding a layer of possible interpretation and compounding the chance for error. The source *you* are reading (*Springfield Gazette*) is at least a third-level (tertiary) source but is probably even more removed. The point here is that you should make every effort to determine how far removed your source is from a primary observation or report.

Now look at the document you've been reading and see if you can find any references to sources, generic or otherwise. You'll see that many publications, especially estimates, make few references to sources. When you read a paragraph that starts out by citing a specific source—or even a generic source—you may find yourself giving a little more credibility to that information than to another paragraph that appears to be nothing but the author's opinion. For instance, compare the two sentences that follow: (1) A team of U.S. soldiers at a border post in northern Panaragua spotted a convoy of about 20 Panaraguan military trucks moving north toward the Nicadorean border. (2) A convoy of trucks was reported in northern Panaragua. Which of the two reports sounds more credible? Why?

Earning Their Keep: Analysts and Their Judgments

Analysts are paid to render judgments in their areas of expertise. So do we expect them to avoid any opinion or judgment when they put something in writing? Absolutely not! If we waited until something was a known fact before we published anything at all, very few intelligence products would be circulating today. We expect authors to provide us the benefit of their insight into the subject of their expertise. The main body of the product is where we expect them to do just that. What we should ask of those authors, however, is that they clearly distinguish between the known and the unknown. Information that has been provided by several reliable sources should be cited as such, and opinions, judgments, or assumptions should be easy for the reader to spot.

How can you, as the reader, differentiate between information that is known and that which is the analyst's judgment? There's no magic formula for this distinction, but some key words and phrases can help you. Note the following examples from unclassified student papers:

"Confidence in performance estimates is high based on Telint and limited amounts of Imint, Elint, and Humint." This student convinced me that he had some pretty good sources—at least four "-INTs"—to corroborate his estimates. Note that these are *generic* sources, not specific ones.

From the introduction of an unclassified master's thesis, "The information contained in this thesis has been obtained principally from Russian open-source publications. The study is based on a consensus among Russian authors." Generic sources are cited again here. Readers' views of this product will depend largely on their perception of open-source Russian material and its credibility.

"The Third Five-Year Development Plan sets out a number of broad policies to be pursued." In this case, the author cited a *specific* source for the information that followed.

All of the above excerpts show you how to recognize primary and generic sources in intelligence writing. They don't, however, tell you how you can know when the authors are relying on their own judgment, analysis, or opinion. That's often easy for the reader to determine, especially when the author uses such phrases as "we believe," "we estimate that," or "in our judgment." Otherwise, unless the author cites a specific source, the reader has no way of distinguishing fact from supposition.

Conclusion: Ending It Right

As you near the end of the main body, you come to the section of the document where the author tries to wrap up the research and tell the reader what it means in terms of a few important conclusions or implications for the future. This last part of the document (before the annexes or appendixes) may be called any of the names listed earlier, including "Outlook" or "Conclusion." Some documents may have both a conclusion *and* an outlook section or paragraph. The important point here is not that you must remember what these sections are called; try instead to concentrate on the content.

Note that this segment has an intended purpose, and if it is used correctly by the author, it will summarize, conclude, wrap up loose ends, and perhaps state any gaps remaining in existing data. There may not always be an outlook as such, but when there is, it should reflect on the future significance of the subject to the reader. In that case, there will probably be a paragraph or a portion of the conclusion termed "Implications for the Future," "Implications for the United States," or "Outlook." You'll frequently encounter these terms in estimative products.

An author must be especially careful at the end of the publication to ensure that conclusions presented are consistent with any that may have been addressed in the summary, key judgments, and main body of the publication. That's another reason why it's so important to write the key judgments or executive summary *last*. There may be nothing more frustrating for an executive reader than to be scanning a document, reading its key judgments and conclusions, only to find contradictory information in the two sections. You wouldn't find that too comforting either, would you?

Don't bury significant conclusions in the text. As you read a document, if you're like most careful readers of an intelligence publication, you're going to be drawing conclusions of your own based on the information being presented by the writer. Indelible impressions will be left on your mind by what the author has said—either because of the way it is said or because of the frequency with which it is said. Either way, you're going to expect those conclusions to show up at the end because this is where the analyst is stressing those final points to be left in the reader's mind. If your own ideas of the most significant conclusions don't show up, your opinion of that product will probably lessen.

Annexes and Appendixes: The Place for the Details

There is no place in the main body of a document for detailed facts and figures, complicated charts, or explanations of complex analytical methodologies. These kinds of details interest only a few readers and should be relegated to a place at the back of the book. Whether these add-on sections are called annexes or appendixes or appendices will depend upon the policy of the publishing organization. All these stipulations are set forth in very specific procedures by the smart people who format publications at the Defense Intelligence Agency, the Central Intelligence Agency, and all the other producing organizations. Even the annexes and appendixes will occasionally have annexes and appendixes (actually, annexes usually have appendixes, and appendixes have tabs).

An important tenet for the writer of intelligence in this case is reader consideration. Readers don't want to wade through pages of tabular data, only to find themselves hopelessly stuck in a quagmire of useless information. All attachments to an intelligence publication must be reader friendly: well organized, relevant, useful, and referred to at least once in the main body of the publication.

If the product you've been reading has appendixes, look over them now. If you have read the entire document without seeing any reference to an attachment (for example, "See annex A for methodology"), then you may be surprised to find a methodological annex. It may be just as confusing to a reader to have unreferenced annexes as it is to have too much clutter in the main body.

Other Considerations

Earlier in this chapter I wrote about making a mental note of the things that tend to interest you in an intelligence publication. Just like a paperback novel or a magazine on the shelf at your favorite bookstore, a national intelligence product should have some attention-getting features. Generally, these will lie in the areas of form and format, discussed earlier. A crisp, clean, uncluttered cover attracts the eye of a reader, then the internal format of the product holds (or loses) the reader's attention.

Graphics are important in attracting and maintaining the attention of a reader. It is essential, when authors choose to use graphics, that they choose relevant and illustrative ones to complement the text. An out-of-place visual aid stands out on the printed page just as badly as a graphic that is needed and not used. Clearly, a writer who describes a geographic location—a city, region, or country, for example—should have an accompanying map. Any geographic location mentioned in the text should be noted on that map, or at least referred to in the text: "The bombing occurred in the town of Garst, 20 miles south of Grossville (see map 3)."

Imagery almost always serves the writer well to illustrate a specific event or situation. A frame of imagery is credible, and if properly annotated and described by the author, it can indeed replace a thousand words. Imagery need not be highly classified. Many open sources are available for pictures of individuals or locations. Even certain satellite imagery is available in the public domain, for a price.

Landsat pictures of the Soviet Union were plastered all over the media after the Chernobyl nuclear accident in 1986; and if you watch the evening news, weather, and sports, you've seen the forecaster showing pictures from weather satellites or the news anchor zeroing in on the location of an event using a satellite image. It takes only a little imagination, a lot of curiosity, and some willingness to work a little harder for the student or intelligence analyst to find some good illustrative pictures to spice up that thesis, report, or study.

Reading for the Sake of Writing

In this portion of the book I've taken you on a guided tour of a national intelligence product. I've stressed that there is no single format common to all strategic intelligence but that there is a definite commonality of pattern among the various substantive intelligence publications: They all have a distinct beginning, middle, and end. Remember that the beginning of an intelligence product is *not* merely an introduction. It is a succinct summary of the entire product, and it is designed to stand alone. The middle part of the product is the more lengthy discussion of the analyst's hard work; and the end wraps up, summarizes, and draws conclusions about the research in the basic document, often forecasting or stating some implications for the future.

Any time you pick up an intelligence product, you should be circumspect. You are, after all, the intended reader of that product. Should you devote your valuable time to it? I hope that this section will help you more critically evaluate your reading material in the future. When you read, keep in mind these factors I've discussed and try to relate the reading to your own writing. If it helps, then you're doing your reading for the sake of better writing.

Exercises in Reading Intelligence

These exercises are designed to stimulate in-class discussion about information, its sources, and its evaluation. While answers appear at the end of the chapter, there is no single answer to any exercise.

Exercise 1: Seminar on Information

This seminar is designed to facilitate discussion in peer groups about where our information comes from and how we look at that information in terms of the reliability of sources and the accuracy of the information. Although the system of letters (A–F) and numbers (1–6) is no longer widely used, it can be useful in evaluating sources.

1. Information: unevaluated material of every description, at all levels of reliability, and from any source, which may contain intelligence information.
2. Intelligence information: information of potential intelligence value concerning the capabilities, intentions, and activities of any foreign power, organization, or associated personnel.

3. Reliability of sources can be denoted by the letters A–F:

   A = Completely reliable

   B = Usually reliable
   C = Fairly reliable
   D = Not usually reliable
   E = Unreliable
   F = Reliability cannot be judged

   Accuracy of information can be represented by numbers 1–6:

   1 = Confirmed by other sources
   2 = Probably true
   3 = Possibly true
   4 = Doubtful
   5 = Improbable
   6 = Truth cannot be judged

4. Consider four levels of sources when evaluating intelligence information: primary, secondary, tertiary, and quaternary.

5. Information is classified for many reasons. Among the most important reasons are as follows: to prevent disclosure, to protect intelligence sources and methods, and to prevent damage to national security.

6. Caveats are used to establish specific criteria for the disclosure of information. Frequently used caveats include Noforn, Wnintel, Orcon, Propin, Nocontract, and certain code words.

7. Compartmentation of information includes formal systems of restricted access. The programs are established and managed by the Director of Central Intelligence to protect the sensitive aspects of intelligence sources, methods, and analytical procedures. The collective products of compartmentation are referred to as Sensitive Compartmented Information (SCI) and must be afforded extraordinary means of protection.

8. Information may be released or disclosed based on access, security clearance, and—importantly—an individual's need to know.

9. Decompartmentation removes information from a compartment *without altering* the information to conceal sources, methods, or analytical procedures.

10. In sanitizing information, we edit and alter it to protect sources and methods, and to permit wider dissemination.
11. In evaluating information and intelligence, we need to continually ask ourselves if the *basic interrogatives* are answered: who? what? where? when? why? how?

Exercise 2: Source Reliability and Information Accuracy

Evaluate the sources below according to *your perception* of the reliability of the source (A–F) and accuracy of the information (1–6). If you choose "A," you need not choose "1"; you may have any combination of the letters and numbers. The sources in each example are admittedly vague and incomplete. This is designed to stimulate discussion about what additional information might be needed—or at least desired—for a more complete evaluation. Use the following matrix for your evaluation:

Reliability of source	Accuracy of information
A = Completely reliable	1 = Confirmed by other source
B = Usually reliable	2 = Probably true
C = Fairly reliable	3 = Possibly true
D = Not usually reliable	4 = Doubtful
E = Unreliable	5 = Improbable
F = Reliability cannot be judged	6 = Truth cannot be judged

1. You read an article in your local newspaper about corruption in government. The article is based on sworn grand jury testimony by an alleged eyewitness.
   A   B   C   D   E   F ——— 1   2   3   4   5   6
2. You have an image of a squadron of fighter aircraft deployed to a tactical airstrip in your area of interest.
   A   B   C   D   E   F ——— 1   2   3   4   5   6
3. You receive a report from a paid informant that a new type of tank is being produced in the country you watch. The source is a night watchman in the tank factory, and this is his first report.
   A   B   C   D   E   F ——— 1   2   3   4   5   6

4. Intercept of a noncommunications electronic emitter near the border suggests that your target country is deploying an air defense system against its neighbor. You have an earlier image of probable air defense artillery in that area.
   A   B   C   D   E   F———1   2   3   4   5   6

Exercise 3: Evaluation of Finished Intelligence

Student Name:
Date: Course/Class No.:
Title of Publication Reviewed:

The purpose of this exercise is to give you, as an intelligence *user*, the experience of critically evaluating a finished intelligence publication. Depending upon your professor's wishes, the completed exercise will constitute a percentage of your course grade. You will be graded on your ability to produce a clear, concise, and coherent written product (50 percent) and on your analytical evaluation of the publication you select (50 percent). To complete this assignment, do the following:

1. Select a publication as defined by your instructor. It might be hard copy or online.
2. Read, and be sure you understand, *all* questions this exercise asks you to answer about the publication, *before* you begin your evaluation.
3. Carefully read the publication.
4. Answer each of the following questions. Show how you arrived at your conclusions (that is, *don't* answer any question "yes" or "no").
5. You may write or print your answers, as long as they are legible, or prepare your evaluation on a computer. In your answers, refer only to the question number and the parenthetical short title given for each question; for example: "1. (Length)." *Do not* rewrite or retype the entire question.

Front Section (Key Judgments, Summary, or Introduction)

1. (Length) The "front section" of your publication may be called any number of titles, as above. Describe the front section and answer the following questions about it: Is it short (about 10 percent of the length of the basic text)? Does it get directly to the point? Is it complete enough to stand alone?

2. (Purpose) Is the purpose of the publication clear to the average reader? Does the front section contain enough information for a reader to see how this product fits into the "big picture" of U.S. national security or to otherwise determine why the product was published?

Main Body

3. (Sources) Does the author identify sources, generic and/or specific? (Examples of generic sources include "satellite imagery," "special intelligence," or "a reliable source.") Is the reader able to clearly distinguish between information provided by these sources and the author's opinion or judgment? Give examples.

4. (Judgments) Are judgmental statements quickly followed up with the evidence or rationale that apparently led the author to make the judgment? Are assumptions clearly stated as such?

Conclusion (Outlook, Prospects, Implications, or Summary)

5. (Summary) The concluding section of your document may also have any of the above names, or even another. Are information gaps, future projections, or implications summarized at the end of the publication?

6. (Conclusions) Are the conclusions at the end of your publication consistent with the main body and key judgments? Were any conclusions that you considered significant left buried in the text?

7. (Appendixes) Are appendixes used to present historical or highly technical supporting material or methodology, rather than the main text? If appendixes are not used, comment on whether you feel they might have been helpful to the average reader of the product.

Other Considerations

8. (Form and Format) Comment briefly on the author's organization of the document—the form and format used. Is the publication well organized? What might have improved its structure and/or readability, in your opinion?
9. (Graphics) Were graphics used effectively? If none or only a few were used, *could* they have been better used to help the average reader? How?
10. (Readership/Other) What type of readership do you feel would derive the most benefit from this publication (for example, analysts at the national level, scientific and technical analysts, armed forces and commanders)? Make any other comments you might wish to make concerning the publication and/or this evaluation exercise.

Answers to the Exercises in Chapter 1

Exercise 1: Seminar on Information Sources and Evaluation

Because this seminar is designed to facilitate classroom discussion, there are no answers.

Exercise 2: Source Reliability and Information Accuracy

Answers will vary on this exercise but usually not much. One student might say "A" and another insist on "B," but seldom will the range be from A to E or from 1 to 5. The comments below are not intended as "answers" but are designed to provide food for thought as you evaluate these sources and, later, other sources you use in your work. After each question below, parenthetically, I have added the results of a faculty survey I conducted on these questions. The response shown is the *mode* for each faculty response.

1. You read an article in your local newspaper about corruption in government. The article is based on sworn grand jury testimony by an alleged eyewitness. (Faculty Mode: C/3)
   a. What is your *local newspaper*? In my case, it is the *Washington Post* or the *Washington Times*. But it might also be the *Fairfax Journal* or the *Arlington Sun-Gazette*. Determine that point first, then decide how you usually evaluate information from that newspaper.
   b. When you hear about "corruption in government," chances are you have an immediately negative reaction. You probably dislike the idea of someone taking advantage of the taxpayers who pay his or her salary.
   c. "Sworn grand jury testimony" is closed and held in secret to determine whether there will be an indictment. How has this information leaked? Was it from a member of the panel who had an ax to grind? Was it from the "alleged eyewitness"?
   d. The "alleged eyewitness" carries at least two connotations: First, the word "alleged" itself can be a minefield. Think about that word; define it and discuss it among your peers. Second, you've probably heard or read of events where eyewitnesses to the same event gave conflicting testimony. Human powers of observation are such that it is common.
2. You have an image of a squadron of fighter aircraft deployed to a tactical airstrip in your area of interest. (Faculty Mode: B/2)
   a. Whenever you have "an image," credibility usually soars. People love to look at pictures, even if they're not entirely sure of what's there.
   b. Notice that the report didn't say "18 aircraft" or "24 aircraft"; it said "a squadron of fighter aircraft." How many airplanes in a squadron? That number varies

among countries and even among services in one country. Someone has already done some evaluation of that photograph and has applied an organizational designation to a certain number of planes. What type of fighters are they? That might also be of great interest, since it could conceivably be "friendly" aircraft in the photo.

   c. The "tactical airstrip" would also be a consideration in determining what types of aircraft could be supported there. In addition, you'd need to know the length of the runway and any other characteristics of the strip.

3. You receive a report from a paid informant that a new type of tank is being produced in the country you watch. The source is a night watchman in the tank factory, and this is his first report. (Faculty Mode: F/3)

   a. Most intelligence professionals—our faculty included—are inherently suspicious of "paid informants." Cutting right to the chase, 83 percent of faculty respondents assigned an "F" rating to the source (reliability cannot be judged). Weighing heavily in that decision, I'm sure, were the words "this is his first report."

   b. Even assuming that the night watchman source was not an "expert" in armored vehicles, he at least seems able to recognize "a new type of tank." Perhaps the source is a former tank driver. Consider that many security guards in U.S. Government installations are former military. Could that be the case in your area of interest as well?

4. Intercept of a noncommunications electronic emitter near the border suggests that your target country is deploying an air defense system against its neighbor. You have an earlier image of probable air defense artillery in that area. (Faculty Mode: B/2)

   a. Like item 2 above, the image was instrumental in the faculty's response. Another consideration, though, is the report by two different sources, because the Elint source appears to be in the same area. It's always helpful in the

intelligence profession to have two separate disciplines
—two "-INTs"—reporting on the same item.

b. You should also look at points that may have led
someone to report "an air defense system." Would it
help you to know exactly what electronic emitter had
been intercepted? Why, or why not?

Exercise 3: Evaluation of Finished Intelligence

This exercise is self-explanatory.

2

Basic Tools of Writing with Intelligence

Summary

Writing is a basic skill required of intelligence professionals. We learn to write by writing, observing, and learning from our own mistakes and the mistakes of others. All writing, including intelligence writing, should communicate something.

- The basic principles of *all* writing are clarity, conciseness, and correctness. Clarity ensures that you are understood. To be concise in intelligence writing, say what you need to say in as few words as possible, and then stop. Correctness includes both precision and mechanical correctness. The most common errors are misspellings, usage, punctuation, and subject-verb agreement.
- Other important considerations in your writing include appropriateness, completeness, and coherence. Appropriateness means considering your audience and their needs. To be complete, be sure you've said everything you need to say. A coherent paper is a unified whole, focused on a central theme.
- There is no magic formula for becoming a good writer. Common components of most good intelligence writing are hard work and perseverance.

Writing is an interesting and challenging part of the intelligence profession. Master the basic skills of writing with intelligence, and you will be a step closer to mastering the tools of the trade. Commanders, war fighters, decision makers, planners, and force developers depend on intelligence. The way you communicate that intelligence to them in writing may be the key to success in accomplishing the mission.

Why Write?

The most basic skill required of the intelligence professional is the ability to write. Some students claim they can't write because they "just weren't born with the ability." Are we to infer, then, that the capacity to write well is genetically transmitted? Don't you believe it! Look in the reference section of any library or book store and you'll find scores of "How To" books dealing with writing. Obviously, a lot of writers out there believe they can help aspiring authors do a better job. My aim is to help you do a better job disseminating the results of your research and analysis. A basic way to disseminate intelligence is via the written word.

This chapter is illustrated with examples of writing that have felt the stroke of my pen over more than 20 years in the classroom and almost 40 years serving in the intelligence profession. Having examined thousands of papers, I found no shortage of material. Examples are quoted verbatim, warts and all, with no editing except the deletions shown by ellipsis periods (. . .), mainly due to length. In no case have I taken any example out of context. What you see is what we got from a midlevel intelligence professional in a postgraduate or undergraduate program.

We learn from our mistakes and from observing the mistakes of others as well. We learn to write better by noting shortcomings and avoiding them the next time we write. In writing this material, I benefited from the counsel and critiques of my colleagues and my students. I hope that you will find something of use to you somewhere in this chapter.

The reason for all writing is to communicate something: for example, ideas, emotions, or information. This tenet should be immediately obvious to the writer of an intelligence product; yet, too many publications of the intelligence community leave the reader puzzled as to what the author was trying to say. For instance, after Operation Desert Storm, when General H. Norman Schwarzkopf testified before the Senate Armed Services Committee on June 12, 1991, he said, "By the time you got done reading many of the intelligence estimates you received, no matter what happened they would have been right. . . . [T]hat's not helpful to the guy in the field."[1]

Intelligence writers either violate or ignore the simplest, most straightforward principles of writing that they learned when they graduated from finger paint to pencil and pen, and finally, to the computer. These are, for the most part, intelligent people who genuinely want to share their knowledge or their analytical product with an audience. They fall short, not from ignorance, but rather from their failure to consider those basic principles of all writing.

Like skilled carpenters with their toolboxes, ready to tackle a construction project, students must equip themselves with the tools of their trade before tackling a writing project. Writing is hard work. There's nothing more intimidating than a blank piece of paper in front of your face—or, in this computer and word-processing age, a blank *screen*. (Why do you think they call that blinking dot on the screen a "cursor"?) But you can win the standoff and break the ominous "writer's block" by keeping in mind a few basic principles to make your writing smoother, easier to read, and more informative to your reader.

Clarity

Clarity, clarity, clarity. When you become hopelessly mired in a sentence, it is best to start fresh; do not try to fight your way through against the terrible odds of syntax. Usually what is wrong is that the construction

> has become too involved at some point; the sentence
> needs to be broken apart and replaced by two or more
> shorter sentences.
>
> —William Strunk Jr. and E. B. White,
> *The Elements of Style*[2]

Robert Louis Stevenson said it clearly: "Don't write merely to be understood. Write so you cannot possibly be misunderstood." Do that and you'll never have a problem with your papers. What's crystal clear to you may be unintelligible to a reader without your experience or background. One person's "simple" is another person's "huh?" Have someone else read your writing—a classmate, your spouse, or a friend. Ask them for constructive and objective criticism. Don't be thin-skinned. Your masterpiece may be maligned or murdered, but you'll learn more that way.

If you can't have a second set of eyes on your work, reread it yourself. Put it aside first, for as long as you can. Try hard to be objective, and read it as though you have no prior knowledge of the subject. Ask yourself, as often as possible while you read, "Is this clear? Does it make sense?"

After I bought a condo, I tried to find out how much insurance I needed for my unit. In the documents from the association, I found the following 128-word sentence:

> Each Unit Owner or any tenant of such Unit Owner should, at his own expense, obtain additional insurance for his own Unit and for his own benefit and to obtain insurance coverage upon his personal property, for any "betterments and improvements" made to the Unit and for his personal liability, provided that no Unit Owner or tenant shall acquire or maintain such additional insurance coverage so as to decrease the amount which the Board of Directors, on behalf of all Unit Owners, may realize under any insurance policy which it may have in force on the property at any particular time or to cause any insurance coverage maintained by the Board of Directors to be brought into contribution with such additional insurance coverage obtained by the Unit Owner. [Can anyone tell me how much insurance I should have bought?]

A suburban Washington, D.C., apartment complex sent a letter to its residents warning of the likelihood of increased crime during the holidays: "We are sure that you are aware that during the Christmas Season the Police Department is plagued by shoplifting, breaking and entering, and a general overall increase in crime." (It's no wonder crime is so bad in the streets. We can't even keep the criminals out of the Police Department!)

Speaking of crime, how about this item from the Durham, N.C., *Morning Herald*? "Durham police detectives say [the victim] was stabbed repeatedly during an apparent struggle between her car and the side kitchen door." (What a sight that must have been: a car and a kitchen door locked in mortal combat!)

We've all seen our own government's bureaucratic writing. Imagine the drought-stricken farmer who read the following and tried to apply for aid under Public Law 100-387:

> Effective only for producers on a farm who elected to participate in the production adjustment program established under the Agricultural Act of 1949 for the 1988 crop of wheat, feed grains, upland cotton, extra long staple cotton, or rice, except as otherwise provided in this subsection, if the Secretary of Agriculture determines that, because of drought, hail, excessive moisture, or related conditions in 1988, the total quantity of the 1988 crop of the commodity that such producers are able to harvest on the farm is less than the result of multiplying 65 percent of the farm program payment yield established by the Secretary for such crop by the sum of acreage planted for harvest and the acreage prevented from being planted (because of drought, hail, excessive moisture, or related condition in 1988, as determined by the Secretary) for such crop, the Secretary shall make a disaster payment available to the producers. [I wonder if the writer of that 145-word sentence was paid for a disaster.]

An article in a business journal was entitled "Tips for Improving Absenteeism." (Did the article *really* purport to tell us ways we could get better with our absenteeism? On the contrary, it dealt with methods of *reducing* absenteeism.)

In a writing journal I spotted an item entitled "Composition Theory in the Eighties." Anticipating an article that might help me do a better job of teaching that theory, I quickly turned to the piece. Then I read its subtitle: "Axiological Consensus and Paradigmatic Diversity." I read no further. Unclear titles will discourage your reader from proceeding.

Look at the student writing examples that follow. (The snide remarks in parentheses are mine.) Do you think these students reread what they had written?

"The cities of Paris, Rome, London, Brussels and Bonn are on daily alert due to the new term 'Euroterrorism' being practiced throughout the continent." (No they're not! Those cities are nervous because of the *threat* of Euroterrorism, not the *term*. Try this instead: "The threat of Euroterrorism is spreading, and daily alerts are common in Paris, Rome, London, Brussels, and Bonn." (Notice also that I didn't say "the cities of . . ." because most people who can read will know that those are cities.)

"Something has to be said for the quality of an individual which is my personal goal although contrary to any career goals." (Something has to be said for the complete lack of clarity in that sentence.)

"The fact that it is hard to *continue* to impress the public and terrorist is not cheap is evident." (Is that a fact? Emphasis was the author's, although I don't know why.)

"Coordinating actions and attacks leads to the other question raised by the original one but is directly tied to the first part." (Why would this student force the reader to decipher a complex sentence like that one? I suspect that even the *writer* of that sentence would not have understood what he was trying to say.)

Other Considerations of Clarity: Carelessly Chosen or Misplaced Words, Faulty Pronouns, and Jargon

This text has placed special emphasis on saying exactly and clearly what is meant. Sometimes ambiguity results from carelessly chosen or misplaced words; sometimes it occurs when writers fail to connect their thoughts; sometimes it results from a vague pronoun reference; or perhaps it has its roots in jargon. We can avoid much of the ambiguity by keeping our audience in mind.

Carelessly Chosen Words

Not all carelessly chosen words result from a poor vocabulary or careless proofreading. Picture the following scenario. The student has just noted that the freeing of American hostages was subordinate to the funneling of aid to the Contras. Later in the paragraph, he wants to emphasize this point, but being properly concerned about repetition, he does not want to repeat the word "subordinate." A trip to the thesaurus, and voila! "The hostage issue was a second-rate consideration in the sale of arms to Iran." Now I doubt anyone would consider the freeing of these captives an issue with "no value." Furthermore, the adjective "second-rate" is generally used to describe things, not issues. In the future, if you're "fishing" in a thesaurus for a synonym to replace an already carefully chosen word, never use one of the words listed without first consulting a dictionary for its exact definition. The thesaurus lists synonyms, of course; but it also includes words similar in meaning.

Misplaced Words

Misplaced words (covered in greater detail in exercise 4 of this chapter) can also distort meaning:

Misplaced: Led by Chiang Kai-shek, the triumph of the Kuomintang forces was viewed as a victory for nationalism. These forces, however, only controlled eight central and southern provinces. (Does the writer mean that the Kuomintang forces only controlled the people but, perhaps, did not improve their lifestyles? I sense that the writer really meant *just* the eight central and southern provinces were affected. If that's the meaning intended, let's move the word "only," and put it after "controlled.")

Replaced: Led by Chiang Kai-shek, the triumph of the Kuomintang forces was viewed as a victory for nationalism. These forces, however, controlled only eight central and southern provinces.

Careless Transitions

Provide road signs for your readers. Don't bring them to a fork in your writing and make them guess at the right direction:

The ambassador's child eats plaster and chalk. He has a condition known as pica.

(Those of us who are not doctors probably have to ponder these two bits of information. Does the child eat chalk and plaster as a result of some disorder known as pica? Or do his eating abnormalities *cause* pica? Possibly the writer is giving us two unrelated descriptions of the ambassador's offspring: that he eats unusual substances *and* has pica—whatever that might be.)

The reader of the above sentence is forced to make a decision, and perhaps he or she will choose the correct relationship (that the child eats plaster and chalk *because* he has pica, a condition that causes an abnormal desire to eat strange things such as ashes, plaster, and chalk). The point, though, is that the reader shouldn't have to guess at what the writer means. Be clear. Use transitions.

Faulty Pronoun References

The antecedent of each pronoun you use should be clear and obvious. Otherwise, vagueness will occur. Let's look at the problems caused by the imprecise, possibly incorrect, pronoun in the following student sample:

"Japanese investment and trade with Oceania has grown in proportion to its rise in overall economic strength."

Not surprisingly, three people asked to read the sentence offered three different interpretations. Reader A felt "its" referred to Japan. Fine, but the word "Japan" is not in the sentence. "Japanese" is an adjective; pronouns don't replace adjectives. Reader B (a tad more knowledgeable about syntax) felt "its" referred to "investment and trade." Maybe, but *countries*, not investment and trade, "rise in overall economic strength." And isn't the subject "investment and trade" plural? Rise and be saluted, Reader C, who commented that "its" must refer to Oceania, the only singular noun in the sentence and also the noun closest to the pronoun "its." I wonder, though, what the writer would answer. How did *you* read the sentence?

Jargon

Every occupation has its own specialized language. If the writer is certain his readers share his language, then jargon can be effective. The risk, though, is that jargon could make the writing incomprehensible to any outsider who happens to read the memo or report. Recognize jargon. Use it when it is appropriate; eliminate it when it's not.

Don't confuse jargon with pretentious language. Jargon can be effective and acceptable. Words chosen for the number of syllables rather than their clarity are never effective or acceptable. The author of the following sentence risks losing even the most entrenched bureaucrat: "If the present administration is to optimize its strength in the Persian Gulf, it must not set parameters on its infrastructures."

Above All, Be Clear!

I could cite many other examples of similarly convoluted sentences and phrases from my collection. But I suspect that by now you've had enough of this offal. The point is this: in intelligence writing, clarity is second only to accuracy in importance. (I'll say more about accuracy later in this chapter.) Even if you have all the facts, the writing must be clear if you are to get your point across. A reader who spots inaccuracies may lose faith in the writer or question the author's sources; but if the writing is not clear, the reader will be lost. Often the reader will simply discard the publication. So be reader friendly. Be clear.

Conciseness

> Omit needless words. Vigorous writing is concise. A
> sentence should contain no unnecessary words, a
> paragraph no unnecessary sentences, for the same rea-
> son that a drawing should have no unnecessary lines
> and a machine no unnecessary parts. This requires not
> that the writer make all his sentences short, or that he
> avoid all detail and treat his subjects only in outline,
> but that every word tell.
>
> —William Strunk Jr. and E. B. White,
> *The Elements of Style*[3]

If I were more concise, this chapter might have been completed
by now! Henry David Thoreau, while he was "pond-" ering at
Walden, said, "Not that the story need be long, but it will take a
long while to make it short." How true it is. There's work involved in achieving a concise product. But that work will prove
its worth in the reader's satisfaction with your writing.

Don't confuse conciseness with brevity. In *Hamlet*, Polonius
said to the king and queen, "Brevity is the soul of wit." Then he
proceeded to ramble on and on, prompting Gertrude to reply,
"More matter, with less art." That's what we need in intelligence
writing: more matter—the essence of the words—and less art,
the "fluff" of saying the words.

Some long pieces of writing are nonetheless concise because
they say what needs to be said without repeating, then quit.
That's the key to being concise. Each time you write a paper,
prune the deadwood from your phrases and sentences. Cut un-
needed verbiage from paragraphs. Be merciless.

The short quotation from Strunk and White that opened this
section is loaded with meaning, especially the last five words:
"but that every word tell." Papers written in the intelligence
community would mean so much more to our audience if the
writers took the time to ensure that every word is needed to convey the meaning. Of course, we don't have time to linger over
every single word in our writing; but we can and should be sen-

sitive to the most obvious troublemakers, like the ones that follow.

Look at the phrases below, all from student papers. The italicized portions are deadwood, unnecessary to the meaning of the sentence. They do nothing but fill white space and waste the reader's time. Avoid the use of these and similar phrases in your own writing:

"... *the month of* February ..." "... *the city of* Munich ..."
"... *the* 1980–81 *period* ..." "... whether *or not* ..."
"... *a distance of* 20 miles ..." "... at *the hour of* noon ..."

There may be occasions when, for the sake of clarity, you need a few extra words. For example, you might want to be sure that your reader understands you mean the state of Washington, not Washington, D.C. Let the principle of clarity guide you in each case.

Being concise means saying what you need to say in as few words as possible. The two writing examples that follow illustrate clearly that these students had no concern for conciseness. Parenthetically after each example, I've included my rewrite. Compare the two and see if you think the point is still made in the shorter version (in parentheses).

"By way of presentation and because of the instructor it was to me, the most successfully presented, also." (The instructor's presentation succeeded.)

"What has been the impact of the tax cuts on the average U.S. citizen, myself included? Although not an expert in this field, I will attempt to answer this question in subsequent paragraphs. In as few words as possible, I feel that very little was gained by the tax cuts." (The impact of tax cuts on the average U.S. citizen has been minimal.)

The 50-word student dissertation above falls into a common trap: repeating the question and overstating the obvious. The student was asked to write a brief essay on the impact of the president's tax cuts. Many students start out answering a question by rephrasing or simply repeating it. That's the old trick of trying to use as many pages in the examination blue book as possible, to impress the professor with your depth of knowledge.

But believe me, the professor knows the question, and doesn't need it parroted back. If anything, do some redefinition of the problem and restate the question in another form—the form in which you intend to answer it. And do it with conciseness.

Trimming the Fat to Achieve Conciseness

Just as unnecessary calories pad the body with rolls of cellulite, blanketing its defining details and structure, so too do needless words make a sentence obese, obscuring its meaning. Throughout this book I have encouraged you to make your writing concise. Remember, though, a sentence is not wordy because it is long, nor concise because it is short. The information conveyed is what is important. Note the following example:

Wordy: It is a matter of grave importance to the health of any *writer* with a *history* of problems with *lack of conciseness* that he immediately begin a program of very *careful proofreading* in order to whittle away the excess baggage from his writing.

(One hint—if you have trouble trimming down a sentence, try italicizing the important words, as I have done here. Then write a coherent, complete thought using primarily those words.)

Better: Any writer with a history of wordiness should proofread carefully.

If your sentences are not genetically lean, take time during the proofreading stage to trim away the fat. Here are a few "Weight Watcher" recipes for eliminating the sentence bulges (the pages that follow have examples of each and some exercises to help you master them):

1. Eliminate the deadweight—lazy phrases and words that pad a sentence without adding meaning.
2. Use one word for many.
3. Avoid beginning sentences with "there are" or "it is."
4. Rid sentences of "who" and "which" clauses.
5. Beware of the verb "to be," especially if a noun or adjective follows it. Use active voice and vibrant verbs.

6. Eliminate redundancy—any expression that repeats the meaning of another.

Eliminate the Deadweight

Although this list is only partial, it does cover those wordy constructions that frequently plague the out-of-shape writer.

Flabby	Lean
arrive at an agreement	agree
at this point in time; at the present time; in this day and age	now
by means of	by
concerning the subject of; in reference to	about
due to the fact that; in view of the fact that	because, since
feel the necessity/need for	need
for the most part	mostly
in relation to; in connection with	by
in the not too distant future	soon
make use of	use
of great importance	important
subsequent to	after
sufficient amount of	enough
to the effect that	that

Also eliminate intensifiers such as too, quite, rather, really, and very—unless they are really very necessary!

Flabby: Due to the fact that terrorist actions are principally designed to instill fear, terrorist groups *for the most part make use of* blindfolds, handcuffs, and darkness to make their hostages feel helpless. (32 words)

Leaner: Because terrorist actions are principally designed to instill fear, terrorist groups *mostly use* blindfolds, handcuffs, and darkness to make their hostages feel helpless. (23 words)

Use One Word for Many

Be direct, economical. One exact word can say as much as many. Use a single adjective or adverb rather than a phrase. If you don't have the right word on the tip of your tongue, consult a thesaurus. (Word-processing programs make it easy. In Microsoft Word, just right-click on a word and scroll down in the pop-up menu to "Synonyms.") One word of caution: make certain the word you select doesn't carry a connotation that might upset the meaning of your sentence. Consult a dictionary after making your choice if you have any doubt. Be positive, too. You'd be amazed how fattening a negative approach can be.

Wordy: Despite slow escalation *of the war into the realm of aerial bombardment*, U.S. military actions were successful.

Better: Despite slow escalation *of aerial bombardment*, U.S. military actions were successful.

Wordy: The Sino-Soviet split *was not partial* and *was not incomplete*.

Better: The Sino-Soviet split was *total* and *complete*.

(Note how the clarity of the last sentence is improved, as well.)

Wordy: In fact, the feeling is evident in a very real sense among government officials that things are going Mr. Chun's way and that there is little they have to answer for.

Better: Government officials think Mr. Chun is getting his way and they have little to answer for.

Wordy: Amazingly, many consumer goods that have long been taken for granted in the West astonishingly do not exist here at all or are in constant short supply.

Better: Many consumer goods that the West takes for granted do not exist here at all or are in constant short supply.

Avoid Beginning Sentences with "There Are" or "It Is"

"There are" and its relatives can occasionally be used to introduce a list or to enumerate. ("There are three reasons why Kuwait is vital to U.S. interests in the Persian Gulf.") Otherwise, treat them as excess weight and eliminate them.

Weighty: There are economic conditions in Bolivia that are of importance to the United States.

Trim: Bolivia's economy is important to the United States.

Flabby: This was the question Mao wrestled with when he went to Moscow in late 1949 to obtain diplomatic assurance and economic aid.

Leaner: Mao wrestled with this question when he went to Moscow in late 1949 to obtain diplomatic assurance and economic aid.

Heavy: It is suggested in newspaper reports that *there is* an alliance of European terrorist groups.

Lighter: Newspaper reports suggest an alliance of European terrorist groups.

Wrong: There are two alternatives that have been offered to scores of property owners and corporations.

Right: Property owners and corporations have two alternatives.

Rid Sentences of "Who" and "Which" Clauses

Fatty: Any emotional proclamation *which is unsubstantiated* mars critical analysis.

Thinner: Any unsubstantiated emotional proclamation mars critical analysis.

Granted, the reduction of a three-word clause to one adjective is not a significant cut. Eating one potato chip won't add inches to anyone's waist, either. But can anyone "eat just one"? "Who" and "which" clauses are addicting, just like potato chips, and finding a bagful of them on one page of writing is not uncommon. Learn to cut even the leanest phrases. After all, an unnecessary word is an unnecessary word.

A Bagful: The U.S. war on terrorism, *a war which our country would probably not be able to win in a military sense,* is problematic.

More Manageable: The U.S. war on terrorism may be militarily unwinnable.

Notice that here the phrase *in a military sense* becomes an adverb, *militarily,* and *probably not able to win* becomes a noun, *unwinnable.* The phrase "is problematic" becomes unnecessary since the modifying phrase contains the reason the war on terrorism is "problematic."

Beware of "To Be"

Forms of the verb "to be" add excess words (hence weight). They confine even an active sentence—one with working adjectives and adverbs—to passivity. With passive voice the sentence's subject, like a passive person, is acted upon:

Passive Voice: "The universities *have been infiltrated* by terrorists."

With active voice the subject performs the action:

Active Voice: "Terrorists *have infiltrated* the universities."

Excessive use of "to be" forms and passive voice, especially in writing intelligence products, can lead to a credibility gap between writer and reader. The consumer thinks either that the writer doesn't know the answer or that the author is intentionally sidestepping the issue.

Sidestep: Supplies were received by the freedom fighters.

Head-On: The freedom fighters received supplies.

To be fair, I should grant that the passive voice is one way to add variety to a string of active sentences, to provide a period of rest in the midst of activity. Passive voice can also add emphasis by inverting the normal subject-verb-object pattern. Look again at the "sidestep" example above. If you're trying to emphasize the *supplies* rather than the freedom fighters, then you've "supplied" the right sentence. For the most part, though, passive voice puts useless words in a sentence and robs it of its personality.

Eliminate Redundancy

Repetition may be used to emphasize an important point; redundancy, also known as tautology, means unnecessarily saying the same thing twice. Study this list:

Redundant	Concise
advance forward	advance
audible to the ear	audible
each separate incident	each incident
many different ways	many ways
new innovations	innovations
past history	history

Wrong: Because of instances of *mudslinging, insults,* and *verbal abuse* between the two leaders, conflict grew.

I'm impressed with the writer's repertoire of synonyms, but I'm wondering why I'm being told the same thing three times. Am I dumb, ignorant, and stupid?

Right: Because of *mudslinging* between the two leaders, conflict grew.

The following excerpt from a six-sentence paragraph in a student's paper demonstrates the repetition of an idea:

"Mao Zedong knew the only way to strengthen China's weakened condition was to locate external diplomatic support and a suitable developmental model. . . . The Chinese leader recognized that internal development could not be achieved without alignment with an external power."

Sounds good; but has the writer really added anything new with the second sentence?

> That writer does the most, who gives the reader the *most* information, and takes from him the *least* time.
>
> —Charles C. Colton

Correctness

Perhaps you are a gifted writer. You may write the clearest, most concise, coherent, appropriate, and complete paper ever to flow from a computer; but if it is not correct, you will offend your reader. I could devote a separate book to this principle alone, but I hope that the brief summary here and the exercises after this chapter will help you avoid some of the more common pitfalls.

Correctness in intelligence writing has two main facets: factual precision and mechanical correctness. Neither is more important than the other. They complement each other by providing an edge of finesse that makes one person's writing better than another's. Some other considerations of correctness, parallelism and modifiers, are covered later in this section.

Precision

Precision is a cornerstone of the intelligence profession. The term itself is synonymous with *exactness*. Mark Twain said, "The difference between the right word and the nearly right word is the same as that between lightning and the lightning bug." Say precisely what you mean. Go for the lightning. Don't use the all-too-familiar "weasel words" that disguise your intent.

If you're writing about the Fizzle fighter, and no one in the intelligence community has any idea of the aircraft's combat radius, don't write, "The Fizzle is believed to have a substantial combat radius." What in the wide world of wonder does that mean? (Yet you've seen writing like that, haven't you?) Instead, make a positive and precise statement for your reader: "The combat radius of the Fizzle is unknown." Is it such a sin to admit an intelligence gap? Not at all. The most serious intelligence gap we have is the space between analysts' ears when they try to cover up a dearth of knowledge by "writing around it." By admitting the unknown, you may get someone's attention and initiate some seriously needed collection action. Students have unwittingly provided scores of examples of imprecise writing. Three are shown below.

One student wrote of the importance of geographic intelligence to a commander in the field, saying that "it must keep the commander abreast of weather and climatic conditions which can change drastically within a few minutes." (We've all seen wide swings in weather, but climate takes more than a few minutes to change.)

"[They] rely on their command structure for strict control of their aircraft and surface-to-air missiles. This is implemented by communications activity." (*What* is implemented? "Command," "control," or "aircraft and surface-to-air missiles"? By *what* kind of communications activity? Introducing a sentence with the word "this" is an invitation to imprecision. Watch out, too, for other vague openings like "there is" or "it is.")

"Political power is one of eight components of strategic intelligence used to quantify aspects of foreign governments." (Have you ever tried to quantify an aspect? What is this writer trying to say?)

Mechanical Correctness

The final touch a good writer adds to ensure readability is a check for mechanical correctness. Proofreading and editing involve more than "dotting i's and crossing t's." Proofread for correctness and edit for style. Go back over your paper from top to bottom for misspellings, errors in punctuation, agreement of subject and verb, and other common errors. If you have trouble detecting spelling errors in your own writing, welcome to the club! Most people tend too overlook there own misteaks. (Yes, I did that on purpose.) If you belong to that Misstep Majority, try proofing your paper by reading backward. By scanning words out of context, your mind will catch more mistakes. It really does work. A good alternative, of course, is to have someone else proofread your paper—preferably a disinterested observer with little knowledge of your topic. If all else fails, then read your words aloud. The mind's "ear" will catch many errors and problem areas for you.

Virtually all computer word-processing software has a built-in spelling checker. Keep in mind, though, that most of these programs still do not recognize the difference between *form* and *from*, between *complement* and *compliment*, or between *too, to,* and *two.* You'll still need to check for usage errors.

Adeptness at proofreading and editing may be acquired but only through practice, practice, and more practice. Try different techniques to see what works best for you. For example, proofread once from the big picture working down to the individual words: start by looking at form and format for coherence and conformity; then check pages for appearance; next, read paragraphs for coherence and unity, one main idea per paragraph; look at sentences next for completeness and correctness; and finally, check individual words for usage and spelling. It won't take you as long as it sounds. If you're uncomfortable with that approach, next time try it the other way around—from the words, working up to the form and format.

Some errors are more serious than others. We all misuse the most frequently abused punctuation mark, the comma. It's one thing to omit the comma before "and" in a series (experts can't agree on that one, but I prefer to use it); it's quite another matter to use a comma between two complete sentences with no joining word like "and" or "but." (Gasp! A comma splice!)

The most common mistakes I encounter in papers are misspellings, usage and punctuation errors, and agreement of subject and verb. These errors are illustrated by the student writing examples below.

Misspellings

Some misspellings completely change the meaning of a sentence, while others leave the reader gazing quizzically into space. Look at the following examples from our students (which also show errors in usage).

"At the operational level of war, intelligence concentrates on the collection, identification, location, and analysis of strategic and operational centers of gravy." (Isn't a center of gravy in the middle of mashed potatoes?)

"In realty, an integrated Euroterrorist front would stand little . . . chance of success." (Then what about some other business besides real estate? This student strayed from "reality.")

"One serious ommission [sic] from the orientation program was a lack of information on what is currently going on at the DIAC." (Ommit that spelling! Precision is at fault here, too. Do you think the student really was complaining about our omitting a lack of information?)

"In Europe this is relected clerarly by the small groups who use terrorism and revolution as a means of political change." (That sentence is a clerar relection of the student's proofreading prowess.)

Proofread carefully to see if you any words out.

—William Safire, in *Fumblerules*[4]

Usage

In the English language, usage of words is dynamic. Words and phrases are in use today that were unknown to our grandparents. From 500 to 1,000 new words are coined every year in our lively language. One need only listen to the younger generation to learn that "bad" may mean "good," that "rad" has nothing to do with nuclear radiation, and that the admonition to "chill out" doesn't involve refrigeration. While usage rules change over the years, the basic conventions of the language remain intact, providing a framework upon which to build "correct" writing. The better dictionaries in print have usage panels. These august bodies don't lay down rules and tell the population how to write; rather, they advise on the language as it is being used.

Even the usage panels don't always agree. (See, for example, the entry under "data" in *The American Heritage Dictionary of the English Language,* fourth edition, 2000.) The most common usage errors are often clear-cut: affect—effect, it's—its, principal—principle. Four more are cited below, courtesy of students.

"The public has more disposal income." (We're buying more disposals? "Disposable" is the intended word here.)

"I am very weary about speed reading. I feel that I will miss a great deal of information." (The student missed something else here. Maybe he *was* tired of speed reading, but the second sentence led me to believe that he was guarded or cautious—"wary.")

"[Terrorist groups] are small, secretive and extremely security conscience." (And I always thought they didn't have a conscience!)

"On 1 June 1992, the U.S. Strategic Command's Joint Intelligence Center (STRATJIC) was formally established from the ruminants of the 544th Intelligence Wing." (Now there's something to chew on! He meant to say "remnants," meaning "remains.")

Spell-checkers are grate, butt they wont sea awl yore errors!

Punctuation

Punctuation is difficult. Many "grammar guides" give you 72 rules for use of the comma, tack on 144 exceptions to those rules, then tell you to use the comma any time you want your reader to pause briefly. Few writers have problems with the question mark or the period; but the comma, colon, and semi-colon are bugaboos.

"Negative results have occurred also, such as; record trade imbalances." (Don't use a semicolon to introduce a list; that's the job of the colon. Note one common use of the semicolon, as I employed it in the previous sentence. It is used to separate closely related sentences—like a supercomma or a semiperiod. Remember that a semicolon separates, and a colon anticipates.)

"Much the same can be said of the classes that I attended however the instructor made a big difference." (Many students have problems punctuating the word *however*. If there are *complete sentences* on both sides of the "however"—as there are in the example—it must be preceded by a semicolon and followed by a comma. If the "however" is followed by a phrase or dependent clause—not a complete sentence—then it is set off by commas on both sides; for example, "Much the same can be said of the classes that I attended, however, *in which* the instructor made a big difference.")

Subject-Verb Agreement

The subject of a sentence should agree in number with its verb. If you have a singular subject, then your verb must also be singular. Writers seem to have the most problems with this principle when their subject is separated by a lot of words from their verb, or when there is a vague subject. Witness the following:

"The amount of funds available have had an enormous impact." (Because of that definite article, *"the,"* the verb must be "has." If it had been *"an* amount," the verb would be correct, although the sentence would sound awkward.)

"The media has focused more on the negative effects." (*Media*—like *data, phenomena,* and *criteria*—is a plural word. "The media *have*" or "The medium of television *has*.")

"I think the issue of tax raises and cuts are clouded with too much emotion." (I think it are, too. Note that the subject is *issue*, but the writer used the plural verb to match the *raises and cuts*.)

"Each of these areas were administered in a professional manner." (The singular word *each* is the subject of the sentence, not the plural *areas*.)

This chapter briefly discusses subject-verb agreement and cautions the writer to match singular subjects with singular verbs and plurals with plurals. But what if the number of the subject is doubtful?

The president, as well as the chief of staff and the secretary of state, (was, were) at the meeting. (Obviously three people attended the meeting, but in this case the correct verb is *was*. Confused?)

Neither Bush nor Putin (supports, support) this issue. (Still confused about which verb is correct? Read on.)

The number of the subject is often blurred in the following cases. Study them.

1. Mistaken plurals—ignore plural constructions (such as "along with," "in addition to," and "as well as") and prepositional phrases that contain plural nouns that settle between the subject and verb. As a rule, they do not affect the number of the subject.

   The *president*, as well as the chief of staff and the secretary of state, *was* at the meeting.

   Every *ship* in both fleets *is* (not *are*) loaded with nuclear warheads.

2. Collective nouns—words such as army, committee, government, group, kind, mob, and team are called collective nouns. If the noun refers to the group as a unit, use a singular verb.

   The *committee* handling these foreign policy questions *was* abolished by Putin. (In this case the group—as a whole—was acted upon. If the members of the unit act individually, use a plural noun.)

   The *committee* handling these foreign policy questions *were* arguing among themselves. (Although correct, the sentence sounds unnatural. Inserting "members" after "committee" eliminates awkwardness. Keep your eye out for ways of recasting sentences that otherwise seem awkward to you.)

3. Expletives—*it* and *there*—are never subjects of a sentence. ("*It*" may, however, be the subject of a sentence when it is a *personal pronoun* rather than an expletive.) Be careful to spot the sentence's real subject and make the verb agree with it.

   There *are* conflicting *opinions* about providing aid to that country's guerrilla forces. (Don't forget, though, that *there are* and its relatives are often unnecessary and, hence, wordy.)

4. Indefinite pronouns—pronouns such as anyone, each, nobody, none, everyone, everybody, and someone make even the best writer pause. Even though they may run with a crowd (none of them, each of the officers), they demand singular verbs. Note, however, that some style guides are beginning to accept a plural verb with "none."

   None of these plans for disarmament *is* plausible.

   Each of the Russian regiments *is* equipped with the new tank.

5. Correlative conjunctions—neither/nor and either/or are tricky fellows. Usually the words joined by them require singular verbs:

   Neither Bush *nor* Putin *supports* this issue. (That's the correct answer to the poser at the beginning of this exercise.)

   If, however, one of the subjects is plural and one is singular, the verb agrees in number with the subject *closer to it*:

   Neither the revolutionaries *nor their leader was* to blame.

   or

   Neither the leader *nor the revolutionaries were* to blame.

   Verbs has to agree with their subjects.

   —William Safire, in *Fumblerules*[5]

Pronoun-Antecedent Agreement

The pronoun must agree in number with its antecedent—the noun it replaces. If the antecedent takes a singular verb, then the pronoun that refers to it must be singular. Unfortunately, the same traps that cause writers difficulty making subjects and verbs agree also affect pronoun-antecedent agreement. Remember what I just said about mistaken plurals? Collective nouns? Indefinite pronouns? Correlative conjunctions? All of these blur the number of the sentence. Add to that demon list the relative clause.

The relative clause usually begins with *who, that, which, whom,* or *whose* and depends on the number of its antecedent.

There are many South American *leaders who have made money* trafficking illegal drugs to the United States. (Note in this sentence that the relative pronoun *who* is considered plural because its antecedent, *leaders,* is plural. Furthermore, the verb in the dependent clause—in this case *have made*—is also plural.)

You cannot, however, always assume that the last noun prior to the relative clause is the antecedent:

The opposition lodged many *complaints* about the government's present defense system *that were* entirely justified. (Ask yourself, "What was entirely justified?" The correct answer, *complaints,* is plural; therefore, the verb *were* must be plural, too.)

Note again: Many times you can tighten up a sentence and rid yourself of some deadwood by *doing away with* relative clauses and expletives. Check out the following rewrites of the two sentences above:

Many South American leaders have made money trafficking illegal drugs to the United States. (Here I eliminated the expletive opening, "There are," *and* the relative pronoun "who.")

The opposition lodged many entirely justified complaints about the government's present defense system. (In this one I converted the windy relative clause "that were entirely justified" to a simple adverb, "entirely," and an adjective, "justified," modifying the complaints.)

Other Considerations of Correctness: Modifiers and Punctuation

Modifiers: Agents for Change

Modifiers are words, phrases, or clauses that help to limit or qualify other elements in a sentence. Modifiers can lend precision to your thoughts and help to establish logical relationships in your writing.

1. *Words* as modifiers
   Adjectives: *wartime* cooperation
   Adverbs: stay afloat *economically*
2. *Phrases* as modifiers
   In view of Western Europe's latent nationalism, its current unity is attributable to the U.S. presence.
   Unlike the United States, Western Europe, *especially Germany*, has reaped economic gains from detente.
3. *Clauses* as modifiers
   Japan, *which has enjoyed a near monopoly on certain trade items*, is now being challenged to address the U.S.-Japanese trade imbalance.
   Observe how the placement of a modifying adverb can affect a sentence's meaning:
   Only the DoD can approve this contract. (No one else can.)
   The DoD can approve *only* this contract. (This contract, but no others.)
   The DoD can *only* approve this contract. (Two possibilities: the DoD can approve the contract but take no other action in regard to the contract; or, the writer is confident that the DoD's only possible reaction to the contract will be a favorable one—approval.)

Errors in the Use of Modifiers

Squinting modifiers, split infinitives, and dangling or other misplaced modifiers can render your meaning ridiculous and damage your credibility as a writer. It's not important that you be able to identify the particular type of misplaced modifiers; just recognize them as out of place and be able to fix them.

Wrong: Preparing against a possible attack, all windows were secured. (Of course, windows, inanimate as they are, can't really prepare for an attack. The agent here, some unknown person or persons, is doing the preparation. Try rewriting the sentence to rectify the problem.)

Wrong: Eating the hamster, the child watched the snake in horror. (It's unlikely that the child is snacking on his furry pet here.)

Right: The snake ate the hamster while the child looked on in horror.

1. A *squinting modifier* appears to look in two directions at the same time:

   Squinting: The administration was confident last week they would receive word of the hostages. (Was the administration confident last week, or would they receive word last week? You can correct this confusion, as shown below, simply by inserting a "that" either before or after "last week.")

   Clear: The administration was confident last week that they would receive word of the hostages. (They felt confident last week.) *Or*: The administration was confident that last week they would receive word of the hostages. (Word was expected last week.)

   Squinting: The reports of an unauthorized attack by local counterterrorist operatives stunned both Senate and House committees yesterday. (Did the report occur yesterday, or the attack? Or both? The modifier above specifies the time of the stunning and nothing else. Use the modifier precisely to clarify what happened and when it happened.)

   Clear: Yesterday's reports of an unauthorized attack by local counterterrorist operatives stunned both Senate and House committees. (Now the sentence describes when the reports occurred.) *Or*: The reports of yesterday's unauthorized attack by local counterterrorist operatives stunned both Senate and House committees. (Now "yesterday" modifies the time of the attack.)

2. *Misplaced modifiers* can destroy the unity and coherence of a sentence:

   Misplaced: Also situations may develop in a country requiring evacuation of U.S. citizens. (*Two* modifier problems here: The "also" refers the reader back to the previous sentence, which was not the intent of the writer in the original context. The phrase "requiring evacuation of U.S. citizens" seems to modify "country" in this example, meaning that the *country* is requiring U.S. citizens to evacuate.)

Replaced: Situations also may develop that require the evacuation of U.S. citizens. ("Also" is placed correctly, to refer to the additional types of *situations*; and the phrase "require the evacuation of U.S. citizens" also is repositioned to refer to the *situations*, not the country.)

Out of place: Geographic intelligence must keep the commander abreast of weather and climatic conditions which can change drastically within a few minutes.

In place: Geographic intelligence must keep the commander abreast of weather, which can change drastically within a few minutes, and climatic conditions. (The phrase "which can change drastically within a few minutes" applies only to *weather*, not to climatic conditions, which take more than a few minutes to change.)

3. *Split infinitives* happen when you put an adverb between *to* and the next verb form. Note: Except for hard-core grammarians, most writers are relaxing this rule a little. The primary guideline should be how the sentence *sounds*. To precisely demonstrate,

Wrong: I want to specifically and certainly know the answer.

Right: I want to know, specifically and certainly, the answer. *Or*: I want to find a specific and certain answer.

Wrong: Lebanon sought to again shield its government officials from bomb attacks.

Right: Lebanon again sought to shield its government officials from bomb attacks.

4. *Dangling modifiers* are some of the most embarrassing writing mistakes you can make. Their absurdity makes them dead giveaways:

a. *Dangling participle*:
   Wrong: Eating lunch on the lawn, the speeding cars amused the children. (Those hungry cars will make your reader "snicker.")
   Right: The speeding cars amused the children eating lunch on the lawn.
b. *Dangling gerund*:
   Wrong: After working round the clock, the end seemed in sight to the congressional committee. (Is that a tight end on the Baltimore Ravens working so hard?)
   Right: After the congressional committee had worked round the clock, the end was in sight. *Or*: After working round the clock, the congressional committee found the end in sight.
c. *Dangling infinitive*:
   Wrong: To be well prepared, the books covered on the test must be reviewed. (The books don't need to pass the course, but the student does.)
   Right: To be well prepared, you must review the books covered on the test.
d. *Dangling elliptical clause* (a clause from which the subject and all or part of the verb have been dropped as understood):
   Wrong: While sunning in Florida, the Mafia assassinated him.
   Right: While he was sunning in Florida, the Mafia assassinated him. *Or*: While sunning in Florida, he was assassinated by the Mafia.
e. *Hidden modified terms*: Modified terms become "hidden" in a sentence when modifiers are not placed either immediately before or after the modified term. In the following sentence, observe how the word "currencies," the modified term, gets lost in the shuffle:
   Wrong: When grossly inflated, leaders of the Common Market economies met to discuss exchange rates for their currencies. (Are these world leaders filled with air like balloons? Determine *what* is inflated, and either have it follow the modifying phrase, or restructure the sentence to modify the appropriate element.)

Right: In view of the gross inflation of their currencies, the European Common Market leaders met to discuss exchange rates.

Wrong: As a distinguished policy analyst, the public naturally looked to Dr. Kissinger for his opinion on Soviet glasnost. (The public is not the policy analyst; Dr. Kissinger is.)

Right: The public naturally looked to Dr. Kissinger, a distinguished policy analyst, for his opinion on Soviet glasnost.

f. *Absolute phrases*, such as the ones italicized in the sentences below, do not have to be followed by the modified term. An absolute phrase modifies *the rest of the sentence* in which it is found. (As you've learned above, other types of modifiers modify a particular *word* or *part* of a sentence.) An absolute phrase contains a noun and usually a participle, plus modifiers. It adds meaning to the sentence but has no grammatical relation to it. Remember the definition of "modifiers": words that can help to limit or qualify other elements in a sentence. *Warning*: Absolute phrases are useful, but use them sparingly.

Economic reforms behind him, Yeltsin made plans for the next plenary session.

Generally speaking, Poland is culturally more "Western" than any other Eastern European country.

Kelly and Henry separated, *she moving to America and he staying in Germany.*

The woman fell in the airport, *her belongings flying everywhere.*

The decision made at last, the jurors filed back into the courtroom to give their verdict.

He rose from the negotiating table, *his stooped shoulders a sign of discouragement.*

All struggle over, the troops lay down their arms.

Undoubtedly, terrorism must be more effectively deterred by the United States in the future than it has been in the past.

Punctuation: Signals for Your Reader

> Punctuation, to most people, is a set of arbitrary and rather silly rules. . . . Few people realize that it is the most important single device for making things easier to read.

> —Rudolph Flesch

The passage above demonstrates four types of punctuation, all of which signal important messages to the reader. If you can't name them and describe their functions now, I hope you'll be able to after you complete the exercise on punctuation at the end of this chapter.

We can view punctuation as an arsenal of writing signals. Since punctuation, like many other elements of writing, is dynamic, changing with the daily use of our language, the rules that guide our use of punctuation are numerous and complicated. This exercise explains some of the more common punctuation problems writers encounter. Let's examine the following sentence to see how punctuation signals meaning.

An unnamed "senior intelligence official" told the *New York Times*, in an interview published on March 5, 1987, that "most leaks of sensitive intelligence information come out of the executive branch, not from Congress."[6]

Allan E. Goodman, author of the sentence, uses four punctuation signals:

1. Quotation marks surround the phrase "senior intelligence official" to indicate how the *New York Times* described one of its sources. The sentence, "most leaks of sensitive intelligence information come out of the executive branch, not from Congress," is set off by quotation marks to show the language has been borrowed from another source and is not the author's original language.
2. Underlining or italicizing *New York Times* indicates the title of a publication.
3. A pair of commas sets off the phrase "in an interview published on March 5, 1987," a phrase that modifies or

explains the circumstances and time the quotation was made.

4. The period at the end of the sentence, of course, tells readers they have come to the end of a complete thought. *Note: Periods and commas always belong inside quotation marks.*

The following section briefly describes and illustrates the function of certain punctuation marks. They are presented in alphabetical order for ease of reference.

Brackets

Brackets are used to indicate that you are interrupting a quotation with your own words.

"The classification 'peasant' stamped on Joseph Djugashvili's [Stalin's father's] official documents differentiated him from most of his early associates, friends as well as enemies, in political work."

Here the bracketed words, [Stalin's father's], explain the identity of Joseph Djugashvili.

Colons

Colons introduce a restatement (especially to expand, clarify, or emphasize), a formal listing, or a quotation. Other common uses for the colon include separating the hour from the minute in expressions of time; dividing a title from a subtitle; and separating chapter from verse in Bible citations.

1. Restatement. The main problems with student papers are punctuation errors: colons, semicolons, and quotation marks.
2. Listing. Items traded to Panaragua included military equipment: replacement parts for military vehicles, communications equipment, ammunition, grenade launchers, and missiles.
3. Quotation. Gaddis notes the importance of limited financial resources in the Eisenhower administration: "The

mechanism that has most often forced the consideration of unpalatable options in the postwar years has been budgetary."
4. Other. I finished reading his thesis at 10:30 last night. The title, *Lebanon: Through a Glass, Darkly*, was inspired by I Corinthians 13:12.

Note: Like a semicolon, a colon must be preceded by a complete statement; unlike a semicolon, however, a colon can be followed by an incomplete statement (as in the examples above). When a colon *is* followed by a complete sentence, capitalize the first word of that sentence. Check your style guide, though, for definitive guidance.

Commas

The distinguished essayist E. B. White wrote, "English usage is sometimes more than mere taste, judgement [sic], and education—sometimes it's sheer luck, like getting across the street." You may feel that way about punctuating with commas; indeed, commas are the beasties of the punctuation jungle. I've observed two types of comma abusers: those who use too many, sprinkling them liberally throughout the text ("comma-kazes") and those whose arms must be twisted to use a comma ("comma-tose").

1. *Comma splices* occur when two complete sentences are "spliced" together by a comma rather than by other, correct punctuation marks. Comma splices are explained under the section on the semicolon below.
   Wrong: The chairman of the board wanted the merger, so did the majority of the board members.
   Replace the comma here with a semicolon, or insert a conjunction after the comma:
   Right: The chairman of the board wanted the merger; so did the majority of the board members. *Or*: The chairman of the board wanted the merger, and so did the majority of the board members.

2. *Use commas to set off modifying phrases and introductory modifiers.*

Modifying phrase: For many developing countries, *especially the indebted Latin American economies*, the United States has become the buyer of last resort rather than the lender of last resort. (The italicized phrase modifies the "developing countries" idea and is set off by commas.)

Modifying phrase: Kissinger, *at that time an academic*, warned that it is an illusion to regard NATO as the "natural" structure of Atlantic relations. (The italicized phrase provides additional information about Dr. Kissinger; therefore, it is set off by commas.)

Introductory modifiers: The four sentences that follow show examples of short introductory phrases, usually transitional in nature, which are set off by a comma.

Accordingly, I resigned.

In addition, a further drop in the dollar would slow the world economy.

To date, the falling dollar has produced little inflation.

For instance, if import prices were to rise, total inflation would increase.

3. *Commas separate words* that would otherwise run together erroneously.

Confused: Whatever is is right.

Clarified: Whatever is, is right.

4. *Commas divide elements of a date, address, and measurements.*

The debate began Tuesday night, July 1, 2008. Note, however, that the "military" date style requires no comma: Classes began on 2 September 2008.

He gave 1162 Magenta Road, Golden Springs, Maryland, as his permanent home address.

She is five feet, four inches tall.

5. *Practice correct punctuation of restrictive and nonrestrictive elements.* A *restrictive* clause is *essential* to the meaning of a sentence. It answers the question "which one(s)?" and is written *without* commas. A *nonrestrictive* clause usually begins with a "which" or a form of "who." The informa-

tion it gives is *not essential* to the meaning of the sentence. Use commas to set it off.

Restrictive: Countries *that do not belong to the International Monetary Fund* do not have access to loans from that organization. (Look at the difference in meaning of that sentence without the italicized restrictive clause.)

Nonrestrictive: That developing country, *which does not belong to the International Monetary Fund*, does not have access to loans from the IMF. (See the difference?)

Restrictive: Embassies *that are located in high-risk areas* are increasing their security staffs. (Not all embassies are beefing up security. *Which ones* are? The restrictive clause tells you.)

Nonrestrictive: The U.S. Embassy, *which is located in a high-risk area of the city*, is increasing its security staff.

6. Punctuate *nonrestrictive appositives* with commas. An appositive is a noun or noun substitute that stands beside another noun and means the same thing. Appositives, like the clauses we discussed above, may be restrictive or nonrestrictive. Notice that the use of commas in the examples below makes a considerable difference in the meaning of the sentences.

Restrictive appositive: My brother John is a freshman at Memphis State, and my brother Mark is doing postgraduate work at MIT. (The restrictive appositives—"John" and "Mark"—tell which brother is meant in each case.)

Nonrestrictive appositive: My sister, Emma, is a midshipman at the U.S. Naval Academy. (The commas tell the reader that the writer has only one sister, Emma.)

Restrictive appositive: In her short story "The Grave" Katherine Anne Porter describes a profound revelation in the lives of a young brother and sister. (Porter wrote many short stories; the lack of commas before and after the appositive shows that it is restrictive, limiting the reference to just one of those stories.)

Nonrestrictive: In her novel, *Ship of Fools*, Katherine Anne Porter chronicles the voyage of a shipload of passengers to the doomed Germany of 1931. (*Ship of Fools* is the only novel Ms. Porter wrote; the commas indicate this. However, if your sentence was about William Faulkner, who published not one but seventeen novels, your modifying phrase "his novel" would be restrictive, lacking commas: In his novel *Light in August* William Faulkner creates the character of Joe Christmas.)

Dashes

Dashes are the most emphatic way of setting off part of your sentence. See how this writer highlights the main concept of his sentence by using dashes:

"The NATO reformers also are on the right track in prescribing a remedy—Europeanization—for the problems they have diagnosed."

Notice that no spaces are left—on either side—between the words and the dashes.

Ellipses

Ellipses, also called ellipsis periods, show that something has been left out of a quoted passage.

"The strong yen should cut Japan's massive current-account surplus and speed up the outflow of capital. . . . Much of that outflow will take the form of portfolio investment while Japanese remain hooked on instruments like U.S. Treasury bonds."

Three spaced periods indicate that the words following them are from the same sentence. *Four* periods are appropriate when you have omitted (1) the last part of the quoted sentence; (2) a complete sentence or more; or (3) one or two complete paragraphs. Do not use an ellipsis at the beginning or at the end of a quotation.

Exclamation Points

Exclamation points are superfluous in writing for intelligence publications. Make the writing show its strength by using verbs and active voice, not a punctuation mark. Exclamation points might be used in dialogue to record an emphatic or surprised manner in speech; but it's unlikely that you'll use many of them in your college work or in intelligence writing.

Italics

Italics (or underlines) most commonly identify titles of books, magazines, journals, newspapers, plays, films, taped or recorded albums, and radio or television series. Examples follow:

1. Government publications such as the Council of Economic Advisors' 1996 *Economic Report to the President* or the U.S. Government Printing Office *Style Manual*;
2. Professional journals such as *Jane's Defence Weekly* or *Military Intelligence* magazine;
3. Television series such as *The O'Reilly Factor*;
4. Books such as George Tenet's *At the Center of the Storm: My Years at the CIA*; and
5. Newspapers: *Pravda, Washington Post, Baltimore Sun*.

Italics are also used to identify terms from foreign languages that have not yet been adopted as common English expressions (*Vernichtung*), and the names of ships (USS *Stark, Achille Lauro*).

Parentheses

1. Use parentheses to subordinate ideas. Parentheses can suggest that the idea enclosed within them is subordinate to the other ideas in the sentence:
   Hurricane Dean in the Caribbean (with incessant rain and flooding) caused massive damage.
   The parenthetical phrase above can be repositioned in two ways. It can be highlighted with dashes: Hurricane Dean in the Caribbean—with incessant rain and flooding—caused massive damage. *Or*, it can be set off with commas: Hurricane Dean in the Caribbean, with incessant rain and flooding, caused massive damage.

Choose parentheses when the idea within them is less important than what is outside; choose commas as a "neutral" solution; and choose dashes when you want to emphasize the portion you are setting off.

2. Avoid overusing parentheses. They tend to weaken writing. Ask yourself if you are burying in a parenthetical expression an idea that deserves a sentence or more of its own.

In the following excerpt from a student paper on the Tet offensive, the writer has buried material in parentheses that rightly belongs in the text of the paper, with fuller explanation:

In response to U.S. ground actions in Vietnam, Secretary of Defense McNamara speculated that China might enter the war with both air and ground forces (the Chinese hate the NVD. It is unlikely that 10 years after a revolution the Chinese would have risked confrontation with the U.S. on behalf of a traditional enemy).

The writer disagrees with McNamara's assessment and attempts to refute it by cramming opposing evidence into a parenthetical expression. This material needs to be "rescued" from the parentheses and developed in the paper.

Periods

A period signals to your reader the end of your sentence and the completion of your thought. Here are three common errors in the use of periods:

1. *Creating sentence fragments*:
   Wrong: The CIA created and financed several American radio stations. Such as those that broadcast into Eastern Europe and the Soviet Union—Radio Free Europe and Radio Liberty.
   Recognize the problem here? The second "sentence" lacks a subject and a verb; it is a *sentence fragment*. Most

readers feel like they've been "fragged" when they read something like that. Try sentence combining to solve the problem.

Right: The CIA created and financed several American radio stations, such as those that broadcast into Eastern Europe and the Soviet Union—Radio Free Europe and Radio Liberty.

2. *Unnecessary periods*:

Wrong: He made many sacrifices to complete his M.A..

No second period is needed here. The period after the abbreviation is sufficient to signal the end of the sentence. Another solution is to add the word "degree" after the abbreviation.

Right: He made many sacrifices to complete his M.A.

3. Run-on (fused) sentences:

Wrong: "You will die not in battle will you be victorious."

This is every reader's nightmare, a run-on sentence. Where is the reader to pause or stop? This quotation is attributed to the Oracle of Delphi in ancient Greece, who replied in those ambiguous terms when asked by a soldier-statesman if he would be victorious in the forthcoming battle. Place the period after the word "die" and it contains an unhappy prophecy for the warrior; but if the period comes after the word "not," the thought is more positive. Don't make your readers struggle for your meaning.

Right: "You will die. Not in battle will you be victorious." *Or*: "You will die not. In battle will you be victorious."

Possessives

1. Joint possession: make only the last term possessive.
   Example: Gramm and Rudman's bill was passed.
2. Avoid confusion of plurals and possessives, one of the most common and least excusable writing errors.

party = singular noun: The Republican *Party* will hold its convention in Minneapolis.

parties = plural noun: Both political *parties* lack strong presidential candidates.

party's = singular possessive: The *party's* host was exhausted by midnight.

parties' = plural possessive: Both *parties'* caterers produced elegant repasts.

Quotation Marks

Quotation marks acknowledge the use of someone else's words, such as those of the anonymous "senior intelligence official" quoted in the example above. Quotation marks can also be used to show distance from a dubious or offensive expression. In that case, think of the quotation marks as synonymous with the words "so-called." Example: Hitler's "final solution" destroyed six million Jews.

Use double quotation marks (" ") to mark the beginning and end of a quotation. Use single quotation marks (' ') to mark a quotation within a quotation. Example: The speaker then said, "Hitler's 'final solution' destroyed six million Jews."

Words within quotation marks must be *exact*. Show any departure from quoted material by using brackets. (See the earlier discussion under "Brackets.") Errors or usage variations in quotes may be pointed out by using [sic]: "Sir Jonathan Frumbleton was named Minister of Defence [sic]."[7]

Semicolons

A semicolon marks a division *and* suggests a close relationship between the parts it divides. Here are the most common problem areas in the use of the semicolon.

1. *Comma splice*: joining two main clauses with a comma.
   Wrong: Some of those party leaders influenced Stalin, others were influenced by him.

Try one of three methods of repair for such comma splices:

Use a *semicolon* between the main clauses:

Right: Some of those party leaders influenced Stalin; others were influenced by him.

Insert an appropriate *conjunction* after the comma:

Right: Some of those party leaders influenced Stalin, *but* others were influenced by him.

Simply *end* the first clause with a *period*, and begin a new sentence with the second clause:

Right: Some of those party leaders influenced Stalin. Others were influenced by him.

Note: Transitional phrases such as the following often mark the need for a preceding semicolon: therefore; then; thus; hence; accordingly; as a result; likewise; similarly; but; however; nevertheless; on the contrary; on the other hand; yet; further; moreover; indeed; finally; and many others.

Wrong: General indicators of the Tet offensive were abundant, moreover, more specific indicators such as handwritten documents and the testimony of captured enemy were also emerging.

Right: General indicators of the Tet offensive were abundant; moreover, more specific indicators such as handwritten documents and the testimony of captured enemy were also emerging.

2. *Do not follow a semicolon with a sentence fragment.*

Wrong: Negative results have also occurred, such as; record trade imbalances. (Who knows why this student placed a semicolon here? Simply remove it to correct the sentence.)

Wrong: The KGB continued to exercise tremendous power in the Soviet Union; even to the extent of influencing Mikhail Gorbachev.

Right: The KGB continued to exercise tremendous power in the Soviet Union; even Mikhail Gorbachev had to act in concert with this deeply entrenched organization.

3. *Use semicolons in a long series of items, or even in a short series if internal punctuation—especially commas—may cause confusion.*

   Long series: The ambassador's first day in Washington included a visit to the White House, where he met with Vice President Bush; luncheon at La Colline, a favorite restaurant of members of Congress; a briefing on U.S. policy in the Middle East; and a lecture by the ambassador to a graduate class in international relations at American University.

   Possible confusion: Our first day in Washington included a tour of the new facility; microcomputer lab and security orientations; a meeting with the director, Mr. Craft; and a counterterrorism briefing. (Try reading that sentence with commas instead of semicolons and you'll see that it can cause the reader to stumble en route to the meaning.)

Exercises in the Basic Tools of Intelligence Writing

Exercise 1: Clarity and Precision

1. Revise the following sentences to eliminate ambiguity.
   a. Locating indicators that pointed to Tet was not cumbersome.
   b. Iran and Iraq agreed when both sides ceased fire to open negotiations.
   c. Khrushchev's realization of Mao's increasingly ambitious desires for world power was directly responsible for its final curtailment of Soviet economic, military, and diplomatic aid and its determination to prevent China from joining the atomic elite.
   d. Many political figures only had access to the general knowledge regarding the situation in South Vietnam, but not access to the individual source knowledge.
   e. Another thing that the United States can influence is to resolve Peru's international debt repayment problem

on terms favorable to Peru based on their particular problems.
2. Words that have approximately the same meaning frequently suggest meanings that are different. The combinations that follow bring together words with different connotations. Try to pin down those differences. Use your dictionary if you're unsure of the shades of meaning.

a. perseverance
   obstinacy
   doggedness
d. probity
   candor
   frankness
g. request
   solicit
   beg

b. resist
   defy
   oppose
e. antipathy
   aversion
   disgust
h. plead
   argue
   exhort

c. illegal
   unlawful
   criminal
f. imitation
   counterfeit
   sham
i. lie (noun)
   deception
   falsehood

3. In the following sentences, replace the italicized word with one that has nearly the same meaning but a slightly different connotation. Explain how the substitute affects the meaning of the sentence.
   a. With the emergence of Japan, Korea, and Taiwan as economically strong nations, the traditional American *fixation* on Europe began to shift west.
   b. Analysts adhered *religiously* to the idea that the North Vietnamese were following Red China's *prescription* for victory.
   c. Either the intelligence community was *ignorant*, or it did not possess the *innovative* thinking required to distinguish between the two assessment methods.

Exercise 2: Conciseness

The following exercises provide practice in eliminating all types of wordiness. You may want to review the "Weight Watcher" recipes provided at the beginning of this unit. Now, surgically remove the fat from the following sentences (you might call it *logosuction*).

Some Long-Winded Sentences

1. Locating indicators *that pointed to the Tet offensive* was *not difficult*. *There were* general indicators available at the time, such as political resolutions and writings, *which foresaw or recognized the possibility of a Tet-like offensive*. (I've italicized problem areas here to get you started. Can you eliminate the padding?)
2. One of the revolutionary group's tactics is to overload the prisons to the point that the government's very corrupt judicial system is even further overworked.
3. There were also indications subtle in nature of an advance forward, such as handwritten documents and testimony of captured enemy, which were collected by military intelligence personnel.
4. Peru has experienced widespread violence from both rural and urban insurgencies for the past several years.
5. The realities of nuclear war at the present time are such that countries that possess equal power find, when they confront each other, that the weapons that carry the most force are precisely the weapons that they cannot use.
6. The guerrillas have concentrated on enlisting the youth in the villages in order to carry on the revolution in the future.
7. This collection edited by Neil Smith contains secret documents, which detail correspondence between high-ranking military figures and politicians who were influential during that time.
8. Virtually all villages, which have had an effect on the economy and which include in their government land-holding politicians, have been attacked by the guerrilla forces.
9. The Sendero can be expected to strengthen its forces by attracting new, young, unemployed, educated recruits for a long and extended struggle within Lima.
10. Garcia, who is president of Peru, must advance the national economy in order to create new jobs for the young who are growing in number.

Some Longer Passages

Write your condensed version of the following. Be sure to preserve the meaning.

1. A realization by European terrorist groups has taken place, that not only will their survivability greatly improve, but that their impact on Western society can be greatly enhanced by unification and mutual cooperation among each other. (36 words)

2. The modus operandi and ideology indicated by terrorist actions show a solidarity amongst the various groups too strong to ignore. This same connection may not be a strong enough statement to suggest an organization with the stature as would be indicated by the term "international terrorist organization." (47 words)

3. There are several strategic reasons for the United States to be concerned about Peruvian stability. There are five reasons concerning U.S. national security. First, Peru is the only South American country that is extensively equipped with Soviet-made arms. Second, outside Cuba, the Soviets have built up in Peru the largest presence of military advisors in the western hemisphere. The Soviet Union has more military advisors in Peru than the United States has in all of Latin America. With its presence in Peru, the Soviets can directly affect the regional arms race in South America. Third, Peru provides the United States with strategic minerals to include zinc and silver but can also be a backup source for lead, tungsten, molybdenum, mercury, iron ore, gold, silver, copper, and phosphate if South Africa should fall into communist hands. In addition, one of the world's richest uranium cobalt deposits was recently located in the Surckico area. Fourth, the acquisition of docking and repair privileges [sic] at Peruvian fishing ports means that Soviet electronic spying ships can stay at sea for longer periods of time. Finally, with continued efforts to cultivate relations with Argentina and to destabilize Chile, the strategic choke point

of the straits of Magellan is threatened and so are trade routes in the South Atlantic. (212 words)

Exercise 3: Modifiers

Rewrite these sentences to correct problems with modifiers:
1. By putting our Brigade and Battalion S-2's under the pressure of a combat environment, they learn their craft quickly.
2. The Brigade S-2 is also responsible for fulfilling all requests for information and intelligence that may be required from corps and national assets.
3. His aged law school professor, though he was still very inexperienced, believed he saw a political talent in the young law student.
4. Rude, insolent, disrespectful toward authorities, the seminary attended by the young Stalin did little to improve his temper.
5. In the 1970s nationalistic, autonomous terrorist groups plagued various European countries such as the Baader-Meinhof Gang.
6. Escalating the frequency of bombings, the Americans for Non-Violence issued a statement condemning the terrorists' actions.
7. By displaying boldness, the trends in Europe can be turned to Japan's advantage.
8. Once pictured on a magazine cover, readers will pay special attention to this candidate's qualifications for office.
9. When riding horses in public parks, greater consideration is needed.
10. He wanted to exclusively link drug dealers to their foreign sources.
11. They agreed when both sides ceased fire to open negotiations.
12. Several heads of state we know have failed to retain our trust in their commitment to end human rights abuse.

13. A good officer, his superiors recommended a promotion for him.
14. Unquestionably my seminar paper will earn a high grade and impress my professor.

Exercise 4: Agreement

If you need to practice subject-verb and pronoun-antecedent matching, try these:

1. Neither the Arab nations nor Israel (wants, want) yet another all-out war.
2. In 1980 the United States, as well as Canada and several other countries, prevented (its, their) athletes from competing in the Moscow Olympics because of the Soviet invasion of Afghanistan.
3. The future usefulness of such tactics (has, have) been questioned by the government.
4. The threat of further expropriations of U.S. corporate assets (continues, continue) to be a major point of tension with Washington.
5. The Chilean army (was, were) opportunistic; (it, they) took advantage of every weakness in the opposition's attack strategy.
6. None of the industrial development projects (was, were) completed after Gorbachev terminated Soviet economic aid.
7. The committee (has, have) declared a new policy, but each of the Arab leaders (believes, believe) that nothing will change.
8. Democracy, as well as socialism, (has, have) influenced the political and economic systems of many European countries.
9. Neither Iran nor Iraq (depends, depend) on other countries for (its, their) oil needs.
10. There (was, were) subtle indicators of a Tet-like offensive, such as handwritten documents and testimony of captured enemy, which (was, were) collected by military intelligence personnel in Vietnam.

Exercise 5: Punctuation

1. Possessives: Fill in the missing forms in the chart below.

Singular Noun	Plural Noun	Singular Possessive	Plural Possessive
	passes		
annex			
		Kennedy's	
crisis			
	media		

2. Miscellaneous punctuation: Delete and/or insert appropriate punctuation to achieve clarity and correctness.
    a. Inside the dog was growling.
    b. Artemus Ward wrote A writer who can't write in a grammerly manner better shut up shop.
    c. An intelligence background does not limit me to intelligence positions, I may still fill an operations billet.
    d. A staunch Republican follows his partie's line.
    e. After eating the child became sleepy.
    f. An old French proverb claims that A white wall is the fool's paper.
    g. The Achille Lauro, was hijacked by terrorists, an American Leon Klinghofer was brutally murdered.
    h. Robert McFarlane then head of the National Security Council was a trusted advisor to the president.
    i. Highly organized and committed to their cause the terrorist groups live in hiding and are difficult to pinpoint.
    j. He claimed he had no interest in achieving a higher office yet he continued to foster dissent in the military.
    k. First planes were heard in the sky overhead on December 7 1941.
    l. Einsteins assertion that It is characteristic of the military mentality that non-human factors [a few words omitted here] are held essential, while the human being, his desires and thoughts—in short, the psychological factors—are considered as unimportant and secondary, serves as the basis for the Rotary Clubs debate. (Hint: There are four missing punctuation marks here.)

m. My assignment, is to provide abstracts of the following books Dangerous Relations by Adam Ulam a professor of Soviet studies at Harvard, Game Plan by Zbigniew Brzezenski President Carters former national security advisor and White House Years by Henry Kissinger secretary of state under President Nixon.

n. In any case fears of renewed conflict abounded.

o. The American economist, Mark Allen, traveled to the Ivory Coast as a representative of the World Bank.

p. A significant reduction of over 50 percent of regional nuclear and conventional forces in Central Europe might promote change certainly the potential for instability and tension there makes it advisable to structure force reductions carefully.

q. Through testing a need may have been established, however, the testing was conducted by a contractor who may have been biased.

r. The goal of these instructional segments is worthy however the presentations could have been better.

Answers to the Exercises in Chapter 2

Exercise 1: Clarity and Precision

1. a. "Was not cumbersome" is a carelessly chosen phrase. Try replacing it with "easy."

   Locating indicators that pointed to Tet was easy.

   b. The clarity problem in the original is due to a "squinting modifier"—a modifier that seems to look in two directions at once. The revisions place the modifier "when both sides ceased to fire" in positions where its meaning is clearer.

   Iran and Iraq agreed to open negotiations when both sides ceased fire.

   or

   When both sides ceased fire, Iran and Iraq agreed to open negotiations.

c. The possessive pronoun "its" (used twice in the sentence) does not have an antecedent. The writer may intend the pronoun to refer to USSR. Unfortunately, USSR is not in the sentence.

Khrushchev's realization of Mao's increasingly ambitious desires for world power was directly responsible for the USSR's final curtailment of Soviet economic, military, and diplomatic aid and its determination to prevent China from joining the atomic elite.

d. A misplaced "only" distorts this sentence's meaning.

Many political figures had access to only the general knowledge regarding the situation in South Vietnam, but not access to the individual source knowledge.

(I would also ask the writer to clarify what he means by "individual source knowledge.")

e. There are definitely too many "problems" with the original sentence. To whom does "their" refer? All the preceding nouns in the sentence are plural. This writer needs to eliminate unnecessary words and to clarify what "particular problems" Peru is having—if that prepositional phrase in fact modifies Peru.

The United States can favorably affect Peru's economic stability by helping it repay its international debts.

2. Individual responses will vary. Be prepared to defend your decision and to discuss the differences in word meanings. I have offered one approach: a rating of the words in terms of their favorable connotations. One (1) is for the most favorable, two (2) for less favorable, and three (3) for least favorable.

a. perseverance—1   b. resist—2   c. illegal—2
   obstinacy—2   defy—3   unlawful—1
   doggedness—3   oppose—1   criminal—3
d. probity—1   e. antipathy—2   f. imitation—1
   candor—2   aversion—1   counterfeit—2
   frankness—3   disgust—3   sham—3
g. request—1   h. plead—1   i. lie (n.)—3
   solicit—2   argue—2   deception—1
   beg—3   exhort—3   falsehood—2

3. Answers to this section will vary. Some suggested substitutions are shown below.
    a. With the emergence of Japan, Korea, and Taiwan as economically strong nations, the traditional American *preoccupation with* Europe began to shift west.
    b. Analysts adhered *faithfully* to the idea that the North Vietnamese were following Red China's *formula* for victory.
    c. Either the intelligence community was *unaware*, or it did not possess the *creative* thinking required to distinguish between the two assessment methods.

Exercise 2: Conciseness

Answers will vary. The following are examples of how the sentences *might* be reduced.

1. Locating Tet offensive indicators was easy. General indicators available at the time, such as political resolutions and writings, predicted a possible Tet-like offensive.
2. One of the revolutionary group's tactics is to overload the prisons to further overwork the government's corrupt judicial system.
3. Military intelligence personnel collected subtle indications of an advance, such as handwritten documents and testimony of captured enemy. (This revision eliminates "there are," the tautology "advance forward," and the passive voice.)
4. Peru has experienced several years of widespread violence from both rural and urban insurgencies.
5. Because of the present realities of nuclear war, equally powerful countries find, when they confront each other, that their most forceful weapons are precisely the ones they cannot use.
6. The guerrillas have concentrated on enlisting village youth to carry on the future revolution. (This one turns the original's prepositional phrases into adjectives.)
7. Neil Smith's edited collection contains secret documents, which detail correspondence between high-ranking

figures and influential politicians. (The revision reduces the prepositional phrases and the "who" clause to adjectives.)

8. Guerrilla forces attacked virtually all the villages that affected the economy and included in their government landholding politicians. (The rewrite eliminates the "to be" passive verb and reduces the "which" clause.)

9. The Sendero can be expected to strengthen its forces by recruiting unemployed, educated youths for its protracted struggle within Peru.

10. Peruvian President Garcia must advance the national economy in order to create new jobs for the ever-increasing youth.

Revision of longer passages: These exercises, too, had many possible solutions. Compare your rewrite to ours, below.

1. European terrorists realize that both their survivability and their impact on Western society can be enhanced greatly by unification and cooperation. (Original = 36 words; revision = 21 words; savings = 15 words!)

2. The terrorists' modus operandi and ideology show a strong solidarity among the various groups, but this connection may not be indicative of an "international terrorist organization." (Original = 47 words; revision = 26 words; savings = another 21 words!)

3. Peru is important to U.S. national security for several reasons. First, Peru is the only South American country extensively equipped with Soviet-made arms. Second, outside Cuba, the Soviet cadre of military advisors in Peru is the largest in the Western Hemisphere, greater than the U.S. presence in all of Latin America. With such a presence, the Soviets can directly affect this area's arms race. Third, Peru provides the United States with the strategic minerals zinc and silver and could be a backup source for lead, tungsten, molybdenum, mercury, iron ore, gold, silver, copper, and phosphate should South Africa fall into communist hands.

In addition, one of the world's richest uranium cobalt deposits was recently located in the Surckico area. Fourth, access to docking and repair at Peruvian fishing ports means that Soviet electronic surveillance ships can stay at sea longer. Finally, the Soviets' continued efforts to cultivate relations with Argentina and destabilize Chili threaten the strategic choke point of the Straits of Magellan and South American trade routes. (The revision reduces the original 212 words to 171, a savings of 41 words. How did you compare? If you had fewer than 171 words, check to be sure that you included all the information from the original. You may also want to check with your classmates to see how you compared.)

Notice that our three original examples had a total of 295 words, which we were able to reduce to 218 words, saving our readers 77 words and more than 25 percent of their reading time. What might have taken our readers three minutes to wade through will now require only a little more than two minutes. Try in your own writing to save your readers a comparable amount of time and effort. They will appreciate it.

Exercise 3: Modifiers

The corrected modifier problems are italicized below:

1. By putting our Brigade and Battalion S-2's under the pressure of a combat environment, *the National Training Center encourages them to* learn their craft quickly.
2. The Brigade S-2 is also responsible for fulfilling, *from corps and national assets,* all requests for information and intelligence that may be required.
3. His aged law school professor believed he saw a political talent in the young law student *despite his inexperience.*
4. The seminary attended by the young Stalin did little to improve his temper, *which some described as rude, insolent, disrespectful toward authorities.*

5. In the 1970s nationalistic, autonomous terrorist groups, *such as the Baader-Meinhof Gang,* plagued various European countries.

6. *Following the terrorists' escalation of* the frequency of bombings, the Americans for Non-Violence issued a statement condemning *their* actions.

7. By displaying boldness, *Japan can turn the trends in Europe to its own advantage.*

8. Readers will pay special attention to this candidate's qualifications for office *once he is pictured on a magazine cover.*

9. *Riders of* horses in public parks *need to exercise greater consideration for others.*

10. He wanted to link drug dealers *exclusively* to their foreign sources.

11. Negotiations were opened *when both sides had ceased fire.* (Or: They agreed, *when both sides had ceased fire,* to open negotiations.)

12. *We know that* several heads of state have failed to retain our trust in their commitment to end human rights abuse.

13. A good officer, *he was* recommended *for* a promotion *by his superiors.*

14. Unquestionably, my seminar paper will earn a high grade and impress my professor. (Be sure to set off this absolute phrase with a comma.)

Exercise 4: Agreement

1. Neither the Arab nations nor Israel *wants* yet another all-out war.

2. In 1980 the United States, as well as Canada and several other countries, prevented *its* athletes from competing in the Moscow Olympics because of the Soviet invasion of Afghanistan.

3. The future usefulness of such tactics *has* been questioned by the government.

4. The threat of further expropriations of U.S. corporate assets *continues* to be a major point of tension with Washington.
5. The Chilean army *was* opportunistic; *it* took advantage of every weakness in the opposition's attack strategy.
6. None of the industrial development projects *was* completed after Gorbachev terminated Soviet economic aid.
7. The committee *has* declared a new policy, but each of the Arab leaders *believes* that nothing will change.
8. Democracy, as well as socialism, *has* influenced the political and economic systems of many European countries.
9. Neither Iran nor Iraq *depends* on other countries for *its* oil needs.
10. There *were* subtle indicators of a Tet-like offensive, such as handwritten documents and testimony of captured enemy, which *were* collected by military intelligence personnel in Vietnam.

Exercise 5: Punctuation

1. Possessives: The missing forms are italicized in the chart below.

Singular Noun	Plural Noun	Singular Possessive	Plural Possessive
pass	passes	*pass's*	*passes'*
annex	*annexes*	*annex's*	*annexes'*
Kennedy	*Kennedys*	Kennedy's	*Kennedys'*
crisis	*crises*	*crisis'*	*crises'*
medium	media	*medium's*	*media's*

2. Miscellaneous punctuation: Appropriate punctuation is added to achieve clarity and correctness.
   a. Inside, the dog was growling.
   b. Artemus Ward wrote, "A writer who can't write in a grammerly manner better shut up shop."
   c. An intelligence background does not limit me to intelligence positions; I may still fill an operations billet. (A period is also correct.)

d. A staunch Republican follows his party's line.

e. After eating, the child became sleepy.

f. An old French proverb claims that "A white wall is the fool's paper."

g. The *Achille Lauro* [no comma here] was hijacked by terrorists, *and* [add the conjunction, *or* use a semicolon, *or* begin a new sentence] an American, Leon Klinghofer, was brutally murdered. (It is also correct to omit the word "an" and leave out the commas. You may also underline the ship's name instead of italicizing it.)

h. Robert McFarlane, then head of the National Security Council, was a trusted advisor to the president.

i. Highly organized and committed to their cause, the terrorist groups live in hiding and are difficult to pinpoint.

j. He claimed he had no interest in achieving a higher office, yet he continued to foster dissent in the military.

k. First, planes were heard in the sky overhead on December 7, 1941.

l. Einstein's assertion that "It is characteristic of the military mentality that non-human factors . . . are held essential, while the human being, his desires and thoughts—in short, the psychological factors—are considered as unimportant and secondary," serves as the basis for the Rotary Club's debate.

m. My assignment [no comma here] is to provide abstracts of the following books: *Dangerous Relations* by Adam Ulam, a professor of Soviet studies at Harvard; *Game Plan* by Zbigniew Brzezenski, President Carter's former national security advisor; and *White House Years* by Henry Kissinger, secretary of state under President Nixon. (Underlining the book titles would also be correct.)

n. In any case, fears of renewed conflict abounded.

o. The American economist Mark Allen traveled to the Ivory Coast as a representative of the World Bank. (No commas are needed here. There are many American economists, so the modifying phrase "the American economist" is restrictive, identifying a particular economist.)

p. A significant reduction of over 50 percent of regional nuclear and conventional forces in Central Europe might promote change; certainly, the potential for instability and tension there makes it advisable to structure force reductions carefully.

q. Through testing a need may have been established; however, the testing was conducted by a contractor who may have been biased.

r. The goal of these instructional segments is worthy; however, the presentations could have been better.

Notes

1. Quoted in Frederick J. Kroesen, "Intelligence: Now a Two-Way Street?" *Army* (September 1994): 7.

2. William Strunk Jr. and E. B. White, *The Elements of Style*, 4th ed. (New York: Allyn & Bacon, 1999), 79.

3. Strunk and White, *Elements of Style*, 23.

4. William Safire, *Fumblerules: A Lighthearted Guide to Grammar and Good Usage* (New York: Doubleday, 1990), 85.

5. Safire, *Fumblerules*, 58.

6. Allan E. Goodman, "Reforming U.S. Intelligence," *Foreign Policy* 67 (Summer 1987): 133.

7. For an interesting discussion of these principles of usage, see Deborah Howell, "A Dilemma within Quotation Marks," *Washington Post*, August 19, 2007, B6.

3

Other Important Considerations: Appropriateness, Completeness, and Coherence

Summary

The basic principles of *all* writing are clarity, conciseness, and correctness, covered in chapter 2. Other important considerations in your writing include appropriateness, completeness, and coherence. Appropriateness means considering your audience and their needs. To be complete, be sure you've said everything you need to say. A coherent paper is a unified whole, focused on a central theme.

Appropriateness

If you haven't already done so by now, you need to consider your reader. Intelligence professionals seldom know precisely who will be reading their work, but they can generally make a pretty good guess. If an analyst has been tasked to write a paper for the director of her agency or for her commander, you can bet that everyone between her and the intended recipient will read it. But if she is doing a thesis or a study that will receive wide dissemination, she might be less certain. At least she can get her hands on the proposed distribution list for the product and try to gear it toward that audience.

To help you determine whether your writing is appropriate for the intended audience, ask yourself the following questions: Who will read my product? Why will they read it? How will they use the information? It's unlikely that you'll be able to answer those questions every time, but the mere act of asking them may prove useful.

Another important consideration in appropriateness is the use of jargon. The "shop talk" of the intelligence professional saves a lot of time in daily dealings with colleagues. Always try to consider whether your paper will be read by someone without a clear understanding of the jargon you use. If you must use an abbreviation or acronym, that's no problem; just spell it out first, and follow it parenthetically with the abbreviation. Then, when you use the term again, use the abbreviation. If you write more than a page or so without using the term again, spell it out one more time for your reader. When in doubt, spell it out.

These techniques of considering your reader and avoiding jargon will make your writing more appropriate for your intended audience. And they will appreciate your efforts on their behalf.

> Easy reading is damned hard writing.
>
> —Nathaniel Hawthorne

Completeness

The flip side of the conciseness coin is completeness in your writing. When you write concisely, you want to ensure that you've said what you need to say in as few words as possible. With completeness, you want to be sure that you haven't left anything unsaid. Prewriting helps a lot. Chapter 4 will cover some prewriting techniques in detail.

Go back and review your outline or other prewriting, and compare it to your first draft. Have you covered everything you wanted to cover? Are your main points all there? Is there any point you've raised that hasn't been fully resolved, either by answering all the questions or by stating that there are still some unknowns or gaps in information? If you can answer those questions appropriately, then your product is probably complete.

Look at completeness from several angles. The review process I've just addressed provides a "big picture" of whether your product is complete with respect to all the major points to be covered. But you should conduct a more detailed review of your work to ensure that the individual paragraphs and sentences are complete.

Look for the topic sentence in each paragraph and see if all the other sentences relate to it and complete the thought it introduced. Remember that the topic sentence is the main idea or central assertion of the paragraph; but without substantiating evidence in the form of follow-on sentences to expand upon or clarify the assertion it makes, the paragraph may be incomplete. The reader will be confused if the topic sentence introduces a thought and the remainder of the paragraph fails to carry that thought to completion. It's like starting your car, revving the engine, and then just letting it idle. The engine warms up, but you don't go anywhere.

Carry your search for completeness down to the individual sentence. There is a fine line between completeness and correctness in the student writing examples that follow. They could have been used to illustrate incorrect usages, but I chose to use them here in conjunction with the principle of completeness because they are, in fact, incomplete sentences.

"The 1985 killing of French General Rene Audran on January 25th and the killing of German arms executive Ernst Zimmermann on February 1st by members of Direct Action and the RAF." (That sentence started out going somewhere, but it never got there. It is an incomplete sentence because there's no verb. The most common form of incomplete sentence we notice in student papers is the lengthy one without a verb. One of your most basic tasks in reviewing your paper for completeness should be to double-check each sentence for its subject and verb.)

"If cuts provided a badly needed boost in public confidence in this country and slowly seem to be succeeding." (Watch out for the demon sentence that begins with a word like "if," "because," or "although." It introduces what is called a "dependent clause," meaning that it depends on something else for its existence as a sentence. The "if" clause above needed a "then" clause to follow, such as "then the cuts would have been worthwhile." The easiest fix, though, is simply to omit the "if." Read the example again without the "if," and you'll see that it makes perfect sense.)

"Utilizing the assumption that military deception at the strategic and tactical level has been and may again be an effective and efficient technique in armed conflict, one that repays handsomely the minimal investment of resources it usually requires." (This excerpt from a graduate thesis uses lots of big words, but it goes nowhere. There's no verb for the subject.)

Coherence

"The assessment additionally needs to be based on human perceptions and assessment of the problem. Combining the two above factors, the determination of terrorist responsibility may be expedited. Monitoring of the terrorist problem must be continuous and thorough, as well."

The student who wrote that short paragraph wasn't thinking about coherence. There are at least three major ideas: (1) assessing the terrorism problem; (2) determining the responsibility for terrorism; and (3) keeping track of the problem. It may be easier to keep track of shadowy terrorist groups than the main idea of that paragraph.

Think of coherence as a plan, a blueprint for logical continuity in your paragraphs. *Merriam Webster's Collegiate Dictionary*, 11th edition (2003) defines coherence as a "systematic or logical connection or consistency." Our minds have a natural tendency to think logically, always trying to connect one thing to another and make sense of them in terms of things we've experienced in our lifetime. When we encounter something incoherent, our minds immediately say "Whoa!" and shift into neutral, grinding and crunching what we've encountered, trying to bring it into focus. Failing our ability to understand, the inevitable result is frustration.

Parallelism—The Power of Balance

Parallelism, one important consideration in coherence, refers to the balance of words and the balance of phrases in a sentence. Just as architects construct buildings with an eye toward pleasing and practical symmetry, and just as intelligence analysts strive to give neither more nor less than the appropriate weight to information and sources, so do writers strive for balance between the individual elements in a sentence. Look at the following examples of effective parallel construction:

"It is more blessed to give than to receive." —Acts 20:35

"I write entirely to find out what I'm thinking, what I'm looking at, what I see and what it means." —Joan Didion

"The love of liberty is the love of others; the love of power is the love of ourselves." —William Hazlitt

The sentences above would lose their balance and their impact on the reader if they contained faulty parallelism. Look at the results:

Giving is more blessed than to receive. (The writer has changed grammatical horses in midstream. Falsely balancing a participle, *giving*, with an infinitive, *to receive*, is a common parallelism error.)

I write entirely to find out what I'm thinking, the things I'm looking at, seeing and how to interpret it. (This sentence becomes garbled without the parallel signal of *what*.)

The love of liberty is the love of others; people who love power love only themselves. (Here the emphasis is shifted from the emotion, "the love of liberty," to a vague noun, "people." With the loss of balance comes the loss of Hazlitt's vivid contrast and the impact of his statement.)

When a single grammatical device controls two or more parts of a sentence, these parts are structurally *parallel*. Study the examples of structural patterns below.

Patterns of Parallelism

1. either *x* or *y*: either *on-site investigation* or *research*
2. neither *x* nor *y*: neither *Bulgaria* nor *Albania*
3. not only *x* but also *y*: Congress not only can *initiate legislation* but also can *enact it into law*.
4. it is better to *x* than to *y*: It is better *to have loved and lost* than *never to have loved at all*.
5. this paper examines *x*, *y*, and *z*: This paper examines Poland's *chances for economic recovery*, for *genuine political plurality under a communist government*, and for a *higher degree of military autonomy within the Bloc*. (In this example, repeating the preposition *for* is optional.)

Note that the patterns above include sentences that list items in a series or strive to make comparisons.

Common Errors in Parallelism

1. Like elements: The element that starts off the construction should be matched by the next element.
   a. Match adjectives:
      Wrong: The ambassador was both *experienced* and *the recipient of a good education*. (The first term, *experienced*, is an adjective, and the second term should match it.)
      Right: The ambassador was both *experienced* and *well educated*.
   b. Match gerund phrases:
      Wrong: Stalin enjoyed *playing records* on the gramophone and *to shoot rabbits* by the light of his car headlights. (The *x* element here is a gerund phrase—the "-ing" phrase, "playing records"—so the *y* element needs to match it by being a gerund phrase, too.)

Right: Stalin enjoyed *playing records* on the gramophone and *shooting rabbits* by the light of his car headlights. (You can also correct the sentence by rewriting it with parallel infinitive phrases: Stalin liked *to play records* on the gramophone and *to shoot rabbits* by the light of his car headlights.)

c. Match infinitive phrases:

Wrong: U.S. foreign service officers are required *to have* a broad knowledge of world geography and political systems, *receive* specialized training at the Foreign Service Institute, and *speaking* a foreign language is essential. (The series begins with the infinitive, *to have*. The writer can continue to repeat the *to* in order to make the parallel clear, or can supply parallel verb forms to be governed by the original *to*. In this example the third element departs from the infinitive, *to speak*, and takes the gerund form, *speaking*.)

Right: U.S. foreign service officers are required *to have* a broad knowledge of world geography and political systems, *to receive* specialized training at the Foreign Service Institute, and *to speak* a foreign language.

2. Parallel subordinate clauses as objects of the infinitive: "The public needs to realize *that freedom for me is not enough, that in fact it is nothing at all.*" —Charles Rembar

3. Word order: Make sure words are correctly placed to balance your comparison.

Wrong: Kadar not only dominates Hungary's reaction to Gorbachev but also the country's conservative political agenda. (This one is tricky. Read back through it carefully, focusing on the pattern *not only x but y*. *Not only*, as it is placed here, modifies the verb *dominate*, and we would expect the pattern to continue so that *but also* would modify another verb in the second part of the sentence: "Kadar *not only dominates . . . but also controls. . . .*" Instead, it modifies a noun phrase, *the country's conservative political agenda*. The solution is simple: Move *not only* next to *Hungary's reaction*.)

Right: Kadar dominates *not only* Hungary's reaction to Gorbachev *but also* the country's conservative political agenda.

Wrong: National security not only depends on intelligence gathering but also on correct analysis of the information gathered. (Again, the structure here leads the reader to anticipate that national security not only *depends* but also ——, another verb, when the reader really wants to parallel the thoughts *not only gathering* and *but also analysis*.)

Right: National security depends not only on intelligence gathering but also on correct analysis of the information gathered.

4. Compare apples to apples, and oranges to oranges:

Wrong: The embassy in Washington was better equipped than Moscow. (This sentence compares an embassy to a city; this is certainly *not* the writer's intention.)

Right: The embassy in Washington was better equipped than *the one in* Moscow.

Wrong: A security system for a large embassy is technically different from a private residence. (I should think so! The writer tries to compare one security system to another but ends up comparing a security system to a private residence!)

Right: A security system for a large embassy is technically different from *that for a private residence*.

A Coherent Blueprint for Your Writing

You don't want your readers to be frustrated because you failed to follow a coherent organizational scheme in your writing. That's why the topic sentence is so important to intelligence writing. The topic sentence, usually the first sentence of your paragraph, says to the reader, "Hi, there. Welcome to a new paragraph. I'm the main idea here and I'll be your guide through the next few sentences." Pick your controlling idea—your central assertion for each paragraph—and stick to it. When you change controlling ideas, move to a new paragraph with a smooth transition. In that way, you'll ensure a more coherent product for your reader. Chapters 4 and 5 cover the topic sentence and transitions in more detail.

Using the Basic Tools

Having reviewed the basic tools of writing an intelligence paper, you're now ready to proceed with the writing itself. Don't be overwhelmed with rules and regulations to the extent that you shy away from writing. Just try to remember those six basic principles, and review your papers with them in mind. Keep your writing *clear* and understandable; be *concise*, saying only what you need to say in order to get the point across; watch for *coherence* throughout the process, sticking to an orderly, logical procedure; be sure your writing is *appropriate* for your intended audience, as nearly as you can determine that audience; check the final product to ensure that you've said everything you needed to say about the subject—that your paper is *complete*; and finally, edit and proofread as many times as possible to ensure *correctness*.

If you seem to have particular trouble with one or two of the principles, spend extra time on the most troublesome. It's easy for me to tell you these things, but the proof comes when your professor tells you to write a paper and turn it in at the next class session. You can never anticipate all the variables, but you can be sure that there will be some deadly deadlines you'll have to cope with in your writing.

Keep in mind that there's no magic formula for writing and that the ability to write well is not something you're born with. While some writers seem to have a "natural" ability, most of the authors who have written anything about writing have admitted that it's hard work, and they have to struggle with words even after years of successful writing.

> If people only knew how hard I work to gain my mastery, it wouldn't seem so wonderful at all.
>
> —Michelangelo

What We Write, Others Don't Always Read

I wrote a draft description for a new course offering to be placed in the college catalog. My intention was to write that it was based on "an *existing* course," but instead I typed *exiting* course. The spell-checker read that as a perfectly good word, but my boss caught the typographical error. I had left for a two-week trip; so he corrected it to read the way he thought it should: ". . . based on an *exciting* course."

Some Final Thoughts about the Basics

Four Levels of Knowledge

(1) Know what you know; (2) Know what you don't know; (3) Don't know what you know; and (4) Don't know what you don't know.

To be precise as an intelligence writer, you must know the limits of your information and where gaps in the data lie (that is, know what you know and what you don't know). If you know neither of those essential elements, then don't try to disguise that fact by writing imprecisely.

Exercises in Appropriateness, Completeness, and Coherence

Exercise 1: Parallelism

1. Identifying parallel elements: Underline the balancing or parallel components in the following sentences from A. J. P. Taylor's *The Origins of the Second World War* (1961):
    a. The post-war period ended when Germany reoccupied the Rhineland on 7 March 1936; the pre-war period began when she annexed Austria on 13 March 1936.
    b. On 5 November 1937, a conference called by Hitler was attended by Blomberg, the minister of war, Fritsch,

commander-in-chief of the army, and Raeder, commander-in-chief of the navy.

c. The Western Powers, in Hitler's view, would be too hampered to intervene in German expansionism, and far too timid.

d. The arms race, Neville Chamberlain believed in 1937, sprang from misunderstandings between the Powers, not from deep-seated rivalries or from the sinister design of one Power to dominate the world.

e. In the one case, the German ambassador Papen would discredit his unruly rivals; in the other, he would win prestige by advancing the German cause.

2. Constructing parallel elements: Notice in sentences a and e above that Taylor uses a semicolon to divide neatly the terms of his comparisons. Try writing similarly structured sentences based on the following topics. Be specific, but be brief and balanced.

a. Risks and potential gains of military participation in domestic antiterrorism operations.

b. The attitude of Congress about covert operations, before and after Operation Anaconda in Afghanistan in 2002.

c. OPEC's influence on the world oil market.

d. Security problems in U.S. embassies abroad.

3. Finding parallel elements: Find several sentences from your assigned readings in professional journals or college texts that strike you as "success stories" of balance— sentences that make their points more effectively through the use of skillfully balanced elements. Underline the balanced elements and comment on what makes the sentences work.

4. Practicing your balancing act: Choose three of the following sentences, all of which illustrate effective balance. Use them as models to write two sentences of your own about any intelligence subject that interests you.

a. It is as a soldier that you make love and as a lover that you make war. —Saint-Exupery

   b. In America only the successful writer is important, in
      France all writers are important, in England no writer
      is important, and in Australia you have to explain
      what a writer is. —Geoffrey Cotterell
   c. What's the difference between capitalism and social-
      ism? Under capitalism one man exploits the other; un-
      der socialism, it's the other way around. —Russian
      joke
   d. The superior man understands what is right; the infe-
      rior man understands what will sell. —Confucius
   e. All the world knows me in my book, and my book in
      me. —Montaigne
5. Correcting faulty parallelism: Rewrite the following sentences to correct any faulty parallelism.
   a. In its trade relations with other bloc countries, the So-
      viet Union often preferred to buy now and later pay
      the bills.
   b. COMECON, the Council of Mutual Economic Assis-
      tance, spawned numerous committees, achieved im-
      proved results in machinery specialization, and
      garnering influence as trade volume with underdevel-
      oped countries increased.
   c. U.S. foreign aid to Costa Rica can be used either to
      fund farm programs or for purchasing military hard-
      ware.
   d. For his participation in the hijacking and bombing, the
      terrorist would have faced death by lethal injection or
      the hands of the enraged crowd.
   e. Soviet citizens under Gorbachev believed that their
      lives would be different from their parents.
   f. Construction of large aircraft carriers is technically dif-
      ferent from battleships.
   g. Gromyko's wall map helped to focus the mind, refin-
      ing and reinforcing priorities, provide constancy and
      identifying areas vulnerable to Soviet exploitation.
   h. The intent of this paper is to answer this question,
      summarize the development of the ill-fated Sino-

Soviet alliance, and showing that the divergence was caused by an impatient and nationalistic Mao Zedong.

    i. Peru will find it increasingly difficult to resolve its urban development problems within Lima, while at the same time it seeks to reduce its rural to urban migration and actively combating Sendero.

    j. Yuri Andropov not only liked American jazz but also Scotch whiskey.

    k. Albania's political behavior is uncompromising, with much distrust, combative and characterized by centralization.

6. Striking a balance in your own writing: Using a current paper or draft of your own, find three sentences that you can revise to correct faulty parallelism or to achieve a more effective balance. Submit both the original and revised versions.

Exercise 2: The Basic Tools

The exercises that follow are based on items found in appendix A, "A Usage Glossary for Intelligence Writers." They contain examples of most of the basic tools of writing with intelligence. Some of the sentences need no correction, but most do. See if you can spot the errors and correct them. These exercises encompass most of the basic tools of intelligence writing.

1. The Saudi cut in oil production effected Japan's trade balance.

2. All of the flag officers at the conference supported the proposal.

3. The Israelis have deployed approximately 112 of these new systems.

4. Electronic surveillance data indicate increased rebel activity at the higher altitudes of the western mountains.

5. The Direct Action terrorist organization has posed some very unique problems for French police.

6. At least one congressional liaison officer visits the majority leader's capitol office everyday during the work-week.

7. The historical conference at Yalta had major effects on Europe.

8. Little change in the Chinese policy toward India seems likely in the foreseeable future.

9. Most members of the study group feel that the Oto-Melara weapon system is likely to have fewer maintenance problems than any alternative.

10. In his speech to the Press Club this morning, the president implied serious problems in regards to the modified MX deployment plan.

11. If the Iranians follow past practice, those regiments which are fully equipped will be used in the attack on Basra.

12. The terrain in northern Italy is relatively mountainous.

13. On the other hand, the Catholic sector of the population strongly favors the revised policy.

14. Nuclear power represents over 40 percent of France's electric generating capacity.

15. The planned rates of ammunition usage cannot be supported by one C-130 airdrop daily.

16. Only 17 reservists were granted wavers for reasons of financial necessity.

17. The pending military pay raise, announced verbally by the prime minister this morning, will raise army morale.

18. Landing craft delivered personnel and material to the beach at Inchon.

19. Although the technical manual calls for stowing the test kit with a restraining strap, most senior technicians consider it alright to wedge the kit under the gunner's seat.

20. By their close coverage of the operation, the media were making it difficult for the military to optimize their security arrangements.

21. In such a situation, the best policy is to duck first and ask questions afterwards.

22. All together, 47 bombers were shot down over Feldkirch in May and June.
23. More Grenadans have emigrated into the United States in the last five decades than now live in Grenada.
24. Yesterday's discussion centered on whether NATO should reduce it's reliance on U.S. intelligence.
25. Aircraft in the Iranian inventory include the F-4, the F-14, and the French Mirage 2, the latter being the most used in recent operations.
26. Though Colonel Muhabbi is a forthcoming individual, he is not one who flaunts his power.
27. In constant dollars, Nigerian imports are down 26 percent from last year, while rising oil prices have increased their exports 31 percent in the same period, but only the future will tell if the government's fiscal policy is really correct.
28. Mujaheddin swimmers attempted last night to attach an explosives charge to the hull of a Kuwaiti tanker.
29. The demonetization of pre-1986 currency insures chaos in the Ethiopian economy.
30. The wing headquarters is colocated with the Marine Amphibious Force Liaison Office in a large reinforced-concrete building at the south end of the runway.
31. Because the criteria is very strictly applied, the average recruit scores only 2.30.
32. About 43 YANKEE-class submarines have been equipped with the new sonar array.
33. Quickly adopting to the demands of the advanced training program, over 80 percent of the students scored "Excellent" or better on the first end-of-cycle test.
34. On both days, the admiral's testimony was continuously interrupted by comments from his lawyer.
35. Traffic across one of London's busiest bridges was stopped while the special squad inactivated the bomb.
36. Alienating the Conservative Nationalists was bad enough, but firing Demarais was an even more fatal mistake.

37. Various tribes, like the Wambia and Dodatse, have claimed the eastern part of the plain.
38. The reoccurrence of wheat rust every few years has severe economic effects; more important, it has several times resulted in overthrow of the government.
39. The data make it clear that the Nicaraguan Air Force has at least 23 less fighters than the opposing forces.
40. The 4077th Wing was deactivated last month.
41. Colonel Khaddafy has in recent months seemed reticent to continue his previous program of supporting terrorists.
42. The overall result of our enhanced electronic surveillance system has been better detection and 50 percent fewer false signals.
43. It is necessary to keep the two processes discrete.
44. The islanders grow taro and breadfruit chiefly for domestic consumption, with copra as their primary export crop.
45. Each of the eleven major political parties has their own method of selecting a leader.
46. The negotiators had an implicit understanding not to raise the issue of immigration quotas.
47. Either one Aegis cruiser or two frigates are assigned to each group.
48. San Felipe is 17 kilometers further south on the A24 highway.
49. Though the population is still predominantly Catholic, the country's divorce rate has increased steadily over the past five years.
50. According to General Mazzeno, ". . . the Fifth Division's training program in explosives handling is vastly superior to that of any other division."
51. Comparing the rubble-strewn road with a posied path, the captain urged his men forward.
52. Dumarais, Laval, and Robeau are the principle architects of the new Common Market tariff policy.
53. Germany must get her agricultural program in order before she can increase defense spending.

54. The premier's remarks with regards to a cutback in chocolate import quotas were not well received.
55. In the majority of cases, transits of the disputed territory by UN observers have been without incident.
56. In an effort to break the four-month stalemate, General Langostino has opened secret negotiations with President O'Hara.
57. Unfortunately, the whereabouts of the other three hostages is completely unknown.
58. Japan withdrew its proposal due to the strong objections of Germany and Great Britain.
59. According to Coburn, "the bomber's ECM gear . . . is first-rate" and clearly superior to anything now operational in the Soviet bloc.
60. In the past, though nothing has been said on the matter, the media has kept an implicit agreement not to publish such stories without first calling us about them.

Answers to the Exercises in Chapter 3

Exercise 1: Parallelism

1. Identifying parallel elements: The balancing or parallel components are italicized in the following sentences from A. J. P. Taylor's *The Origins of the Second World War* (1961):
   a. The *post-war period ended when* Germany reoccupied the Rhineland on 7 March 1936; *the pre-war period began when* she annexed Austria on 13 March 1936. (Look at all the parallel elements in this sentence. The main two are the sentence openers, "period ended," "period began," but there are many others: Germany = she, reoccupied = annexed (notice how verb tense stays parallel); direct objects are also parallel: Rhineland = Austria; and the dates are given in the same order, day-month-year.)
   b. On 5 November 1937, a conference called by Hitler *was attended by* Blomberg, the minister of war, Fritsch,

commander-in-chief of the army, and Raeder, commander-in-chief of the navy. (The phrase "was attended by" governs the three objects, Blomberg, Fritsch, and Raeder; notice that their titles are also parallel.)

c. The Western Powers, in Hitler's view, *would be too hampered to intervene* in German expansionism, and *far too timid*. (Here the adjectives "hampered" and timid" are parallel. "To intervene" is understood after "far too timid.")

d. The arms race, Neville Chamberlain believed in 1937, sprang *from misunderstandings* between the Powers, *not from deep-seated rivalries or from the sinister design* of one Power to dominate the world. (The modifying clause beginning with *from* governs the sentence; its skeleton is *"from x, not from y or from z."*)

e. In *the one case, the German ambassador Papen would discredit* his unruly rivals; *in the other, he would win* prestige by advancing the German cause. (Note the parallel elements: *In the one case* is paralleled by *in the other* (*case* is understood); *the German ambassador Papen = he; would discredit = would win.*)

2, 3, and 4. Student responses will vary. A faculty member can review your work if you wish.

5. Correcting faulty parallelism: The following are possible corrections to the faulty parallelism. The parallel elements are italicized.

a. In its trade relations with other bloc countries, the Soviet Union often preferred *to buy now and pay later.*

b. COMECON, the Council of Mutual Economic Assistance, *spawned* numerous committees, *achieved* improved results in machinery specialization, and *garnered* influence as trade volume with underdeveloped countries increased.

c. U.S. foreign aid to Costa Rica can be used *either to fund* farm programs *or to purchase* military hardware.

d. For his participation in the hijacking and bombing, the terrorist would have faced *death by lethal injection or death at the hands* of the enraged crowd.

e. Soviet citizens under Gorbachev believed that *their lives* would be different from *the lives of* their parents.

f. Construction of large aircraft carriers is technically different from *that of* battleships.

g. Gromyko's wall map helped *to focus* the mind, *to refine and reinforce* priorities, *to provide* constancy, and *to identify* areas vulnerable to Soviet exploitation.

h. The intent of this paper is *to answer* this question, *summarize* the development of the ill-fated Sino-Soviet alliance, and *show* that the divergence was caused by an impatient and nationalistic Mao Zedong.

i. Peru will find it increasingly difficult to resolve its urban development problems within Lima, while at the same time *seeking* to reduce its rural to urban migration and actively combating Sendero.

j. Yuri Andropov *not only liked* American jazz *but also enjoyed* Scotch whiskey. (The sentence might be rewritten: Yuri Andropov *liked not only* American jazz *but also* Scotch whiskey.)

k. Albania's political behavior is *uncompromising*, with much *distrust, combativeness,* and *centralization.* (Or, Albania's political behavior is *uncompromising, distrustful, combative,* and *centralized.*)

6. Student responses will vary.

Exercise 2: The Basic Tools

Brackets [ ] are used in the answers below to show words to be removed. Words substituted or added to the answer are shown in *italics*.

1. The Saudi cut in oil production *affected* [not effected] Japan's trade balance.

2. All [of] the flag officers at the conference supported the proposal. (The "of" is unnecessary. You may also say "All flag officers. . . .")
3. The Israelis have deployed [approximately] 112 of these new systems. (There's nothing "approximate" about 112.)
4. Electronic surveillance data indicate increased rebel activity at the higher [altitudes] *elevations* of the western mountains. (Yes, "data indicate" *is* correct. Remember that "altitude" describes something in the air.)
5. The Direct Action terrorist organization has posed some [very] unique problems for French police. ("Unique" is unique. Don't add more qualifiers to it.)
6. At least one congressional liaison officer visits the majority leader's capitol office [everyday] *every day* during the workweek. (The adjective "everyday" means ordinary or usual. It's not interchangeable with the two words "every day," meaning daily.)
7. The historical conference at Yalta had major effects on Europe. (Nothing is wrong with this one; "effects" is the word we want.)
8. Little change in the Chinese policy toward India seems likely in the [foreseeable future] *next ten years*. ("In the foreseeable future" is one of those imprecise phrases a good intelligence writer tries to avoid. Be more specific if you possibly can. Also, pay close attention to the spelling of "foreseeable.")
9. Most members of the study group [feel] *think* that the Oto-Melara weapon system is likely to have fewer maintenance problems than any alternative. (It would be better if the study group restrained their emotions and *think* or *conclude* rather than "feel.")
10. In his speech to the Press Club this morning, the president implied serious problems [in regards to] *with* the modified MX deployment plan. (Avoid the cumbersome "in regards to." Use "with" or "in.")
11. If the Iranians follow past practice, those regiments [which] *that* are fully equipped will be used in the attack on Basra. ("That" is preferable to "which" in this case,

but it would be even better to say simply, "the fully equipped regiments.")

12. The terrain in northern Italy is [relatively] mountainous. (Relative to what? Vague language.)

13. On the other hand, the Catholic [sector] *portion* of the population strongly favors the revised policy.

14. Nuclear power [represents] *provides* over 40 percent of France's electric generating capacity.

15. The planned rates of ammunition [usage] *use* cannot be supported by one C-130 airdrop daily. (If we expend or employ ammunition, we are talking about *use*; if we consider which is the correct word in the sentence, our subject is *usage*.)

16. Only 17 reservists were granted [wavers] *waivers* for reasons of financial necessity. (Perhaps the reservists' eagerness was wavering, but they wanted *waivers*.)

17. The pending military pay raise, announced [verbally] *orally* by the prime minister this morning, will raise army morale. (Unless the prime minister used sign language, the more correct word is *orally*. Omitting "verbally" or "orally" is okay, too.)

18. Landing craft delivered personnel and [material] *materiel* to the beach at Inchon. (Assuming a military operation is being described, the correct word is *materiel*.)

19. Although the technical manual calls for stowing the test kit with a restraining strap, most senior technicians consider it [alright] *all right* to wedge the kit under the gunner's seat. (Perhaps it is *all right* to stow the test kit that way, but "alright" is not a word.)

20. By their close coverage of the operation, the media were making it difficult for the military to [optimize] *maintain* their security [arrangements]. ("Optimize" is one of those words usually best avoided. "Arrangements" is not incorrect, just excess baggage. "Media were" is correct.)

21. In such a situation, the best policy is to duck first and ask questions *afterward*[s]. (A good grammarian will ask questions *afterward*.)

22. [All together] *Altogether*, 47 bombers were shot down over Feldkirch in May and June. (Since they were shot down in May and June, the 47 bombers did not go down *all together*—at the same time; the word we want is *altogether*—in sum.)
23. More Grenadans have [emigrated] *immigrated* into the United States in the last five decades than now live in Grenada. (They would have *emigrated from* Grenada but *immigrated into* the United States.)
24. Yesterday's discussion centered on whether NATO should reduce [it's] *its* reliance on U.S. intelligence. (Remember that "it's" *always* means "it is" or "it has." In this sentence we want the possessive form, "its.")
25 Aircraft in the Iranian inventory include the F-4, the F-14, and the French Mirage 2, the [latter] *last* being the most used in recent operations. ("Latter" applies only to the second of two items.)
26. Though Colonel Muhabbi is [a forthcoming] *an outgoing* individual, he is not one who flaunts his power. (Unless he became a colonel in the womb, he is better described as "outgoing" than "forthcoming.")
27. In constant dollars, Nigerian imports are down 26 percent from last year, while rising oil prices have increased [their?] exports 31 percent in the same period, but [only the future will tell?] if the government's fiscal policy is really correct. (This sentence has two problems, shown by the bracketed question marks above: [1] the pronoun "their" has no suitable antecedent; and [2] "only the future will tell" is one of those fuzzy phrases a careful intelligence analyst will avoid. Give yourself a pat on the back if you got them both. A possible rewording of the sentence: In constant dollars, Nigerian imports are down 26 percent from last year, while rising oil prices have increased *the country's* exports 31 percent in the same period, but *the government's fiscal policy remains untested.*)
28. Mujaheddin swimmers attempted last night to attach an *explosive*[s] charge to the hull of a Kuwaiti tanker.

29. The demonetization of pre-1986 currency [insures] *ensures* chaos in the Ethiopian economy. ("Insures" applies to Prudential, Geico, and the like. "Demonetization" is not my favorite word, but it fits this sentence perfectly.)
30. The wing headquarters is [colocated] *collocated* with the Marine Amphibious Force Liaison Office in a large reinforced-concrete building at the south end of the runway. (Correct spelling is the problem here.)
31. Because the criteria [is] *are* very strictly applied, the average recruit scores only 2.30. (The correct verb for the plural "criteria" must be "are." The singular form is "criterion.")
32. [About 43] *Forty-three* YANKEE-class submarines have been equipped with the new sonar array. (You might say "about 40," but 43 is a precise number. Also, spell out numbers, as we have done, when they fall at the beginning of a sentence.)
33. Quickly [adopting] *adapting* to the demands of the advanced training program, over 80 percent of the students scored "Excellent" or better on the first end-of-cycle test. ("Adopt" plans, or policies, or children if you wish, but "adapt to" a situation.)
34. On both days, the admiral's testimony was [continuously] *continually* interrupted by comments from his lawyer. (If the original sentence were true, the admiral would not have spoken a word. Probably the lawyer interrupted *continually*—over and over again.)
35. Traffic across one of London's busiest bridges was stopped while the special squad [inactivated] *deactivated* the bomb. (See the glossary entry at "deactivate/inactivate.")
36. Alienating the Conservative Nationalists was bad enough, but firing Demarais was *a*[n even more] *fatal* mistake. (Either something is fatal or it isn't. It's inappropriate to write of something as more fatal than something else.)
37. Various tribes, [like] *such as* the Wambia and Dodatse, have claimed the eastern part of the plain. (The original

sentence permits the persnickety reader to assume that the tribes in question *resembled* the Wambia and Dodatse but did not *include* them. The more precise term here is "such as.")

38. The [reoccurrence] *recurrence* of wheat rust every few years has severe economic effects; more important, it has several times resulted in overthrow of the government. ("Reoccurrence" means only a second occurrence. The wheat rust obviously is "recurring.")

39. The data make it clear that the Nicaraguan Air Force has at least 23 [less] *fewer* fighters than the opposing forces. (Since we count the fighters one by one, the word should be "fewer." See the glossary entry at "fewer/less.")

40. The 4077th Wing was [deactivated] *inactivated* last month.

41. Colonel Khaddafy has in recent months seemed [reticent] *reluctant* to continue his previous program of supporting terrorists. (Khaddafy may indeed have become reticent—quiet or restrained—but the appropriate word here is "reluctant.")

42. The [overall] result of our enhanced electronic surveillance system has been better detection and 50 percent fewer false signals. (Does the word "overall" really serve any purpose?)

43. It is necessary to keep the two processes discrete. (The word "discrete," meaning separate and distinct, is correctly used. It is necessary, however, to rewrite this sentence to eliminate the wordy phrase "it is necessary." For example: The two processes must be kept discrete.)

44. The islanders grow taro and breadfruit chiefly for domestic consumption [,]; [with] copra [as] *is* their primary export crop. (The use of "with" in this sentence is vague and wordy.)

45. Each of the eleven major political parties has [their] *its* own method of selecting a leader. (Remember that "each" is singular and requires a singular verb and pronoun reference.)

46. The negotiators had an implicit understanding not to raise the issue of immigration quotas. (There's not a thing wrong with this sentence.)
47. Either one Aegis cruiser or two frigates are assigned to each group. (This one, too, is correct. *If,* however, the sentence read, "Either two frigates or one Aegis cruiser . . . ," then the verb would be "is," taking the number of the nearer noun.)
48. San Felipe is 17 kilometers [further] *farther* south on the A24 highway.
49. Though the population is still predominantly Catholic, the country's divorce rate has increased steadily over the past five years. (This one is another correct sentence.)
50. According to General Mazzeno, "[. . .] the Fifth Division's training program in explosives handling is vastly superior to that of any other division." (The ellipsis [. . .] should not be used at the beginning or end of a quotation. It is correctly used *within* a quotation to show that one or more words have been omitted.)
51. Comparing the rubble-strewn road [with] *to* a posied path, the captain urged his men forward. (Unless a posied path is right in front of the captain so that he can examine it closely, he should be comparing the road *to* the path.)
52. Dumarais, Laval, and Robeau are the [principle] *principal* architects of the new Common Market tariff policy. (Remember that "principle" is always a noun, not an adjective.)
53. Germany must get [her] *its* agricultural program in order before [she] *it* can increase defense spending. (The preferred style in modern intelligence writing is to speak of a country as an "it" rather than a "her.")
54. The premier's remarks [with regards to] *about* a cutback in chocolate import quotas were not well received. ("With regards to" is flab.)
55. [In the majority of cases] *Usually,* transits of the disputed territory by UN observers have been without incident. (Same meaning, fewer words.)

56. In an effort to break the four-month [stalemate] *impasse,* General Langostino has opened secret negotiations with President O'Hara. (If the general can resolve the situation, it is not really a stalemate but rather a deadlock or impasse.)

57. Unfortunately, *we are not aware of* the whereabouts of the other three hostages [is completely unknown]. (Presumably the hostages' captors know where the missing three are, so "completely unknown" is not accurate.)

58. Japan withdrew its proposal [due to] *because of* the strong objections of Germany and Great Britain. (Unless the proposal was formulated in reaction to the strong *objections* of the other two countries, "due to" is a phrase to avoid here; "because of" is better.)

59. According to Coburn, "the bomber's ECM gear . . . is first-rate" and clearly superior to anything now operational in the Soviet bloc. (The ellipsis is used correctly here. Presumably Coburn said something like "There is no question that the bomber's ECM gear, developed by Widgetron and manufactured by Boeing, is first-rate, especially for the price." However, note the term "Soviet bloc," which is best avoided.)

60. In the past, though nothing has been said on the matter, the media [has] *have* kept an implicit agreement not to publish such stories without first calling us about them. (Remember that "media" is plural. A newspaper or television is a medium; the media are more than one source.)

4

Prewriting:
Getting Ready to Write

Summary

Prewriting is a distinct phase of the writing process. It is the time and place where you identify precisely the topic you'll be writing about. Then devote time to narrowing and focusing that topic. While you are prewriting, avoid the temptation to move into either the writing or revision phases.

- Getting organized is an early step in prewriting. Zero in on your subject; focus on the external form and the internal format your product will take; organize your time and space requirements in advance, using a milestones list and considering your readers; gather the necessary reference materials such as a good dictionary, a thesaurus, and a sample format of your product; search for relevant materials, then research thoroughly.
- Before you start writing the first draft, use one or more of the prewriting tools: *freewrite*, letting the words flow as quickly as you can write them for 10 minutes without stopping, then stop; *write an outline* of your paper, using either words and phrases (topic outline) or complete sentences (topic sentence outline); *use a balloon map* to tap into your "creative right brain" and get more ideas on paper;

and *try an idea tree* to organize the writing, point where more information is needed, and reveal organizational problems.

Every minute you spend prewriting will earn a dividend of *at least* one minute in the writing and revision stages. It is always time well spent.

Finding Your Subject

In the early stages of writing, it's important to identify clearly the subject, topic, or theme you'll be writing about. That sounds like it should go without saying; but you'd be surprised at the number of students and intelligence analysts who are assigned a vague, general task and who charge off to their computer keyboards without the foggiest notion of where they're going. The important idea here is to do it *early* and to be certain that it's *clear* to you, your fellow students, your co-workers or subordinates who may be helping you, and even your supervisors.

> Writing is no trouble; you just jot down ideas as they occur to you. The jotting is simplicity itself—It is the occurring which is difficult.
>
> —Stephen Leacock

In college your writing assignments come from your professors. Many (most?) writing tasks for others in the intelligence community come down through the chain of command. Often they are generated by a casual remark in a briefing or meeting. "The general" finds something of interest and muses. "I wonder what would happen if...." Next thing you know, there's a tasker on your desk telling you to write a five-page fact sheet for the general on the subject. There's no easy way around this problem, but there are some techniques for clarifying the problem. The best one is probably prewriting.

Focusing on Form and Format

Once you've managed to clarify your task, or at least to redefine the problem in manageable terms, you must identify the form of the product you'll be writing. Nail down its external shape precisely. Is it to be a thesis? A research paper? A fact sheet? An estimate? A current intelligence product? Don't allow yourself to fall into the trap of being tasked to write "a paper." Find out early exactly what kind of paper is wanted. If you have latitude for creativity in the selection of the product's form, congratulations. It is rare indeed that kind of leeway is allowed the poor student or analyst.

Generally speaking, there are three broad types of products in the intelligence community: scheduled, initiative, and ad hoc. The scheduled products are the ones programmed months, even years, in advance for publication on a regular recurring or non-recurring basis. Consumers of intelligence products can consult catalogs to get an idea when certain products will be published. Initiative products are the dream children. The lucky student or intelligence analyst who has the chance to sit back and think about something that really needs to be written is the exception in our business. But it does happen, and products are generated through initiative. By far the most prevalent product type in the intelligence business is the ad hoc one. The phone rings and your friend over in the other command or agency needs some information for an important briefing the next day; the resulting research takes you two hours. In the middle of that project, the boss lays a "hot one" on your desk—a paper for the deputy director, who needs an answer by yesterday. And so goes the analyst's day.

Once you've determined the type of product you'll be doing and you've pinned down its form, the format should come a bit easier. Whereas the form was the *external* shape of the paper, the format is its *internal* content. Administrative personnel can be extremely helpful in guiding you through the myriad formats in the intelligence community, or in the office procedures of your command or agency. Ask the secretaries, the administrative

people, or the intelligence technicians to lend you a hand in determining the exact format of a fact sheet, background paper, or
whatever you're tasked to produce. Many organizations now
post their report formats online.

Where answers are not readily available, consult with your
professor. In the long run, it makes everyone's work easier if you
submit your draft in the correct format.

Finding the Time and Space

One of the most difficult tasks faced by students and intelligence
analysts every day is finding the *time* to do everything they want
to do. But when you have a writing assignment—whether it's as
an analyst or a student—you must find the time to do it.

In this stage, while you're still getting organized to do the actual writing, you need to sit down and work out a *plan* for your
writing. Again, prewriting will help here; but the important
early problem is to identify milestones in your writing requirement. Start with the due date and work backward.

Take the example of a paper due next Monday to the general.
It's now Tuesday morning. Including today, you have four
weekdays to finish the project. You know that you have to allow
time for the administrative preparation. Calculate early how
much time it will take you to prepare the paper in the proper format. Then rest assured that each person in the chain of command
between you and the general will want to see the product before
it goes to him. Build that time into your schedule. *Write down
your expected milestones!* Then try to stick to them as closely as
possible. Recognize that when one milestone slips, all the others
will, too, *except one*—the general. Your handwritten milestones
list might look something like this:

Drop-Dead Dates for Fact Sheet to General Payne:
    Monday noon—Paper on Payne's desk
    Close of business Friday—Final Division/Office approval
    Noon Friday—Final draft finished
    Friday a.m.—Polish final draft
    Thursday p.m.—Rewrite

Thursday a.m.—Draft to division/office chief
Wednesday p.m.—Rewrite
Wednesday a.m.—Draft to branch chief
Tuesday—Write fact sheet

If you're more comfortable reading from top to bottom, you can always reverse your list; but construct it working backward from the due date. The process works exactly the same way in planning for a term paper or a master's thesis.

Your consideration of time should include not only what is available to *you* but also your anticipated *reader's* available time. In general, the higher the rank, the shorter the paper should be. Most commands and agencies have specific formats for succinct products like fact sheets, background papers, and talking papers. Know ahead of time what will be expected of you in the staffing process. It's usually not enough just to write a one-page fact sheet, even if it is clear, concise, coherent, appropriate, complete, and correct. Often you'll be required to accompany the fact sheet with a staff summary sheet or some other explanatory paperwork that tells all the intermediate supervisors what you're doing and why you're doing it, then asks for their coordination or signature. All these "extras" take *time*. Allow for them when planning your milestones.

The *space* available to you is another reader consideration. Higher-ranking readers want concise papers without all the detail you might include for a colleague or peer. The product's form and format generally predetermine the number of pages. Consult your format guides. The best bet is to have a "successful example" of your product to use as a guideline. Nothing succeeds like success, and if you can find a paper that has already run the gauntlet and acquired all the necessary signatures, then you're ahead of the game.

Finding the Right Reference Materials

During your preparation and organization for writing, you'll want to be sure that you have all the appropriate reference materials. I'm not talking about substantive, database-type materials here. At this point I'm referring to the essential references every student—every writer—needs to have at hand: a dictionary and a thesaurus. There are many others, but those two are the most basic and necessary to the writer.

In these days of sophisticated computer software, you'll find dictionaries and thesauruses (or thesauri, if you prefer) readily available online. Learn to use these tools if they are built into your software. They are fast, convenient, and valuable resources. But don't use them until you reach the *revision* phase of your writing.

Many people think of the dictionary only in terms of looking up a word they can't spell. (And you've probably heard someone say, "How can I look it up if I can't spell it?") But the dictionary is much more than a simple speller. It gives precise definitions and points out proper usage for words and terms—especially important when usage in the language is changing; it gives a word's part(s) of speech, etymology (where it came from), syllabication, pronunciation, plural(s), and alternate forms (if any). Many good dictionaries also have special sections on the English language and on usage, style, punctuation, grammar, biographies, and geographical entries. It's well worth your time just to thumb through the front pages of your dictionary and get acquainted with all it has to offer. You might also thumb to the *rear* of the dictionary because many have extra added attractions there. A dictionary is not for everyone; it's just for those who use the English language in written or oral form.

A second basic reference is the thesaurus—a book of synonyms. The most familiar name in thesauruses is "Roget," but there are other excellent ones as well. Use your thesaurus to help you find exactly the right word for a given sentence, especially when you're "stumped," or when the word is "right on the tip of your tongue." The thesaurus will help you find that word—or a better one. Whatever you do, avoid using the thesaurus just to look up bigger words. Usually the simpler of two words will be the preferred one. Remember, too, that most modern software programs have built-in synonym finders.

If you are a country analyst, a regional desk officer, or the like, you'll want to have immediate access in your office to a world atlas, a gazetteer, and perhaps an almanac. For those who do a *lot* of writing, it's helpful to have a style manual handy. Federal workers need to use the *U.S. Government Printing Office Style Manual*, often referred to as the *"GPO Style Manual."* It's an excellent reference, with especially good sections on abbreviations, capitalization, compounding, and punctuation—areas that seem to be particularly troublesome to students. That style manual is also available online. At this writing, the URL address is www.gpoaccess.gov/stylemanual/index.html.

Some Prewriting Tools: Building a Foundation

Earlier I told you about equipping yourself with the "tools of the trade" for writing, like a skilled carpenter with his toolbox. That carpenter may be a master tradesman, but you'll never see him build a house without a foundation being laid first. Trying to write without first laying your own foundation or framework—that is, without prewriting—is the same principle. Words are the tools of the writer's trade, and they must be laid out thoughtfully, precisely, and with great consideration for the reader, if the writer is to be successful.

Everything you do before you actually begin to write the first draft might be considered prewriting. But in this case I will address some of the prewriting tools you can use to help you break writer's block and get some words on paper. Among those tools are freewriting, outlines, balloon maps, and idea trees. One of these tools, or a combination of them, may be of more value to you. The important thing is to practice using them and find out for yourself which one is better suited to your writing style.

Freewriting

A student made my day once. I had been working with him for weeks, trying to break the writer's block that had been choking off his writing. I was beginning to share his frustration as I ran out of ideas. I even asked—perhaps only with mock sarcasm—whether he had tried exorcism, acupuncture, and hypnosis. Finally, though, he broke the chains. He attributed his break to a single page in a book I had loaned him.[1] As we talked we both realized that the war of words was still being waged but that at least one huge battle had been won. Finally, we acknowledged that there was still work to do, and we agreed to continue looking into the root causes of the writer's block.

It occurred to me after my discussion with that student that it might be worthwhile to share some of the techniques for breaking writer's block. In fact, that tends to be a real problem for me, and I often break my own writer's block by putting into practice some of the principles I preach every day. I used one of those techniques—"freewriting"—when I wrote the first draft of this section as an article in 1991. The idea behind freewriting is to keep the pen, pencil, or computer keyboard moving, without stopping, for at least 10 minutes. Often that process serves as a mental aerobic exercise, warming up the writing hand or the keyboard and serving to stimulate the creativity that's locked behind the logjam of other words in the mind.

Freewriting is a concept made popular by Peter Elbow.[2] It is designed to "free" the words that may be hung up inside your head. "The goal of freewriting," according to Elbow, "is in the process, not the product."[3] Think of starting the writing process in the same terms as you might think about starting a car on a cold morning. You don't just jump in, start the engine, and speed off. You need a little time to let the engine warm up. That's what freewriting does for you: It starts your creative engines and allows you to warm up your brain and your writing apparatus— the writing hand or the keyboard.

Freewriting is simply writing anything and everything that comes to mind for 10 minutes, without stopping. If you have a subject area in mind, write whatever may flood through your mind about that subject in those 10 minutes. If you're drawing a total blank and can think of *nothing* to write, then write that: "I can't think of a thing to write!" Remember, you're not looking for a finished product here; you're only doing mental aerobics to get the writing process started.

Having gone through the exercise, what do you do at the end of the 10 minutes? Peter Elbow says, "Don't read over your freewriting unless you can do so in a spirit of benign self-welcoming."[4] In other words, if you're not happy with what you've written, at the end of 10 minutes wad it up and throw it in the trash. The idea here is not to be critical of what you have written. But you may wish to read back over your freewriting and see if perhaps some useable idea crept in during those few minutes.

The first two paragraphs in this section on freewriting took me exactly 10 minutes to write in the original draft. I wrote them with only one interruption. What you're reading, though, is not the original version of those two paragraphs. One important aspect of freewriting is that you must not worry about revision, proofreading, spelling, grammar, or any other mechanical stumbling blocks that may lie in your path. The process is as follows: begin writing; write freely *but continuously* for 10 minutes; and stop. You can always go back, spell-check, or edit to your heart's content. But don't let yourself be distracted by those worries during the initial stages of freewriting.

For example, earlier, when I mentioned the book that helped my student, the scholar-researcher in me grabbed my arm and said, "Stop! Document that reference!" But my freewriting free spirit slapped me in the back of the head to regain my attention and reprimanded me: "Never mind that for now. Keep writing!" I at least acknowledged the scholar-researcher's admonition by inserting a simple parenthetic "(footnote)" in the text. That took maybe three seconds, including the fistfight between scholar and free spirit, but it reminded me to clean up my act during revision.

I wrote the original article that now constitutes this section on freewriting, start to finish, in just over half an hour. Notice, however, that I said I *wrote* it in that amount of time. By the time you read these words, they will bear only a passing resemblance to the original ones that poured out in my earlier freewriting. My scholar-researcher will have gone back and done his thing, ensuring proper documentation; my editor will spill his or her ink all over a printed version, whipping it into shape for your consumption; and my wife will have had a shot at it, as well.

What's the bottom line? There is no magic solution to getting started with your writing. If, like the student in the first paragraph of this section, you find yourself hopelessly mired and without a word to commit to paper, try freewriting.

Again, keep in mind that your goal is to write nonstop, unconcerned with details of grammar and spelling. If you find that hard to do, turn off your monitor, or cover the computer screen with something. If you're writing longhand, cover the writing with a blank piece of paper as you proceed. That simple mechanical process will physically prevent your going back and rereading and revising during this important warming-up phase.

Outlining

Everyone writes differently. Freewriting may be of little help to you. If that's the case, then maybe some organizational tool will help translate your thoughts into words and get you started. Try outlining if you tend to think in a logical, well-organized, but *linear* fashion. Mind mapping—also called clustering or balloon mapping—can help you think *spatially*, envisioning many other aspects of a problem and focusing your topic to a manageable one. I'll talk about mind mapping after this discussion of the outline.

I frequently encounter opposition from students on the idea of an outline. Those who seemed to oppose it the most were those who had been experts in their field and felt that an outline was superfluous; they could simply construct the paper in their minds. I can't deny that this type of expertise exists, and after a number of repetitive writing assignments in the same area, one might well be able to *dictate* a paper to a stenographer. After all, how many fact sheets can you write in three months on the capabilities of the Fizzle fighter?

For the most part, though, I recommend that you start any project with an outline. It helps you organize your thoughts and maintain your focus on the topic at hand. Sometimes the more you know about a subject, the more you need the outline to assist you in narrowing your focus. Otherwise, you'll find your writing frequently going off on a tangent.

An outline can also help to serve you and your superiors as a management tool. For example, if you've been tasked to write "an estimate on the future of the Fizzle fighter," you may find that you need to narrow that topic down after you start working on it. Outline the paper and proceed with a more narrowly focused perspective. After you review your first draft outline, you may discover that you've redefined the problem to read, "An Estimate of Fizzle Fighter Production in the Second Decade of the 21st Century."

Looking at your redefinition, you decide that's a problem you can handle. But what about the person who tasked you to write the paper in the first place? Will he or she be satisfied with the way the paper is going? Now is the time to find out—*before* you've wasted a lot of time writing a vague, undefined paper that no one wanted in the first place. Take your outline, clean it up a little, and pass it along with a note to the assigning authority. It's always better, of course, if you can discuss the matter face-to-face, to avoid any possible misinterpretation as it moves along command lines.

There are two basic types of outline: the *topic* outline and the *topic sentence* outline. The type you use is entirely up to you. Usually, you will be the only one who sees the outline, unless you choose to use it as a management tool. The topic outline uses only words and phrases for its major headers, like this:

Estimate of Fizzle Fighter Production, 2010–2020
I. Current Production Estimates
  A. Assembly plant at Cutchernosoff
  B. Parts and shipping capability
  C. Assembly technology and available skills
II. Projected Production Capability by 2020
  A. Prospect of additional assembly plants
  B. Increased parts supply
  C. Improved shipping
  D. Better technology and improving skills

Do you need to use the Roman numerals, the capital letters, etc.? No, you don't. Use what is comfortable to you, even if it amounts to asterisks, hyphens, bullets, and dashes. Just keep in mind these two principles about your outline: (1) Entries at the same level should be accorded equal treatment in your paper; that is, the Roman I should equal the Roman II, and the A's, B's and C's should be of comparable importance; and (2) be consistent throughout, using the same system from start to finish. You'll avoid confusing yourself that way.

The topic sentence outline, on the other hand, is one step more advanced. It is probably the best type of outline for use by an experienced analyst in the subject because the act of "fleshing out" the skeletal topic sentences will complete the paper. Each sentence in this outline should be a heavyweight idea that will be the basis for a paragraph or even a section within the final product. Compare the topic sentence outline below with the earlier topic outline.

An Estimate of Fizzle Fighter Production, 2010–2020
I. We estimate current Fizzle production rate is 200/year.
  A. Only one assembly plant, at Cutchernosoff, is operating.
  B. Capability to manufacture and ship parts is excellent and improving.
  C. Assembly technology is well developed, and necessary skills are available for sustaining production rate.
II. By the year 2020, we estimate production will be in excess of 400 units per year.
  A. Additional assembly plants are under construction at Glasnost and Gudenov.
  B. Parts supply is already improving after recent aid agreement signed with Panaragua.
  C. Shipping is expected to improve when the new rail lines open in 2010.
  D. Technology and available skills are improving as a result of technology transfer and improved training.

The difference between the two outlines is obvious, and I won't belabor that point here. Notice, though, the commonality of form between the two: the same numbering system, the same relative positions of the points made, and the title at the top of each outline. I strongly recommend that you use the technique of writing your subject at the top of the page when you outline. It will be another means of keeping your attention riveted on the relevant topic.

If you use a computer in preparing your papers, you might want to look into some of the excellent software programs for outlining. They take a lot of the tedium out of the process, save a bundle of pencil erasers, and are smart enough to know when and where you insert something so that they can change everything after the insertion to conform. If you like composing your paper at a keyboard instead of wielding a pen or pencil, then the computer outlining programs may be of great benefit to you.

Mapping

I wrote earlier that outlining will be comfortable to you if you tend to think in a logical, well-organized, but *linear* fashion. Mapping—also called mind mapping, clustering, or balloon mapping—helps you think *spatially*. It taps the right side of your brain to free some of those locked-up ideas, allowing you to envision other aspects of a problem that may not occur to you if you follow the rigid structure of the left-brained (logical) outline. The mind map also helps you focus your topic and make it more manageable.

I have read numerous student papers. The single most troublesome problem that I see is a lack of focus. Granted, there may be some difficulty in the student understanding the writing assignment; but the most common reason for the shotgun approach is a lack of attention to prewriting. The writer has bypassed that important phase of the writing process and has gone straight to the drafting stage. When it comes to focus, few prewriting tools can match the mind map for its ability to help you trade that shotgun for a rifle.

So how can you tell when focus is lacking? Let's look at an example: In one week I read more than 30 student papers that compared and contrasted strategic and tactical intelligence analysis. Some students tried to cover three or four components of strategic intelligence in 750 words or less. Ask yourself, Is that really possible? If you give some thought to that question, your answer should be an emphatic, "No way!"

Then where do you go from here? You have your topic: compare and contrast strategic and tactical intelligence analysis. Now you need to narrow that topic to something that can be handled in 750 words. The components of intelligence might provide you a good starting point; but notice that I said *starting point*. Even if you choose to focus on the components, you must narrow that focus down to no more than one component. For the sake of this discussion, let's say that you choose geographic intelligence as your theme. Now you have at least confined the scope to one of eight components of intelligence.

You still should recognize, though, that you cannot adequately discuss in 750 words geographic intelligence as a consideration in tactical and strategic intelligence analysis. The topic must be further defined, and some issue must be derived from the topic to lend focus to the paper. At this point, however, you are ready to begin mapping. Using "geographic intelligence" as the focal point, draw the first balloon and begin thinking on paper. (Refer to figure 4.1 as I discuss this point.)

You know that geographic intelligence, in broad terms, has two major "subcomponents": physical geography and human or cultural geography. Put each of those in its own circle. Then consider whether you can address either of those subcomponents adequately in a short paper. (You will not have the space to discuss both.) Let's say that you are more comfortable with physical geography, having studied more about that in your undergraduate years. From that circle, then, you draw two more circles that zero in on the subject of this paper: "strategic" and "tactical," representing the two major elements of the assigned topic.

Now you must begin to be as specific as possible, to avoid having your writing labeled "generic." At this point in your prewriting, ask yourself a question like this one: "What specific examples can I use to make my points clear to the reader?" Your mind whirls with possibilities. Since you are writing about

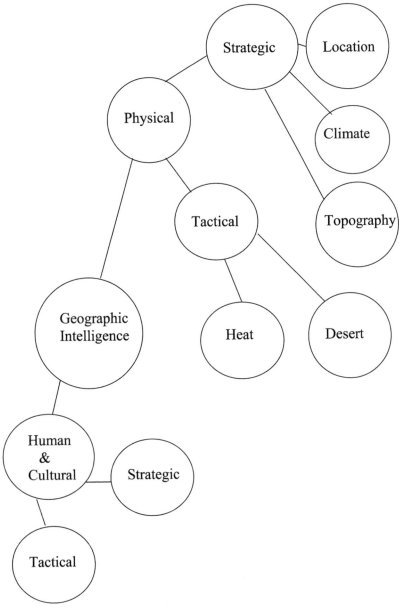

Figure 4.1.   Balloon map

geographic intelligence, you have (pardon the expression) a *world* of possibilities out there. But perhaps one area comes more readily to mind because of your own experience. Because this short paper does not require outside research, your personal observations will help to focus the topic.

Let's assume that your experience came in Operation Desert Storm. Returning to your balloon map you note again the two subtopics where you have focused your attention: strategic and tactical intelligence. Now continue to ask yourself questions about each "balloon" in turn, aimed at narrowing your topic and adding focus to your discussion: "What can I say about physical geography in Operation Desert Storm that might relate to strategic intelligence?" Jot those ideas down, one per circle, as they come to you.

In figure 4.1 you see that I listed only three aspects: regional location (of Kuwait), topography (of the theater of operations), and climate. Certainly there are many more; but as you will see, I might need to narrow these topics even further to confine myself to 750 words.

After listing your ideas for the impact of physical geography on strategic intelligence, you move on to the next major balloon, tactical intelligence. Ask the same question about this topic: "What can I say about physical geography in Operation Desert Storm that might relate to tactical intelligence?" I have listed only two ideas, simply to confine the subject to manageable proportions: desert terrain and heat.

Looking again at the balloon map in figure 4.1, you can get a good idea where this paper is going. It may still be too soon, though, to begin the drafting process. First, do some math to determine whether you have too much—or too little—to cover. Recognizing that your paper is to be no more than 750 words, you can estimate that it will be about three pages (using a planning factor of 250 words per page). Figure two or three paragraphs per page, each with four to six sentences. (You may have a few subheadings, too, but don't worry about them for now.) Your paragraphs, then, should average about 100–125 words each.

The first paragraph will be the all-important introductory one where you set forth your topic clearly and concisely, highlighting the major points your paper will cover. Your final paragraph will be the conclusion, wrapping up and summarizing your discussion as well as projecting any assessment you may have about the topic. That leaves you with only four paragraphs in the main body of the paper. At the far right of the balloon map, you have already identified five major subtopics to be discussed: three under strategic intelligence and two under tactical intelligence. Can you reasonably expect to cover those topics completely in less than a paragraph each, using Operation Desert Storm for your examples? Once again, you should have concluded that such broad coverage is unlikely to be clearly focused.

This short discussion will not solve all the problems you may encounter with organizing your thoughts early in the writing process; but I hope it reinforces for you the importance of narrowing your topic and doing some mapping. Focus early, and keep your focus throughout the paper. The process works equally as well on a 750-word paper, a 15-page term paper, or a 100-page thesis. The mind maps or outlines may get more complicated, but the *process* is the same.

Planting an Idea Tree

You've used a balloon map to help you decide on your subject, organize your thoughts, and get some ideas down on paper. Now you need something to help organize your writing, to point out areas where more information is needed, and to reveal any organizational problems you may encounter. Welcome to the idea tree.

The idea tree is designed with just those purposes in mind. Look back at figure 4.1, the balloon map, and assume that you have mapped the subject to your heart's content. (Of course, your final map would be considerably more complex than the simple example I've shown here.) Now you want to explore that subject in more detail. One way to do that is to ask a question about it, then to transpose that question to an idea tree.

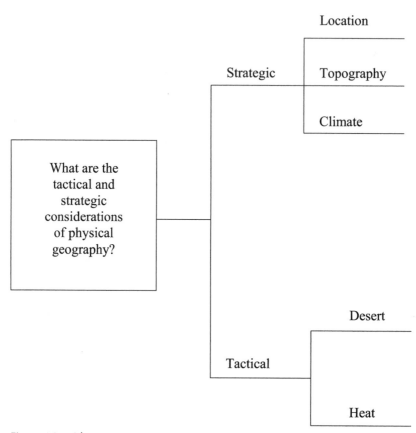

Figure 4.2. Idea tree

Figure 4.2 shows that I've asked the question, "What are the tactical and strategic considerations of physical geography?" The first two "branches" of the tree are then obvious, and after that, the continued branches will contribute more detail to the subject and move toward answering the question. At the very least, you should get a good idea of the areas where you need more information.

The tree in figure 4.2 has the same information as did the balloon map in figure 4.1. That need not be the case. For example, you might ask a different question: "What are the physical limitations imposed by desert heat on tactical operations?" You would then proceed in the same way along your own branches to identify those limitations. It works the same way with any subject you might be exploring.

Prewriting: Maps and Trees

The two prewriting aids discussed above—the balloon map and the idea tree—are summarized below. Refer to this page whenever you have a problem getting started with your writing. Don't wait for "inspiration." When you feel a tap on the shoulder, it won't be the creative muse. It will be your professor or your boss, asking you for the overdue paper!

Balloon Map

How: First zero in on a central topic. Then let your mind leap from thought to thought. Even before you know what you want to write, you are jotting down ideas as quickly as they come. Don't try to think step-by-step; doing so may stop the free flow of ideas.

Why: Decide upon a subject; organize your thoughts; make choices; make connections; get started/break the ice.

Idea Tree

How: Start by putting your main idea in a box to the left. If you don't know what to say about your subject, jot down a question about it. Next, look for topics that will help you explain your big idea. Now look for details that will tell more about your topics. Review your ideas. If some don't belong together, erase them and put them in new places. Stick-on notes make the whole process easier.

Why: Organize writing; show where more information is needed; reveal organization problems.

Searching, Researching

You're almost ready to start writing now; so don't get impatient. The last thing you need to do in preparation for the actual writing phase is to research the subject thoroughly. The amount of effort you put into this phase will vary depending upon time available to you, resources immediately at hand such as other recent studies, and your depth of knowledge in the subject area. Even if you are the world's greatest expert in the subject, though, you should make one last check to ensure that you've included all the latest available data. That's especially important if you're working in an area of current intelligence interest.

Avoid the "Syndrome of the Analyst's Reach" as you do your research. That is, don't assume that if the information is not within your reach as you sit at your desk, it's not anywhere to be found in the community. You're the one who's been following events or keeping up with developments in your area of expertise, so you'll be expected to have current knowledge of the subject; but don't assume that all that knowledge is within arm's reach. Sometimes you might have to dig for it. That means checking with other commands or agencies that may have some current tidbit of information; it means scanning the latest unclassified sources like newspapers, magazines, and journals to see if the media have printed anything about the subject lately; and it means considering all possible sources of information such as analysts or perhaps other individuals in your command or agency who may know what's going on.

The word "research," as you might suspect, means "to search again." So search out all your sources, consider them, and then search again to ensure thorough coverage. On a "short-fuse" requirement, that whole process may be limited to a few hours, but they'll be hours well spent. After you've searched and researched, you'll be ready to write and rewrite. And that will be the subject of the next chapter. But first, try your hand at the following exercises.

Exercises in Prewriting

Exercise 1: Thinking Logically and Critically

Of Course You Can! What's that you say? You don't have the *talent* for writing? No *original ideas* to contribute? Nothing *important* to say? I hope this chapter will convince you that you can write a better analytical paper by using some basic tools to plan, focus, and organize your thoughts ahead of time. The thought processes you exercise in getting ready to write will pay big dividends on the other end, when it's time to commit words to paper. This exercise covers the following thought processes:

1. *Thinking logically and critically.* Before you begin to write, think about what you are going to write. Ask yourself reflective questions that help you understand what you want to write, and why.
2. *Finding a focus.* Narrow your thinking down to a manageable topic, and find the issue within that topic.
3. *Freewriting.* Employ this form of "mental aerobics" to conquer the nemesis of writer's block.
4. *Using a mind map.* Mind maps can help you get organized, zero in on your topic, maintain coherence, analyze information, and arrive at conclusions.

These processes are discussed in detail on the following pages, with exercises to serve as discussion points in class or to help you progress in a self-paced mode.

> Writing is nothing more mysterious than the logical arrangement of thought. Writing is thinking on paper. Anybody who thinks clearly should be able to write clearly and vice versa.
>
> —William Zinsser

Start your writing process by thinking clearly and logically. List on a separate piece of paper some ideas to help you do that.

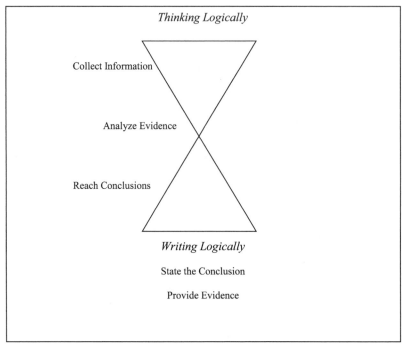

Figure 4.3. Thinking and writing logically

Questions for Discussion (Refer to Figure 4.3)

1. Why is the hourglass so much wider at the "collection" end than in the middle?
2. By looking at the shape of the hourglass and what it portrays, what can you conclude about its narrowest point?
3. What is the relationship between a statement of your conclusions and a topic sentence?

Thinking Critically about Intelligence Writing

Critical thinking in the prewriting stage amounts to little more than asking yourself a few questions before you start writing. Reflect thoughtfully on your subject for a few minutes; twist it; turn it; hold it up to the light for illumination; look at it in the mirror to see another side of it.

Some Reflective Questions

If you're not disposed toward the intuitive kinds of things that I discussed above, try this more practical exercise instead:

1. Pick a topic—any topic. If it's a paper or a thesis you're already working on, then you're ahead of the game. Otherwise . . . pick a topic—any topic.
2. State the topic in one declarative sentence, no more than 30 words long. (Example: The April 1995 bombing in Oklahoma City foreshadowed more terrorist activity on U.S. soil.)
3. Now answer as many questions as you can about your topic. Keep answers short, to the point. (In the sample questions below, I've added in parentheses some answers to the questions about my own topic that I generated as an example above.)
   a. *Who* are the main "actors" in my topic? (The terrorists. Their sponsors. Counterterrorist and antiterrorist organizations worldwide, especially in the United States.)
   b. *What* is my main point? (That there is more to come.)
   c. *Where* is my focus—geographically or thematically or both? ("On U.S. soil." May also of necessity have to look at foreign support/sponsorship of terrorism as well as foreign efforts to help the United States or to counter their own threat.)
   d. *When* is the concern of my topic most evident? (In the immediate future and into the early 21st century.)
   e. *Why* am I writing about this subject? (Terrorism, especially on U.S. soil, is a topic of immediate and high interest to policy makers and decision makers, therefore to the intelligence community as well.)

f. *How* will I write about this topic? (Seek evidence of a trend toward more terrorism. Compare and contrast the Oklahoma incident with others.)

g. What are the *key terms* that must be defined for my reader? ("more," "terrorist," and "activity." Possibly "on U.S. soil"—to include U.S. embassies, for example?)

h. What are the *implications and consequences* for the United States and/or for the intelligence community? (The lack of security for U.S. citizens in the workplace; the need for the intelligence community to devote more resources to monitor the problem.)

i. Other question(s) related to your topic but not listed above.

Exercise 2: Finding a Focus

Begin in your earliest stages of writing to narrow your topic to a manageable focus. Remember that one of the basic premises of intelligence analysis is to break a complex topic down into its components, look at those components individually, then put the pieces together so that they mean something.

"The Middle East" is not a topic. It is a vast geopolitical entity. What do you want to examine about it? "The Middle East situation" is a broad, general topic involving many nations and complex problems of history, geography, economics, ethnicity, and others. What about the situation?

Look at the list of general topics below. Choose one, and take notes on how you would narrow that topic to something that might be covered in a 15-page analytical paper. You might want to use one or more of the components of strategic intelligence (below right) as guidelines.[5] Be prepared to discuss your topic in class.

General Topic Areas	*Components of Strategic Intelligence*
1. Instability in Eastern Europe	Biographic
2. Unrest in the Russian Armed Forces	Economic
3. Prospects for the Korean Peninsula	Sociological
4. The Resurgence of Japan since 1945	Transportation and Telecommunications
5. Crisis in Iraq	Military Geographic
6. The Palestinian Question	Armed Forces
7. Panama since Operation Just Cause	Political
8. South America's Economic Prospects	Scientific and Technical

Exercise 3: Freewriting

"Freewriting" has nothing to do with money. It is a concept designed to "free" the words that may be hung up inside your head. Review the discussion of freewriting earlier in this chapter. Then, on a separate sheet of paper, freewrite for 10 minutes on your own topic. If your topic still lacks focus, then move on to the next exercise and practice mapping.

Exercise 4: Using a Mind Map

A basic prewriting warm-up can help get your creative engines started. Try one or more of the ideas below when you need a jump start on a cold paper.

The Balloon Map

A balloon map is a prewriting tool that can help you answer the question "What am I going to write about?" It can focus and

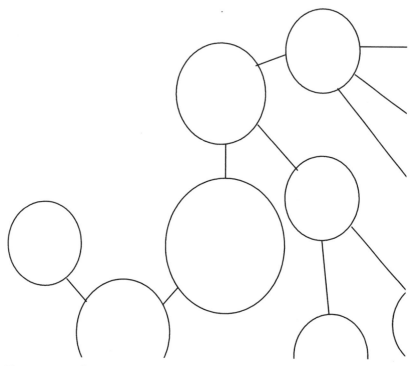

Figure 4.4.   Balloon map

organize your thoughts, help pin down your subject, and give you a graphic, spatial representation that makes choices and connections easier to see. It's important with the balloon map that you allow your thoughts to flow freely, without stopping to judge them or to evaluate their relevance or validity. Consider your own topic and map it.

The Idea Tree

An idea tree is a great tool for organizing your thoughts. It points out areas where you might need more information, and it readily reveals problems you may have with organization in

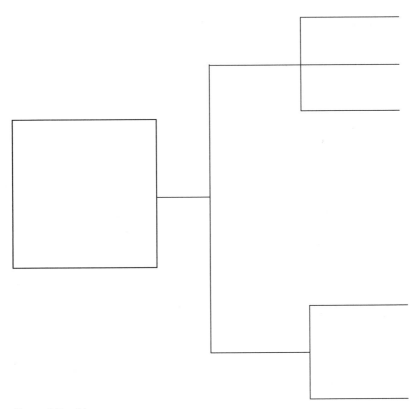

Figure 4.5. Idea tree

your writing. Often you can transfer your prewriting work back and forth between a balloon map and an idea tree, first to focus and then to organize. Transfer your topic from the balloon map you've drawn to an idea tree.

Answers to the Exercises in Chapter 4

Exercise 1: Thinking Logically and Critically

The *best* way to start the analytical writing process clearly and logically is with some sort of prewriting—the subject of this introductory chapter. Your answers may differ, but I suggest the following:

1. Prewrite
2. Narrow your topic
3. Reach conclusions

Questions for Discussion

1. Q: Why is the hourglass so much wider at the "collection" end than in the middle? A: We *always* collect far more information than we are able to analyze and use.
2. Q: By looking at the shape of the hourglass and what it portrays, what can you conclude about its narrowest point? A: The conclusion will be clearly focused—a synthesis—as a result of the earlier body of collection, research, and analysis.
3. Q: What is the relationship between a statement of your conclusions and a topic sentence? A: The statement of your conclusions *is* a topic sentence and is likely to be the first sentence in your paper. It may also be called your thesis statement or a key judgment.

Note: The other exercises in this chapter have multiple answers and are designed to be done in the classroom.

Notes

1. Victoria Nelson, *Writer's Block and How to Use It* (Cincinnati, Ohio: Writer's Digest Books, 1985).
2. Peter Elbow, *Writing with Power: Techniques for Mastering the Writing Process* (New York: Oxford University Press, 1981).
3. Elbow, *Writing with Power*, 13.
4. Elbow, *Writing with Power*, 17.
5. As a mnemonic device, note that the first letters of the components of strategic intelligence, as I have listed them here, spell out the acronym "best maps."

5

Writing the First Draft

Summary

The second distinct phase of the writing process is the drafting itself—writing a first draft of your product. To get started with the writing phase, work on good writing habits: use your prewriting to guide you; consider your reader throughout; keep in mind the products you have read, and look to improve on them.

- Remember the *style* of intelligence writing: keep the bottom line up front; use only enough background and history to ensure that your reader will understand the problem or issue; and get right to the point, without defining your methods.
- In the drafting process, choose a time and place best suited to your writing style; set realistic goals; write any sentence first but write continuously. You can always rearrange paragraphs during revision.
- Organize your first draft by considering the orders of time, space, and logic. An order of *time* is chronologically organized. *Spatial* organization looks at where the elements fit in the structure of your paper. There are seven possible orders of *logic*: increasing importance, decreasing

importance, comparison, components or "analysis," inductive reasoning, deductive reasoning, and cause and effect.
- The actual process of *writing the first draft* involves building complete sentences and paragraphs onto your existing outline or map. Stay focused on your topic throughout the writing. Use strong verbs and as few prepositions as possible.
- Write the main body first, then the conclusions or outlook. Finally, extract the important *key judgments* you've made in the paper and place them *up front*. Those key judgments are a complete summary of your paper, and they should stand alone for the busy reader. Remain objective in the writing by evaluating both your sources and the arguments that they—and you—are making.
- "Dress up" your paper by using meaningful headings and subheadings, and by creating an eye-catching title.

Keep the writing phase separate and distinct. Avoid the temptation to revise as you go along. That's the *next* phase of the process.

Getting Started: Good Writing Habits

I've already told you that writing is hard work; that it requires a great deal of time and effort if it's to be any good; and that writing skills can be developed through study and practice. If that hasn't scared you away from this chapter, then I hope you'll bear with me for just a few more pages as I get you started on a writing project, walk you through it, and help you polish it to perfection.

Probably the best writing habit you can practice from the start is prewriting, which was the subject of the previous chapter. In addition to prewriting, though, you should develop some other good habits in your writing. Among those habits are considering your reader, being aware of your own reading and writing, the style you use, and visual aids.

Reader Considerations: Some Basic Truths

Meanings Sent Are Not Always the Same Ones Received

Toward the end of the workday the plant manager walked through the factory. As he passed one of the welders, he remarked, "I think we should clean up around here." The welder immediately began to tidy up his work area. The manager said the same thing to the next three welders he passed. The second man was embarrassed and decided he was probably due a shower. The third wondered how the boss found out he had been telling dirty jokes. And the fourth one smiled and thought, "Yeah, we're making a pile of money."

Meaning Is in the Mind

Words are just the symbols we use to communicate. Meaning arises as a receiver filters the words, the linguistic symbols, through his or her experience. Let's work through an example together. When you hear the word steed, what do you think of? Write your answer on a separate sheet of paper.

Some people don't know what a steed is. Some may have said it is *just* a horse, or something to that effect. Some may have recalled a poem about a chivalric knight proceeding into battle upon his spirited steed and thus attached a romantic connotation to the word. Yet another may have fallen from a steed and been trampled by it. Unless he is a masochist, *steed* would not conjure up any romantic imagery in this receiver. Finally, someone who just watched a rerun of *The Avengers* on television might picture the dashing gentleman in the bowler hat, John Steed.

Communication Is Imperfect

Words are limited. *Dog* refers to a countless number of sizes, shapes, colors, and breeds of this four-legged animal. Some of you may have had blind dates with the infamous two-legged variety of this species. I live in a house rather than an apartment, but do you know what it looks like? Is it a mansion or a shanty? A colonial style or a bungalow?

Discuss the meanings the words below could have under various circumstances (consider them not only as nouns—they all are—but also as verbs, which they can also be):

bug   draft   drive   frame   form   file

Meeting the Needs of Your Audience

Before drafting and during the revision stage as well, you need to crawl into the socks of your reader. Ask yourself two basic questions:

- What does my reader need to know about this subject?
- What does my reader already know?

I first addressed reader considerations in chapter 1. Remember that you want to think about *who* will be reading your product, *why* they will be reading it, and *how* they will *use* the information you give them. This simple act of thoughtfulness toward the reader will pay dividends in the final product. It will be more readable and probably will have a greater impact on your audience.

Reader considerations will also have an important influence on the way you write your paper. Generally, the higher the rank of the intended recipients, the more formal your product will be. If it's a fact sheet or background paper for a flag rank officer or senior civilian, you'll want to be sure that you adhere to the proper format, and keep it short. If it's a "think piece" to be circulated among peers in your section or division, then you can afford to be less formal. As a student, you'll want to be certain that your thesis or your papers meet the criteria of your institution and the individually imposed requirements of your professor. Don't use the excuse of not knowing those requirements. You can always ask.

Reading: A Basic Complement to Writing

Your *reading habits* are basic to the way you will write. The Greek philosopher Epictetus said, "If you would be a reader, read; if a writer, write." In the intelligence profession, I might paraphrase that to read, "If you would be either, do both!" If you want to write a readable intelligence product, then you must spend some time reading the publications of other intelligence writers. Look for the details that make their products most readable, and try to emulate those things. At the same time, avoid the techniques that cause you to lose interest in the writing or simply to consider it bad writing. The subject of reading intelligence publications is so important that I devoted the first chapter of this book to the topic. Review that chapter again if you want to refresh your memory on the importance of good reading habits.

The Style of Intelligence Writing: Bottom Line Up Front

By now you might have noticed that each chapter in this book begins with a "Summary" section. That summary is intended to encapsulate the main points made in the chapter. Such a style conveys to my audience those elements of the chapter that I think are most important. And that is a key point in writing with intelligence.

The relationship between a writer and the audience determines the basic style of communication used. Some possible styles include formal versus informal; direct versus indirect; and authoritative versus cooperative.

In a *formal* writing style, the writer carefully chooses words, remains objective, and writes for the record. Academic papers and most government correspondence fall into this category. With an *informal* style, the writer uses a conversational, relaxed approach. Contractions and even slang may find their way into the writing. Personal emotions may be expressed. Personal letters, e-mails, and even some interoffice correspondence are written informally.

With a *direct* style, the writer gets straight to the point, with no fluff or unnecessary words. Well-written intelligence papers should employ a direct writing style. Using an *indirect* approach, the writer tries to prevent hurt feelings and is careful not to ruffle feathers. Peer critiques of writing often fall into this category, as do papers written to superiors by subordinates.

In an *authoritative* style the writer speaks as an expert or as the boss. Journal articles, directives, and regulations are written authoritatively—and often incomprehensibly. When writers use a *cooperative* style, they consider themselves on an equal footing with their readers. They may be co-workers or peers. A peer writing critique is written in this style.

What Is Style?

I've used the term "style" 15 times already in this chapter without defining it. The *American Heritage Dictionary of the English* Language (fourth edition) defines *style* as "the way in which something is said, done, expressed, or performed."[1] For intelligence writing, that translates, quite simply, as "bottom line up front." That means you lead with your knockout punch, putting your most important information in the first sentence of the first paragraph on the first page.

Defining Methods

I am often asked about one of the toughest parts of any paper: the introduction. Faculty members and students alike have trouble getting started and telling the audience what the paper is all about. Typically their approach is the familiar academic lore of defining methods. Student writers spend much of the first page or two telling readers what they are going to tell them in the pages ahead.

A Description of What I Will Tell You Later

You have no doubt read classic lines like these:

The purpose of this paper is to discuss the recent events in Iraq. I will attempt to show, through a levels-of-analysis approach, how government policy has changed in that country over the past decade. The paper also will examine in detail the character traits of the late Saddam Hussein, and will show the relationship between his personality and the current crisis in the Persian Gulf. Finally, I will attempt to provide a forecast for the next six months in the region.

Having read those opening lines, see if you can answer the following questions: What recent events in Iraq will be discussed? Will the paper deal only with internal events in Iraq, or will it relate those events to the Persian Gulf region? How *has* government policy changed? What aspects of Saddam's personality will be examined? Is there, in fact, some relationship between his personality and the crisis? What does this writer believe will happen in the next six months?

You probably can't answer *any* of the questions posed. All this writer has done is to define methods. That is, he has told you what approach he will take in the paper, but he has not given you a clue about its content. My example above may seem far-fetched, but I have seen introductions like that more often than I like to admit. These types of introductions to intelligence or academic papers often tend to be laden with stodgy, plodding prose. If you are a student, though, keep in mind that you are writing academic papers *with the mindset of an intelligence professional.* Once the distinction is clear in your mind, you should have few problems with this approach.

Making the Distinction Clear for Students

The most difficult point for most students (and faculty members as well) to understand is that you are writing intelligence papers in an academic environment. For that reason we need to ensure that students leave the course with a clear idea of what constitutes a well-written intelligence paper.

The focus on the past so common in many academic papers is one reason students tend to linger so long in the introduction. They feel honor-bound to cover the "historical background" of the Gulf crisis, beginning with the conquest of Persia in 333 BC by Alexander the Great. Before you know it, their introduction alone to a paper that was to have been no longer than 10 pages is already 15 pages. The intelligence paper, on the other hand, looks toward the future. Certainly it has its contextual roots in history and experience, but the analytical thrust of the intelligence discipline calls for a forward-looking paper.

Since you are writing papers for professors who are experts in their field of scholarship, you may perceive a need to provide great detail about the methods you are employing. Perhaps you see that as a "safety valve," so that the professor will not be convinced too early that you do not really know what you are talking about. More often, though, the early and strong statement of your conclusions will be more convincing. That technique also will keep you in tune with the "real world" of the intelligence community out there, where your readers are *not* subject-matter experts, and where they must have the most important points up front so that they can make decisions, determine policy, or command their organizations.

The details are important. Don't think that you have to boil every paper down to a set of bullets. Your professor must be able to determine your depth of knowledge and your understanding of the subject of your paper. So provide that information, but do it by sticking to the essentials. Don't bog the professor down with superfluous detail. Focus on your topic; narrow it down to its essence; and stay focused on the topic throughout the paper. If your subject is the crisis in the Persian Gulf, you probably do not need to talk about the history of the region unless it bears directly on your conclusions. *Begin* with those conclusions, and then follow through with your assessment of what it means.

What's It All About?

A colleague told me of a friend who worked with him at the CIA years ago. Behind his desk was a huge sign that read, "So What?" We must find the meaning in all our intelligence writing. Zero in on the essence of the topic, and then state that essence up front in the paper. With that in mind, take a look at a fresh introduction to the paper I showed you earlier, rewritten in terms of what I have talked about here:

Events in Iraq since August 1990 have altered dramatically the situation in the Persian Gulf. A level-of-analysis approach shows that the Iraqi government, under the dictatorial hand of the late Saddam Hussein, became increasingly hard-line both domestically and internationally. Individual role analysis suggests that Saddam's stubbornness and his intense nationalistic pride had a direct bearing on the ability of the United States and its allies to convince him to withdraw peacefully from Kuwait and to renounce his pursuit of weapons of mass destruction. The next six months will be crucial as decisions are made to turn over more responsibility to the Iraqi government, with serious implications for the entire Persian Gulf region.

See the difference? Now at least you know what the writer is going to talk about. You still know that the method used will be the levels of analysis, but you also know the substance of the analysis and its conclusions. It is still an academic paper, but you are writing it with style—intelligence style.

Drafting

Now that you have done the research, focused your topic, and engaged in planning, prewriting, and audience consideration, you are ready to draft that thing. Some writers waste enormous amounts of time pondering first sentences, believing if they get that one just right, everything else will flow from it. Wrong! Many a writer has paused for an equally long time over the second sentence. Although we all will discover ways of drafting that work best for us, some reminders might streamline the process.

Choose the Right Place and Time

You've probably dashed off a sentence or two flying across country or sitting in your favorite Starbucks. Writing gets done in some surprising places. Nevertheless, drafting will be a much smoother process if you can eliminate interruptions from your coworkers, your classmates, and the telephone. Seek a place that suits you well for thoughtful, uninterrupted work. Write when you are the most relaxed, creative, and productive. That may be the early morning (as it is for me) or late at night over a cup of coffee (as it *was* for me in more youthful times). Once you have found the right place, try to return to it whenever you have to write.

Set Realistic Goals

If you are facing a 15-page term paper or report, aim for *part* of it. Write a few pages at a time. Large goals are intimidating and may encourage you to postpone any of the work until you have several days, a weekend, to do the work. We all know those "free" weekends never come.

Write Any Sentence First

Don't tear out your hair trying to craft that perfect first sentence. If you have trouble with introductions, start with the body or, better yet, the section of the body you know best. If you get stuck or run out of steam, work on another section of the paper. Like a patchwork quilt, your paper can be pieced together later. That's become easier these days with computers that enable us to cut and paste to our hearts' content.

Write Continuously

The first draft is not the place to revise, to censor thoughts, to worry about word choice. Everything need not be perfect in this working draft. In fact the quest for perfection itself often causes writer's block, disconnected ideas, and the omission of important material.

The most valuable lesson I learned when I started teaching writing to intelligence professionals in the 1980s was to write first, and *then* to revise. With my strong urge toward perfection, I had found myself constantly stopping, reviewing what I had written, and revising as I wrote. That not only ate up my writing time but also required that I reread a good deal of my previous writing after I "lost my place" in revision.

As I put into practice what I preached, I found that my writing output increased immensely. The hardest part was learning to ignore those little green and red squiggly lines my word processor sprinkled throughout my drafts. Of course they could be disabled; but I chose to note them, ignore them, and return to them during the revision phase. Sure enough, they were still there awaiting my attention. So that's my writing style. How about yours?

The Way *You* Write

The way you write is something that has been instilled in you since the day you picked up your first crayon and scrawled something that resembled "wonwu," proudly proclaiming it to read "Mommy." Even today, you may proudly consider your writing to be clear, concise, correct, and appropriate for your reader; but that reader might be seeing no more than "wonwu." There is no greater learning experience for the writer of intelligence than to write intelligence. I see it frequently: A student writer is overwhelmed by the task of writing an intelligence paper in the first term of school; yet, by graduation day, that student is a competent and proficient writer. What happened? Nothing more than a few months of experience in writing. And that same experiential factor applies to intelligence professionals on the job.

There's no simple formula for overcoming the difficulties of getting started with your own writing; it's something that requires patience, perseverance, and the willingness to learn from one's own mistakes. Sure, there will be mistakes. But take them to heart and don't make the same ones twice. If conciseness is your problem, then work on that aspect twice as hard next time. You will see improvement.

More about Style

Style is an attribute of writing that is unique to individuals. The basic elements of your writing style include usage, composition, and form. The way you use words in your writing, the manner in which you compose your products, and the form your writing takes are all integral components of the style you display for your reader. Is it important to change your style to conform? Not always. If you have a relaxed, informal way of writing, you may need to adopt a little more formal mode for some writing requirements like a master's thesis or an intelligence estimate; but you will find that an informal style does not automatically equate to a "bad" style of writing. Every style has its time and place, and the trick is adapting your own techniques to suit the task at hand and the intended reader of your product. How is that done? Only through practice, which means writing every chance you get.

Visual Aids

Not all intelligence publications use visual aids, but it's a good writing habit to give some thought to illustrating your work graphically. The use of visual aids alone cannot rescue an otherwise foundering intelligence product. Clearly, the graphics employed by a writer should do more than just "dress up" the page. They should be effective in making some point more clearly or concisely than words alone could do it.

Let's take the example of our old standby, the Fizzle fighter. If you're assembling an estimate of Fizzle production in the years 2010–2020, your reader would appreciate seeing early in the publication a picture of the aircraft. An ideal site for such a picture is on the left-hand page opposite the opening segment of the publication. You might also want to accompany your text with some bar graphs, charts, or other visual data to graphically portray your assessments.

The same principle applies to a product dealing with a geographic region or a particular country. Have a map where your reader can refer to it early. Before final publication, go through your text one last time and check for place names. Every time a place is mentioned, look to see if it is noted on the map.

Many maps, illustrations, photographs, and other graphic materials are readily available online. Check out the "images" section of your favorite search engine and you'll find hundreds, if not thousands, of examples to spice up your work. Be certain, though, that the downloaded version of the graphic image is not degraded in quality, resulting in a grainy or otherwise unsatisfactory image. Also, keep in mind the copyright restrictions that govern many online materials.

Organizing the First Draft

One of the most basic considerations in the style of any product is its organization. Before you get too deeply into the writing process, you should think about the organizational form you want your product to take. This procedure is essentially a mental process that enables you to outline and then write in a more orderly manner. It's a good idea to consider organization as you do your prewriting. The fundamental organizational structures in writing are the orders of *time*, *space*, and *logic*.

Time to Get Organized

If you choose the order of *time*, your subject should lend itself to a chronological coverage. Ideal topics for this organizational form would include historical subjects. Temporal (time) organization is easy to map or outline. Just start with the earliest date you want to cover, and work your way up to the most recent date or event. Some periods will emerge as more important than others. Those years should be given additional emphasis in your paper. If, for instance, your paper deals with the rise of Islamic Fundamentalism in Iran, you might start with the emergence of Islam during the Mohammedan years, but you would certainly want to devote a good deal of space to the return of the Ayatollah Khomeini to Iran after the fall of the Shah in 1979.

Lost in Space?

Spatial organization refers literally to the way elements of your subject relate to each other: up to down, in to out, north to south, east to west. You might want to consider a spatial organization in writing about a geographic region: Cover all aspects of the region starting in a given place, and then proceed in a fixed direction throughout the remainder of the region, covering the same points for each step.

For example, in writing a historical assessment of the threat to Western Europe posed by the former Warsaw Pact, you might start with a more detailed examination of Germany, since that country is the linchpin of NATO's Central Region. You could start by examining the geographic regions from north to south—from the North German Plains to the Bavarian Alps; then you could cover aspects of the terrain that make certain regions particularly vulnerable to attack, such as the Northern Plains and the "Fulda Gap"; and so forth until you had addressed each component of the threat. Then you could proceed to other Western European countries and do the same thing for each.

That Sounds Logical (You Hope!)

There are at least seven orders of *logic* that might be employed in writing an intelligence paper. I'll discuss each of those briefly to give you some ideas for logically organizing your writing.

Increasing Importance

This order of logic is a common technique used by mystery writers, but *not* in the intelligence profession. As you might expect, this organizational structure builds from the least important information to the most important. In the case of the murder mystery, the punch line is the "whodunit," and if the writer has managed to keep you in suspense until the last page, then you're happy with that mystery. But you would never make it to the end of an intelligence product if the author were to use that method. Remember that as a writer of intelligence, you must pull no punches. It is your obligation to the reader to tell everything you know *up front*.

Decreasing Importance

Conversely, the order of *decreasing importance* leads with the punch line and follows up with the supporting material. That wouldn't make for a very funny joke, but it might save some time if the listener has already heard it. Obviously, you don't want to have all your most important points in the first few lines and then trail off to nothing in the rest of the paper. The point is to put the vital information at the front of your product in the form of "Key Judgments" or an "Executive Summary"; then keep the important points of each paragraph and each section toward the start of that paragraph or section. If there's a mound of supporting data or analytical methodology to back up your writing, put it in an appendix or annex at the end, so that it doesn't distract the busy reader.

Comparison

A third order of logic is called *comparison*. This form involves arriving at a conclusion based on comparing the unknown to something that is known. You would probably want to use the comparison method in writing about that newly discovered fighter aircraft, the Fizzle. You could find the fighter that most closely resembles the Fizzle and compare its characteristics side by side; or, if the readers are not familiar with foreign aircraft, compare the Fizzle to a U.S. plane. In that manner, readers are able to grasp the significance of important features of the new aircraft in terms of other equipment already familiar to them.

Components

The *components* or *"analysis"* order of logic entails breaking a topic down into its component parts, looking at each of those parts, and arriving at a conclusion based on those components. This technique is one you've used many times in buying a "big-ticket" item like a new car, when you consider factors such as style, size, gas mileage, safety, repair costs, and comfort. In the intelligence business, it's a method that might work well on a complex piece of equipment or a complicated subject such as terrorism.

Inductive and Deductive Logic

The next two organizational structures are closely related and can be discussed together: *inductive* logic and *deductive* logic. When you examine something *inductively*, you look at a specific point and move to a generality. You might know, for example, that the Fizzle aircraft is armed with a type of missile that makes it particularly suited for air-to-ground operations. You might conclude, then, that its principal purpose is close air support of ground forces. *Deductive* logic, on the other hand, starts with the generality and moves to a specific conclusion. If you have noted the Fizzle in a close air support role, then you might conclude that it is armed with a particular type of weapon system. The most important point to keep in mind about using either inductive or deductive logic is this: be certain that your starting point, whether specific or general, is defensible. If you start from a position that your reader will disagree with, you've lost the argument before you go through your process of reasoning.

Cause and Effect

The last of the seven orders of logic I will discuss is the *cause-and-effect* method. You can start with the cause and work forward to the effect, or you can look first at the effect and work backward to the cause. It doesn't matter. Think about the impression you want to leave in the reader's mind. If you're writing about Islamic fundamentalism in Iran, do you want the reader to be left with the effects this upheaval has had on Iranian society, or would you rather leave the reader with a clear picture of the root cause of the Islamic resurgence? If the cause is most important, go from cause to effect—always keeping the most important points toward the front.

It is not necessary to choose and then adhere to only one organizational structure. Some subjects will lend themselves to treatment by several different methods. You might easily employ in one paper a combination of a chronological order of time and a logical order of decreasing importance, and even include a dash of comparison and a pinch of deductive reasoning thrown in for good measure. Whatever type of organizational structure you choose, remember these basic points: be consistent by not switching back and forth between opposing structures; and use these organizational methods as guidelines to help you methodically and logically construct both your prewriting and your finished product.

Writing That First Draft

Let's review briefly where our discussion of writing has taken us so far. We've considered the basics of clarity, conciseness, and correctness; we've looked at the other important factors of appropriateness, completeness, and coherence. We've gotten organized by identifying the form and format our product would follow, thinking about the time and space available to us and our readers, and doing our homework in the form of thorough research. Finally, we've sat down to write our first draft. But do we have a written product yet? Not quite.

Back to the Prewriting

If you've followed all the steps up to now, what you *do* have is a well-organized outline or mind map of what your product is going to look like. You've built the foundation of strong stuff, deciding on the structure you'll follow and meticulously outlining your thinking on the subject. The rest is a piece of cake. All you have to do now is build on that established framework and complete your written product.

Review your prewriting one more time before you start writing, and keep it in front of you throughout the final process. Remember that your subject should be boldly inscribed at the top of the page to remind you to maintain that focus and not stray onto other topics unnecessarily.

If you've written a topic outline, the first step is to develop those words and phrases into topic sentences. Just follow through on the thought in each topic and subtopic, and turn each of them into a complete sentence. Those topic sentences will become the basis for your paragraphs in the final product. By zeroing in on the ideas you advanced during the outlining phase, you'll be surprised at how quickly the paper takes shape. If your outline is already in topic sentence form, you're almost home.

If you chose mapping as your prewriting form, look over your map at this point and decide whether you can write directly from the map. Some writers prefer to go through a quick intermediate step, converting the map to an outline to add structure to the paper before beginning the writing process. That's a good approach because it satisfies both sides of the brain. The right brain has been soothed by being allowed to roam unhampered through a free flow of ideas onto paper; now the left brain can be satisfied by lending structure and organization to that free expression.

Your Main Points and the Topic Sentence

If you still have a problem envisioning the concept of a topic sentence and exactly what it means, compare the writing in hard news stories in your daily newspaper. Notice that you can read the first one or two paragraphs in a news story and derive the meaning of the entire article. The item itself may go on for a half-page or more, but by reading only those first two paragraphs you can answer the following questions about that article: who, what, where, when, and sometimes why and how. That's how intelligence writing should be. The reader should be able to know at a glance what the writer is trying to say; and the best way to ensure that happens is to put your main ideas early in the paragraphs.

Importance of the Topic Sentence in Intelligence Writing

The *style*—form and format—of intelligence writing demands that we put the important ideas or information *up front*.

Why? The *topic sentence* is the most important idea or information that we want to convey in each paragraph and should be the *first sentence* of each paragraph.

As you develop your topic sentences into paragraphs, you're really adding flesh to the bone of each skeletal idea. You'll find that you can review your product, reading only the first sentence of each paragraph, and understand the major thrust of the information being offered. Your reader should be able to do that, too.

Think of your paragraph as a MOBILE.
The TOPIC SENTENCE is that piece at the top
that holds the whole thing together.

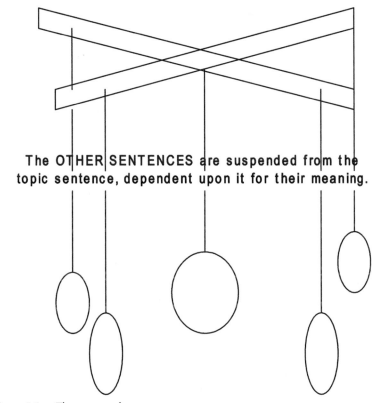

The OTHER SENTENCES are suspended from the
topic sentence, dependent upon it for their meaning.

Figure 5.1. The paragraph

Remember that I discussed in chapter 1 some of the techniques for reading intelligence publications. I stressed at that time the importance of being able to recognize the key judgments in intelligence writing and how they should stand alone as a summary of the entire paper, leaving out no major point. Those key judgments are the last words that should be written in your paper. The key judgments—or executive summary, or whatever else the substantive front section of your product might be called—are the most important part of your product. They are the words that will be read by more readers than any other part of the document. So you should spend a little more time developing those key judgments.

The Body of Your Writing

The main body of your product will follow a prescribed form or format, or you may have the flexibility to dictate your own terms for this part—a rare occasion. *Write this section first*, following the framework of your map or outline and revising as you go. Make revisions first on your prewriting, then follow through in the written product. This may seem like a tedious process, but in the long run it will actually save you time by lessening the need to rewrite the main body. The prewriting—usually seen, remember, by you alone—is a better place to do early revisions than in the text of your product.

If you find yourself "bogging down" in facts and figures somewhere along the way in the main body, try to detach yourself from the writing for a moment and look at the "big picture" of your work. Is the text becoming too cluttered with statistics or methodology, detracting from what you have to say? Then maybe it's time to shift some of that excess baggage to an annex. If Writer's Brain Cramp sets in along the way, take a break. Unless you're driven by a tight deadline, you will only frustrate yourself if you sit and stare at the blank paper or blinking cursor waiting for the words to flow.

Many authors advise that "writer's block" may be overcome by writing something—writing *anything*—and then going back later and cleaning it up. If that suits your style, then go for it. You may prefer, though, to divert your attention for a few minutes. Stretch your legs; have a cup of coffee or a soft drink; listen to some pleasant music. When you feel more refreshed, return to your writing.

Before you know it, you'll be through with the main body and ready for your conclusions. Remember that these conclusions must be consistent with what you've written earlier. This, too, is the section where you'll provide some forecast or outlook for the reader concerning your subject.

Last, but Assuredly Not Least

Finally, you come to the last part of your writing: extracting the key judgments. If everything else in your writing has proceeded according to plan, the key judgments should be obvious to you when you reread the paper. If they don't smack you in the middle of the forehead as you scan each paragraph, they should at least tap you on the shoulder or whisper in your ear. In some cases, you will be able to use topic sentences verbatim as the key judgments; but the preferred method is to rewrite them. A particularly keen reader will notice the similarity between the key judgments and the main body and will feel cheated that you didn't think enough of the product to do a little extra work. The less astute reader may simply feel that he's read the product before, and will toss it aside without finishing it. Usually you can combine one or two topic sentences into one key judgment. Compare the summaries of each chapter in this book to the text. Notice how I have extracted main ideas without repeating sentences verbatim.

Don't make the mistake that some students have made with the key judgments. Having followed directions to the letter, they write the key judgments last; then they leave them as the last portion of their paper. Remember that the key judgments or the executive summary is always the first part of your intelligence product. That's the part busy readers will want to see, and they certainly don't want to turn to the last page to find it.

The Bottom Line: Focus

What's it all about? Do you ask yourself that question after reading a paper you have just written? When a professor or your supervisor asks that same loaded question—"What's your paper about?"—do you answer, "About 10 pages"?

Every paper written in the intelligence community should have some central focus—a guiding theme that takes the reader through the paper and provides a point of reference. Previous discussions dealt with various aspects of finding and narrowing that focus. Now let's look at some ways to *energize* the writing that goes into that paper, to make it more readable and to make your reader more likely to remember something besides "it's about 10 pages."

The first step in energizing a piece of intelligence writing is to have its theme up front. Don't bury the main topic under a sea of words and phrases like these: "The purpose of this paper is to describe the aspects of strategic and tactical intelligence as they relate to geographic intelligence," or "This paper will examine the role played by Yeltsis Borschtin in the attempted Russian coup." Start right off with the key point.

Look at how much more energetic those two boring examples are in the following: "Geographic intelligence is a key consideration in both tactical and strategic intelligence, especially in terms of topography, weather, and location." "Yeltsis Borschtin played the pivotal role in the 25 February coup that toppled the Russian government." See the difference?

It is often difficult for us, as writers of intelligence, to avoid the temptation to succumb to the Agatha Christie Syndrome. Like the great mystery writer, we want to keep our readers in suspense until we can deliver that "punch line"—the "whodunit," in murder mystery parlance. After all, we have worked hard on this analysis, and we want the reader to know all the wonderful facts and all the great analytical methods that have gone into our conclusions. I hope this does not come as too much of a shock, but most of your readers really will not care about all those bells and whistles that went into the analysis. *They want the bottom line,* and that is what we as intelligence professionals are paid to deliver. Of course, professors expect you to provide those details. They will read them and evaluate your knowledge of the subject accordingly. But by putting that bottom line up front, you are delivering the goods and *energizing* your writing, too.

Use the Energizers: *Strong Verbs*

Verbs are the strongest parts of speech in the English language. They carry the action of the sentence, and they can be energetic or dull. You might write, "Russian tanks came to Putinville and quickly put an end to the demonstration." That sentence conveys meaning, but is it energetic? It just sits there and yawns back at you as you read. Now look at this one: "Russian tanks roared into Putinville and quickly crushed the demonstration." Doesn't that sentence convey a more vivid impression in your mind?

Of course, there is a tradeoff here. You need to be careful not to overdo this type of writing. It is terribly easy to get caught up in the spirit of energetic writing and lose sight of the fact that you are still just trying to convey a meaningful thought to your reader. Before long you can begin to sound like you are writing a techno-thriller or, worse, a comic book: "Smash! Bam! Holy Squash, Batman, look at those Russian tanks!" So temper your energy with a healthy dose of common sense.

One way to check for energetic verbs is to look for the number of times you use the verb "to be" or any of its conjugations: *am, are, is, was, were, be, been, being.* That verb is one of the weakest in the English language, simply because it does no more than portray a state of being. Usually you can find another verb to take its place and make your writing more vigorous in the process. Here is an example: "Relief workers at the scene of the earthquake were unanimous in their praise of the International Red Cross." Try one of these on for size instead: "Relief workers at the scene of the earthquake unanimously praised the International Red Cross" or, "At the earthquake scene, relief workers unanimously praised the International Red Cross."

Another problem with the "to be" verb is that it often leads to the passive voice, which almost always saps the energy from your writing. Let's look at a variation of our earthquake sentence above: "The earthquake scene was visited by the Red Cross." That sentence is in the passive voice because the *doer* of the action, the Red Cross, is not in the position of the subject. The sentence is not wrong. In fact, it highlights the object of the sentence, the earthquake, which might be your intent. But the sentence would be stronger in the active voice, like this: "The Red Cross visited the earthquake scene." Note the position of the subject and object now, and the elimination of the prepositional "by" phrase from the previous sentence, saving us a few words in the process. That brings us to another means of energizing your writing: avoiding the weak prepositional phrase.

Watch Out for the Wimps: *Prepositional Phrases*

If the verb "to be" and its permutations are the 98-pound weaklings of our language, then prepositional phrases are the ones that get sand kicked into their faces by the 98-pounders. While some prepositions are unavoidable, there is a tendency to string them together in long sequences—boring! Look at this phrase from a student's paper: "The chief of one of the tribes involved in the resistance movement in Afghanistan. . . ." If your tendency is the same as mine, you will find yourself reading these kinds of sentences in a rhythmic, singsong voice. As a result, you lose your train of thought. Look at my rewrite of that phrase: "A tribal chief in the Afghan resistance movement. . . ." The second version has 8 words instead of the 14 in the original, almost a 50 percent savings. It still conveys the same meaning, doesn't it? Yes, it still has one prepositional phrase; but the original had four of them. If I had gone to extremes to eliminate *all* prepositions, the rewrite would have sounded awkward: "An Afghan resistance movement tribal chief. . . ." Stacking adjectives like firewood is a poor alternative to eliminating prepositions. Again, use discretion and common sense.

Still-l-l Go-o-oing . . .

You have probably seen the battery commercial where the little pink bunny marches across the screen beating a drum while the voiceover says, "Stil-l-l Go-o-oing." The point is clear: those batteries have the energy to keep going after their competitors wear down. We have to write like that: keep an energetic tone in the writing that makes the reader *want* to keep going. Energize your writing in three ways: put your most important points early in the paper; use strong verbs; and spare the prepositional phrases.

Remaining Objective

Another important consideration in writing intelligence is *objectivity*. As human beings, managing our own lives and the lives of others, we make hundreds of informed decisions daily. Will we need an umbrella today? To find out, we listen to our local weather forecast. We are on a diet. Do we buy "I Can't Believe It's Not Butter" or "Smart Beat" margarine? We read the labels to see which is lower in fat.

Generally these decisions are easy to make. The facts on which we base them are as close as the television or radio or a product's packaging label. But all of us have carried an umbrella around all day only to find it did not rain as our weather forecaster predicted. We have all been fooled by packaging descriptions: One brand, for example, may list grams of fat in one teaspoon. The other brand measures the amount of fat in one tablespoon. Even if we read the labels carefully, can we trust them?

Now step from the world of mundane decisions to the world of the intelligence professional. The intelligence professional who draws the wrong conclusion or makes an incorrect forecast may not simply inconvenience people with a burdensome umbrella. Inaccuracies can snowball into more inaccuracies and into catastrophe—nor are the facts easily obtained. The intelligence professional cannot rely on leaders like North Korean president Kim Jong-il to provide a blueprint outlining his plans. Even if facts are available, they may not be accurate. Furthermore, the more serious the decisions are, the greater the chances that emotions will cloud judgment.

Evaluating Sources

One of the first steps in writing a credible report or assessment is to ground it in support that is objective and current. This support may be from primary or secondary sources. (See chapter 1 for a more detailed discussion of source levels.) Primary sources could be surveys and interviews you conduct, historical documents (treaties, maps, laws) that you interpret yourself, or imagery you examine. Secondary sources consist of the work of other people—their fieldwork or data, their analyses or studies. Bear in mind that, if both primary and secondary sources are available, you should use both. Once gathered, you will need to evaluate who wrote the article or made the statement (if you conducted an interview), the date, and the publisher (especially for articles from current magazines).

The Originator

Yes, the person you interviewed or read may be an expert on your topic. President George W. Bush no doubt listened to many experts regarding Iraqi weapons of mass destruction. But they were not all reporting the same facts or offering similar interpretations of those facts. Researchers must go one step further. On what basis has the originator arrived at his or her point of view? Has that person approached the subject with a preestablished attitude and interpreted the evidence in light of that attitude?

Now examine your own views. Why did you select this source? If you share the source's interpretation, why do you do so, and in what ways do your views differ from the source's? Consider the student who interviews a previous commander now stationed in a prominent Pentagon position that gives even more credence to his words because he knows that source shares his own convictions on the subject. Objectivity will be skewed. The researcher may hear what he *wants* to hear but not what he *needs* to hear.

The Date

All researchers should strive to acquire the most recent data, although the latest is not necessarily the best. Again, remember to read both primary and secondary sources. In a paper on Soviet military strategy, Carl von Clausewitz's *On War* would be a primary source (and do make sure you get the best translation of primary works written in foreign languages). Next, read interpretations of his ideas that include the experts and cover the span of history up to the present. Do not assume that all the work on Clausewitz ended definitively with Michael Howard. For example, a December 6, 1990, *Washington Post* article dealt with how Clausewitz's writing applied to decision makers determining Persian Gulf strategy. Primary sources can take on new meaning as they are applied to new situations or viewed through the eyes of a different generation.

The Publisher

Most major book publishers (Scribner, McGraw-Hill, Random House, and others) cannot afford to appeal to a particular readership, but weekly magazines target a specific segment of society. The researcher needs to identify the owner or managing editor's biases. Articles in the *Weekly Standard* will interpret events with the conservative slant of its editors. Do you know who puts out the *National Review*? *New Republic*? *The Nation*? As a researcher trying to achieve objectivity, you should.

Evaluating Arguments

Now that you have evaluated the source itself, you need to assess the arguments put forth in or by that source. Evaluating

arguments—those we read, see, and hear, and those we construct ourselves—is challenging. We may be generally wary of
statistical evidence, perhaps because numbers can be easily dis-
torted or because we do not understand complex statistical tables. At the same time, though, we may be suckers for
emotionally charged arguments. Show me pictures of helpless
animals being subjected to scientific experimentation, and I become an animal rights activist—for the moment anyway.
Whether such reasoning is deliberate or accidental, it is deceitful,
and we have all been swayed by it. The vigilant reader who
catches such arguments, though, is not likely to take the work seriously. As writers of credible reports and assessments, we must
write for the vigilant reader. Watch for common fallacies of hasty
generalization, either/or hypothesis, post hoc fallacy, appeals to
emotions, and statistics.

Hasty Generalizations

Hasty generalizations are conclusions based on insufficient
evidence. Stereotypes are examples of this fallacy. Not all
teenagers and elderly people are bad drivers, nor are all ac-
countants boring. Not all military officers are conservative. Beware of any reasoning that has roots in sexual, racial, ethnic, or
religious bias.

Either/or Hypothesis

Either/or reasoning, like the hasty generalization, almost always oversimplifies the evidence. This reasoning demands that
we accept one of two extreme positions. The committee that pro-
claims either private health companies or a federal agency
should manage a national health insurance program has failed
to consider other viable options.

Post Hoc Fallacy

This reasoning assumes that, because event B happened after
event A, event A caused event B. Superstitions are based on this

fallacy. The black cat that crossed your path did not cause your flat tire. The person who runs over broken glass carelessly dropped by a garbage truck, has a flat tire 10 minutes later, and automatically assumes the broken glass caused the flat is also guilty of the post hoc fallacy. The assumption may be correct, but the driver must be able to prove his conclusion in a court of law if he is to receive compensation from the waste management company.

Appeals to Emotion

Who thinks about the human lives being saved by scientists when pictures of maimed beagles are shown graphically? Who thinks of air pollution and health problems linked to cigarettes in an advertisement picturing a robust, tanned cowboy enjoying the fresh air and glory of space in Montana. Photographs, direct quotations from famous people, music, name-dropping, and loaded words—all can mask central issues. We have seen the bruised faces of abused POWs and listened to their ordeals; we could not help but be outraged.

Statistics: Buy the Numbers?

How to Lie with Statistics and works similar to it have exposed the problems rooted in statistical evidence. Statistics can be based on unrepresentative data or on unreliable data (data that cannot be or have not been validated). What is the size of the database? What is its composition—people or laboratory animals? Consider the following polls surveying Americans' response to Operation Desert Storm: a television survey that invites viewers to register their opinion on U.S. action in the Persian Gulf by calling one of two telephone numbers flashed on the bottom of the screen, and a telephone survey by a neutral pollster who randomly selects names from current voting lists. Which results would you rely on? Consider the factors that might affect accuracy. Does the television poll have any way to screen multiple votes from one caller? How does each poll verify voter eligibility? Were "no opinion" votes counted? Were all geographic sections of the United States represented? Were both Democrats and Republicans polled? Men and women? Eighteen-year-olds and retired?

Where Are the Truths in This Ugly Business?

The Quarterly Review of Doublespeak asked the following question: "When is an invasion not an invasion? When it's a 'pre-dawn vertical insertion,' as the Reagan administration called the invasion of Grenada. Or when it's called 'Operation Just Cause,' as the Bush administration called its invasion of Panama."[2] Advocates call themselves "pro-choice," while their opponents speak of "pro-life" or criticize the "baby killers." The answers are never easy. Henry David Thoreau maintained that when a person confronts the truth he will know it; it will cut through him like a scythe. Keep looking for that scythe.

Final Dressing: Titles and Headings

As you near the end of the drafting phase of your paper, look for a place to add a final "dressing" to make your work more pleasing to the reader's eye and, indeed, to catch the reader's eye in the first place. That final dressing might be your work's title, along with its headings and subheadings. One thing I notice in my review of papers is that the best ones are not only well organized and well written. The most excellent papers I see are also more interesting because they give the reader a clear road map in the form of well-thought-out titles and headings. I suspect that having a title that reflects a subject properly narrowed and focused, and using subheads that have been carefully and painstakingly constructed, benefits the writer as much as the reader.

The Title: Promise Only What You Can Deliver

I once reviewed a student paper titled "The 600-Ship Navy: National Strategy or Personal Mission?"[3] The minute I saw the title I wanted to read the paper, and my interest never waned throughout the paper's 15 or so pages. The writer had done a good job of narrowing the subject to something he could discuss in a paper of that length. In other words, he did not promise more than he could deliver. And he kept his promise. He discussed what was relevant to the title, and only that; he kept the reader's interest throughout; and he answered the question he had raised in the title (the answer was "Both").

A typical paper that I review is 10 to 20 pages long. Of course, the thicker the paper, the broader the subject can be. Look at the proposed title, "Japan: A Study," in the outline below for paper A. Even a PhD candidate submitting a proposal for a dissertation of hundreds of pages would never be able to get a subject like "Japan: A Study" approved. It would be much too broad. Think, then, how much more difficult it would be to cover "Japan" adequately in a paper of 10 to 20 pages. It simply cannot be done.

Headings: Signposts for Writers and Readers

Headings are, quite frankly, fundamental to an organized, readable paper. They serve both the writer and the reader.

How Headings Help the Writer

Headings help writers organize all the data they have collected. Consider these two sample outlines for papers on Japan:

Paper A (Japan: A Study)
- I. Background
- II. Discussion
- III. Conclusion

Paper B (Japan: The Power to Our West)
- I. Background
  - A. Political History
  - B. Demography
  - C. Geography

II. Discussion
    A. Present Political System
    B. Japan's Economy Today
III. U.S. Interests
IV. Conclusion

Clearly, making decisions about what information to include and where it should go is much easier if, as in paper B, the student has isolated some specific areas he wants to cover. Thus, even before beginning the research, the writer will probably want to do a broad outline with generic headings similar to those in paper B's outline.

At this stage of the writing process the outline controls the paper; later, the paper more or less controls the outline, as evidenced in paper C below. The headings in paper C's outline most likely were tailored to the text and thus created after the paper was written. Such descriptive headings often pick up key phrases or ideas from the text and spotlight them as text headings—signposts for the writer as well as the reader.

No paper writes itself, but if writers are flexible and open to new ideas, their papers will evolve, perhaps into something quite different from what they had planned. Outlines and headings, like text, can be drafted and changed, redrafted and changed again, depending on the direction the research and writing take. The writer must beware, however, of giving the research and writing too much control and straying too far from the paper's original plan.

How Headings Help the Reader

For all the help headings give the writer, they are really there for the reader. They jump off the page to announce the topic. Without them, readers have to rely on the writer's transitions to carry them from point to point. Imagine reading the "Discussion" section of paper A. Not only does it cover Japan's political makeup, population, and terrain, but it also spans a huge period of time, reaching back into Japan's past, tracing its rise to economic power, and projecting where it will go in the 21st century.

Furthermore, because the generic "Discussion" heading established no boundaries, it invited the writer to sprinkle throughout facts on Japan's military, religious, and educational systems. Let's face it: there are no transitions that can carry a reader through such a morass.

I also should emphasize that headings enable the reader to locate easily only those parts that interest him. Imagine a researcher interested in facts on Japan's agriculture picking up a 300-page book on Japan that has no chapters. Let's hope the book has an index. I personally glance at the headings to see how the paper approaches its topic, to get a feel for what the paper is about before I begin reading it.

Lest you assume paper B is the epitome of heading excellence, examine paper C's outline as follows:

Paper C (The Threat of the Rising Sun)[4]
I. Economic Health in the International Environment
II. Japan: Vitamins or Bad Medicine?
III. The Benefits of Competition
IV. Political Help or Interference
V. Godzilla in Proper Perspective
VI. Deterrence—Japanese Style
VII. Japan, Not Camelot
VIII. It's a New World out There

Just from the headings, I know the paper focuses on Japan as an economic force. Should we view it as a threat, a Godzilla rising from the sea to destroy those in its path? The last two headings remind us that Japan faces problems and experiences failures. If Japan is not Godzilla and not Camelot, then the final heading suggests that obsolete attitudes and perspectives must change—"It's a new world out there."

Descriptive Headings versus Generic Headings

Some writers either are not creative enough or do not wish to take the time to construct headings that are catchy or contain allusions (Camelot, Godzilla), and for some papers such headings are neither possible nor appropriate. But in all honesty, headings like "Introduction" and "Conclusion" are meaningless.

I must acknowledge here that some instructors provide all the headings a student needs for a paper such as a country study; I have seen some excellent papers built from outlines such as the following:

  I. Historical Background
 II. Current Situation
III. U.S. Interests
IV. Scenarios That Could Threaten U.S. Interests
 V. Indicators to Watch

Even prescribed headings, however, can often be supplemented by an interesting, focused title and descriptive subheads.

Marketing analysts would tell us packaging is vital to a product's success. If that were not the case, then you would see considerably more plain wrappers on your grocer's shelves. The color, the bold lettering, and the product brand names all catch our attention as we wander the aisles of our supermarket. We likewise are less inclined to "buy" an argument packaged in generic titles or headings. If we are going to invest our money or time in a product, we want a little glitz. This is not to say that packaging necessarily makes the quality of one product better than another. Most generic brands are just fine and can even save you a few pennies. But I will say this: I did not have to search through the hundreds of student papers on hand looking for one with descriptive headings. From memory, I went immediately to the student folder containing paper C. That says it all!

One Final Note

It's not easy to turn a blank piece of paper or a dark monitor into an outline or a mind map and then to develop that prewriting into a rough draft. Some writers have no problem at all sitting at a computer screen and turning out thousands of words at a sitting; but those same writers often fail in the important process of revising their work. You've heard that "the project is never completed until the paperwork is done." That paperwork, for the intelligence writer, is the process of polishing and revising the writing until an acceptable finished product is the result. "Finished intelligence" means not only all-source, analyzed, evaluated intelligence but also proofread and edited intelligence. That's the subject of the next chapter.

> The Moving Finger writes; and, having writ,
> Moves on: nor all your Piety nor Wit
> Shall lure it back to cancel half a Line,
> Nor all your Tears wash out a Word of it.
> —*The Rubaiyat of Omar Khayyam*

Exercises in Writing the First Draft

Exercise 1: Approaches to Writing Styles

Study the following pairs. How do the two approaches differ? What relationship does each set up between the writer and the audience? What are the advantages and disadvantages of each style?

Pair A

- The commander wants to meet with us to review the results of the latest joint exercise. How about 0900 on 22 April 2008?
- The latter part of April seems to be a good time to review the results of our joint exercise with the commander. Let me know if 0900 on 22 April 2008 is open.

Pair B

- This is a joke, right? This report is clearly not the work of a professional. Where did you learn how to write, anyhow?
- This style of writing does have a place in intelligence, but usually not in the analytical report. I'm all in favor of conversational style. Usually it is in active voice and easily

understandable. You do take chances with stuffed shirts who have no sense of humor, though. Please rewrite this report, modifying its tone, wording it more appropriately.

Exercise 2: Finding the Topic Sentence

A good piece of intelligence writing has an identifiable topic sentence. That sentence contains the essence of the paragraph, and all other sentences—four or five of them as a general rule—will relate directly to it. No other sentence in a good paragraph could be the topic sentence. Look at this paragraph, for example. Could any but the first one be the topic sentence?

One way to check for a topic sentence is to scramble the order of the sentences in a paragraph. Computers make that an easy job. Simply type a paragraph and then use a cut-and-paste function to shift the sentences around. No matter how they are mixed up, the topic sentence should still be obvious to the reader. Let's test that hypothesis in some exercises. Find the topic sentence in the paragraphs below. Assume that each is the first paragraph of a longer paper.

Paragraph 1

As a result, the Cold War reached new heights of tension. Nations all over the world began "taking sides" with the superpowers, and the battle lines were clearly drawn. The Soviet Union invaded Afghanistan in December 1979. President Jimmy Carter, in a move of defiant bravado, withdrew the U.S. team from the 1980 Olympic competition. The crisis threatened to escalate into one involving worldwide alliances.

Paragraph 2

Some people would rather work alone, while others like to work with other people. The intelligence analyst examines information and makes decisions about that information. There are, however, additional ways in which personality influences how we do our jobs and our degree of job satisfaction. Some people, for example, enjoy making decisions while others are reluctant to decide because of perceived information inadequacy. Those two tasks form the core of the intelligence profession. Another aspect relates to our decision-making style.

Exercise 3: More Topic Sentence Exercises

A topic sentence is the main idea—the central focus—of a paragraph. In intelligence writing the topic sentence should usually be the first sentence of each paragraph, in keeping with the principle that intelligence writers place the most important ideas early in their papers. The following sentences are extracted from essays submitted by graduate students. Read the sentences carefully. Determine the topic sentence of each paragraph. Then renumber the sentences so that the paragraph flows smoothly. Use the blank space after each sentence for the new number.

Topic Sentence Exercise No. 1: George H. W. Bush's Qualifications to be President of the United States

1. Under President Ford, George Bush was the Director of Central Intelligence (DCI).____
2. In that capacity, he has been a member of the National Security Council and, therefore, worked closely with the U.S. intelligence community and the foreign and national policy process.____
3. George Bush is exceedingly qualified to make decisions about the National Foreign Intelligence Community.____
4. He has been the Vice President of the United States for eight years.____
5. Mr. Bush was also a congressman, and his total federal government service exceeds 25 years.____

Topic Sentence Exercise No. 2: Peace in the Persian Gulf

1. The Iran-Iraq war has hindered the ability of other Middle East nations to export crude oil.____

2. From a U.S. domestic perspective, peace in the Persian Gulf will signal the return of higher gas prices._____
3. Additionally, since Iran and Iraq will no longer be selling oil at reduced prices to finance their war efforts, oil price indexes will rise as these two nations compete in the OPEC community._____
4. The absence of a need for U.S. warships escorting oil tankers in the Persian Gulf will mean a return to higher volumes of oil shipments._____

Topic Sentence Exercise No. 3: Cuts in the Defense Budget

1. Like people crowding through a door, some programs will have to wait, or turn sideways, presenting skinnier profiles to the funding door, and taking longer to get through._____
2. Many of these programs are reaching the "fattest" part of their funding profile, finished with research and development, and should be entering series production at economical procurement rates._____
3. The Defense Department stubbornly continued funding programs authorized in the euphoric rearmament of President Reagan's first term._____
4. Given that the defense budget, far from growing at 5 percent per year after inflation, is in fact not growing at all, these "fat" programs cannot all squeeze through the narrow funding door._____
5. This means longer, slower production runs at higher unit prices or less bang for the buck._____

Topic Sentence Exercise No. 4: Venezuela's Economy

1. Mid-2007 reports estimated Venezuela's yearly inflation rate at almost 20 percent, with a monthly increase forecast for the near future._____
2. This debt burden forces the Venezuelan government to make certain choices—choices that almost invariably make life harder for the average worker._____

3. Although Venezuela enjoys the most evenly distributed and one of the largest per capita incomes in Latin America, individual Venezuelans have seen their wealth eroded by runaway inflation.____

4. Venezuela owes so much in interest payments alone that no matter how much it earns via a vigorous export sector, all new funds will merely find their way into the asset accounts of North American banks.____

5. Venezuela's inflation problems are compounded by its huge external debt.____

Topic Sentence Exercise No. 5: Cuban-Soviet Relations

1. Though U.S. hostility toward his regime is often blamed for Fidel's initial move into the Soviet camp, it is more than likely that his global ambition and fanatical hatred of the United States had already precluded any other path.____

2. The enduring relationship that developed between Castro's Cuba and the Soviet Union was not a natural progression from Soviet support for the Cuban revolution but rather a subsequent development.____

3. Instead, the relationship gradually developed in the early 1960s as Castro became increasingly estranged from the United States and actively sought Soviet sponsorship.____

4. The subsequent growth of the ties has resulted in Cuba's economic dependence on and importance as a strategic asset to the Soviet Union.____

5. In contrast to their immediate embrace of the Sandinista regime in Nicaragua, the Soviets did not instantly welcome or recognize the Castro regime.____

Exercise 4: The Style of Intelligence Writing

The *Random House Dictionary of the English Language* (second edition, unabridged) defines *style* as "those components or features of a literary composition that have to do with the form of

expression rather than the content of the thought expressed."
With that definition in mind, list at least six words that you think
might describe the *form* of good intelligence writing.

Style—Or the Lack of It!—In Writing

Can you sometimes recognize the style of an author? What
elements of a writer's words on paper make those words recognizable or unique to that particular author?

1. And nothing can we call our own but death,
    And that small model of the barren earth
    Which serves as paste and cover to our bones.
    For God's sake, let us sit upon the ground
    And tell sad stories of the death of kings.
2. Deep calleth unto deep.
3. Why do you hate the South?
    I dont hate it . . . I dont hate it. . . . *I dont hate it* he
    thought, panting in the cold air, the iron New England
    dark; *I dont. I dont! I dont hate it! I dont hate it!*
4. The great masses of the people . . . will more easily fall vic-
    tims to a big lie than to a small one.
    The words a writer uses and the way those words are
    used in sentences and paragraph's define that writer's
    style.

Do Your Words Make Sense?

'Twas brillig, and the slithy toves
Did gyre and gimble in the wabe;
All mimsy were the borogoves,
And the mome raths outgrabe.

In the excerpt from "The Jabberwocky's Song" above, what
part of speech is the word "slithy"? What about the word
"wabe"? What were the toves doing? Where? How did the borogoves feel?

Now look at the introduction to a graduate student's thesis, reprinted below. "The Jabberwocky's Song" makes just as much sense, doesn't it?

Excerpt from a Graduate Student Thesis on "Deception," Fall 1987

> The purpose of this thesis is to examine deception in depth and provide accurate assessment of key factors effectively utilized for successful implementation. Utilizing the assumption that military deception at the strategic and tactical level has been and may again be an effective and efficient technique in armed conflict, one that repays handsomely the minimal investment of resources it usually requires. The nature of this information presented will enable a unique insight into those special situations which generally attribute to the deceptive operation.
>
> The task of identifying prominent characteristics within the framework of case studies will not be limited to strategic deception, but also include examples from tactical deception. Because of the wide scope of this requirement, the infrastructure for methodology will be based upon broader considerations of analyzing and scrutinizing data accurately to assess the capabilities and possible courses of action. The process used to formulate will remain essentially the same, regardless of peculiarities of presentation of case study aspects. Furthermore, the visualization of principles peculiarities which are relevant in planning and supporting deceptive operations will be identified in each particular case.

With only a minimum investment of time and effort, I condensed that 183-word monstrosity to its 26-word essence, below. That's an *86 percent savings* of a reader's time and energy—not to mention the frustration of wading through that plodding prose. My rewrite follows:

> Deception pays handsome dividends for a minimum investment of resources in war. Case studies of both strategic and tactical deception show the peculiarities of each type.

Notice in the rewrite that I took special pains to avoid what I call "defining methods." That's a common practice in the community of scholars, and it's one reason academic papers often read like—well, academic papers. You define your methods when you use terms like this writer did to open his introduction: "The purpose of this thesis is. . . ." Other common method-defining phrases include the following: "This paper will examine . . ."; "My thesis will discuss the topic . . ."; and "I will attempt in this paper to prove. . . ." Those are empty words that do little more than fill space. We try to avoid that kind of writing in the intelligence community.

Note also that this student's method defining led him to use the weak passive voice over and over again: "The task . . . will not be limited . . ."; "the infrastructure . . . will be based upon . . ."; and "the visualization of principles peculiarities [whatever the heck that means!] . . . will be identified. . . ." When any writing style causes the writer to resort to passive voice so often, it is a weak writing style.

Answers to the Exercises in Chapter 5

Exercise 1: Approaches to Writing Styles

Pair A

The distinctions between these two styles of writing are subtle but noticeable. The first example appears to be from one person to another of equal or lower rank or status. Notice the informality of the question, "How about 0900 on 22 April 2008?" An informal, relaxed approach in correspondence between peers can produce favorable results. The second sentence in the second example, on the other hand, is an imperative: "Let me know. . . ." This note was probably written by a superior to one of his or her subordinates. There are advantages to using moderate language, even with imperatives. "Let me know" is considerably less forceful than "Be in my office. . . ." At least the superior in this case has offered consideration of the subordinate's schedule.

Pair B

These two examples are taken verbatim from comments that instructors penned on student papers. Imagine writing a paper and having a professor comment, "This is a joke . . . . Where did you learn to write, anyhow?" That kind of negativism spawns resentment and bitter feelings but seldom produces better writing. On the other hand, it certainly caught the attention of the writer, who came directly to the Writing Center for help. The second example responded to a paper that was assigned a grade of C-, but the professor let the writer know *both* the strengths and weaknesses of the writing. That student learned considerably more about his shortcomings—and strengths—than did the first one.

Exercise 2: Finding the Topic Sentence

Paragraph 1

The Soviet Union invaded Afghanistan in December 1979. As a result, the Cold War reached new heights of tension. The crisis threatened to escalate into one involving worldwide alliances. Nations all over the world began "taking sides" with the superpowers, and the battle lines were clearly drawn. President Jimmy Carter, in a move of defiant bravado, withdrew the U.S. team from the 1980 Olympic competition.

Paragraph 2

The intelligence analyst examines information and makes decisions about that information. Those two tasks form the core of the intelligence profession. There are, however, additional ways in which personality influences how we do our jobs and our degree of job satisfaction. Some people would rather work alone, while others like to work with other people. Another aspect relates to our decision-making style. Some people, for example, enjoy making decisions while others are reluctant to decide because of perceived information inadequacy.

Exercise 3: More Topic Sentence Exercises

Topic Sentence Exercise No. 1: George H. W. Bush's
Qualifications to be President of the United States

1. Under President Ford, George Bush was the Director of Central Intelligence (DCI). (4)
2. In that capacity, he has been a member of the National Security Council and, therefore, worked closely with the U.S. intelligence community and the foreign and national policy process. (3)
3. George Bush is exceedingly qualified to make decisions about the National Foreign Intelligence Community. (1)
4. He has been the Vice President of the United States for eight years. (2)
5. Mr. Bush was also a congressman, and his total federal government service exceeds 25 years. (5)

Topic Sentence Exercise No. 2: Peace in the Persian Gulf

1. The Iran-Iraq war has hindered the ability of other Middle East nations to export crude oil. (2)
2. From a U.S. domestic perspective, peace in the Persian Gulf will signal the return of higher gas prices. (1)
3. Additionally, since Iran and Iraq will no longer be selling oil at reduced prices to finance their war efforts, oil price indexes will rise as these two nations compete in the OPEC community. (4)
4. The absence of a need for U.S. warships escorting oil tankers in the Persian Gulf will mean a return to higher volumes of oil shipments. (3)

Topic Sentence Exercise No. 3: Cuts in the Defense Budget

1. Like people crowding through a door, some programs will have to wait, or turn sideways, presenting skinnier profiles to the funding door, and taking longer to get through. (4)

2. Many of these programs are reaching the "fattest" part of their funding profile, finished with research and development, and should be entering series production at economical procurement rates. (2)
3. The Defense Department stubbornly continued funding programs authorized in the euphoric rearmament of President Reagan's first term. (1)
4. Given that the defense budget, far from growing at 5 percent per year after inflation, is in fact not growing at all, these "fat" programs cannot all squeeze through the narrow funding door. (3)
5. This means longer, slower production runs at higher unit prices or less bang for the buck. (5)

Topic Sentence Exercise No. 4: Venezuela's Economy

1. Mid-2007 reports estimated Venezuela's yearly inflation rate at almost 20 percent, with a monthly increase forecast for the near future. (2)
2. This debt burden forces the Venezuelan government to make certain choices—choices that almost invariably make life harder for the average worker. (5)
3. Although Venezuela enjoys the most evenly distributed and one of the largest per capita incomes in Latin America, individual Venezuelans have seen their wealth eroded by runaway inflation. (1)
4. Venezuela owes so much in interest payments alone that no matter how much it earns via a vigorous export sector, all new funds will merely find their way into the asset accounts of North American banks. (4)
5. Venezuela's inflation problems are compounded by its huge external debt. (3)

Topic Sentence Exercise No. 5: Cuban-Soviet Relations

1. Though U.S. hostility toward his regime is often blamed for Fidel's initial move into the Soviet camp, it is more than likely that his global ambition and fanatical hatred of

the United States had already precluded any other path. (4)
2. The enduring relationship that developed between Castro's Cuba and the Soviet Union was not a natural progression from Soviet support for the Cuban revolution but rather a subsequent development. (1)
3. Instead, the relationship gradually developed in the early 1960s as Castro became increasingly estranged from the United States and actively sought Soviet sponsorship. (3)
4. The subsequent growth of the ties has resulted in Cuba's economic dependence on and importance as a strategic asset to the Soviet Union. (5)
5. In contrast to their immediate embrace of the Sandinista regime in Nicaragua, the Soviets did not instantly welcome or recognize the Castro regime. (2)

Exercise 4: The Style of Intelligence Writing

This exercise can have many possible answers because the form of good intelligence writing can be described many ways. I had six nouns in mind, though, when I constructed this exercise, and they were the six words I used in chapters 2 and 3 of this book to describe the basic considerations of intelligence writing: (1) clarity, (2) conciseness, (3) correctness, (4) appropriateness, (5) completeness, and (6) coherence.

Style—Or the Lack of It!—In Writing

In this exercise, note that on occasion not only the words themselves but also the *context* suggests the style of the writer. This principle is important to consider in your own writing, too.

1. William Shakespeare, *Richard II*, III, ii, 144.
2. *The Holy Bible*, Psalms 42:7.
3. William Faulkner, *Absalom, Absalom* (New York: Random House, 1936), chap. 9.
4. Adolf Hitler, *Mein Kampf* (Marburg-Lahn, Germany: Blindenstudienanstalt, 1933), vol. 1, chap. 10.

Do Your Words Make Sense?

Volumes of scholarly articles have been written about this nonsensical verse from Lewis Carroll's *Through the Looking-Glass*. Strictly on the basis of syntax (word order) a reader may reasonably be assured that "slithy" is an adjective describing the "toves." We also assume that "wabe" is a noun because of its position as the object of the preposition "in."

Although it sounds silly, most readers can readily determine that the toves were "gyring" and "gimbling." Of course we have no idea what that means, but don't you get a sense of some action from the words? A number of respondents we've tried this on said they pictured something like swimming or bouncing around in the surf. That may be because they associate the word "wabes" with the similar word "waves."

Notes

1. *The American Heritage Dictionary of the English Language*, 4th ed. (New York: Houghton Mifflin, 2000), under the word "style."
2. National Council of Teachers of English, "Doublespeak and the Invasion of Panama," *Quarterly Review of Doublespeak* 16, no. 3 (April 1990): 1.
3. Lieutenant Michael Seitz, U.S. Navy, "The 600-Ship Navy: National Strategy or Personal Mission?" Unclassified seminar paper (Washington, D.C.: Defense Intelligence College, February 1990).
4. Captain Brad Nelson, U.S. Army, "The Threat of the Rising Sun," Unclassified seminar paper (Washington, D.C.: Defense Intelligence College, February 1990).

6

Revision: Polishing Your Writing

Summary

The third distinct phase of the writing process is *revision* or *rewriting*. Here you revisit your writing and clean it up, editing for organization and style, and proofreading for errors.

- After you've written the first draft, set it aside for as long as possible, then return and reread it objectively. Have someone else read it and make comments.
- Polish your first draft by using short words and varying the length of your sentences. Use active voice (subject—verb—object) wherever possible, avoiding the weaker passive voice. Check again for *precise* words and phrases; say what you mean, and be sure your reader will understand precisely what you are trying to say. If you are certain of a judgment, say so; but don't convey the message of 100 percent probability if the analysis doesn't support such a conclusion.
- Prune the deadwood from your writing: redundancies and other excess baggage add nothing to the content. Check your writing for negativism. Try to be positive, and convince your reader that you clearly know what you're

talking about. Use a peer group to help you revise your work.

- To review content, use the "Three R Method": Reread, reenvision, and rewrite. Employ a hierarchy of reviewing and editing concerns as well, moving from organization to words, or vice versa.
- Be sure your paper has a thesis statement in the form of a bottom line up front, and that the reader can easily determine the main point you're trying to make.
- Check paragraphs to be sure that related ideas and details are grouped properly, each paragraph with a topic sentence. Check for *cohesion* of paragraphs by looking for pronoun reference, word repetition, sentence-structure repetition, and collocation. Employ proper *transitions* to help your reader see relationships of logic, time, and space.
- Use your computer's grammar-checker, but don't count on it exclusively for the revision process.

Revision is a final step writers take to polish their words for their readers. It is an essential step in wrapping up the writing phase.

Basic Revision Techniques

In chapter 2, I wrote about the importance of correctness as a basic principle in writing. Correctness in intelligence writing means both precision in word choice and mechanical correctness. Until you have polished your written product to ensure that you have met these criteria, you don't have a finished intelligence product. Well-established procedures will help you clean up your first draft and make it more readable. These techniques take some time and effort but are well worth the final result in terms of reader (and writer) satisfaction. The procedures include the use of short words and sentences, active voice instead of passive, precise language, and the pruning of deadwood in your writing.

Use Short Words and Variable-Length Sentences

For some reason, many writers feel they haven't accomplished their objective unless they have mired their readers in a swamp of big words and long, compound-complex sentences. I've advised you several times already to have a dictionary and thesaurus handy when you're writing; but there should be little cause for you to have to rely constantly on those reference books while you're reading someone else's writing.

The daily working vocabulary of the average college graduate is about 6,000 to 12,000 words, although he or she may have an "inventory" of 60,000 words.[1] An average citizen, however, uses only about 3,000. Common dictionaries in use today list 150,000 or more words, but most of us are familiar with far fewer than that. We are certainly becoming more sophisticated with our vocabularies, and most of us today recognize words that were not in existence when our grandparents learned to speak English; for example, it's unlikely that Gramps ever heard of an "astronaut," a "byte," or a "blog." Our daily newspapers use as many as 6,000 different words. Compare that to the number of words that were used in the Old Testament (5,800) and the New Testament (4,800). Compare it, also, to the number of different words you find in the next intelligence publication you read.

I'm not suggesting, of course, that you count different words in an intelligence product just to make a point. It's usually obvious to the average reader when a writer is resorting to unnecessarily big words to make a point. One of the graduate papers I read was proceeding well in its description of tax reform under the Reagan administration. Then the author threw this gem at me: "Many other factors influenced the U.S. economy during this period and many of those were exogenous, stochastic events." While the meaning of the sentence was discernible from the context, many readers would nonetheless find themselves scurrying for the dictionary on that one.

This sentence came from the key judgments section of a student's paper: "Terrorist ideologues build contrived organizations predestined to relentless combat action." (I wrote in the margin, "Film at 11!" Although the words are generally understandable, they are strung together in an almost comical attempt to use the biggest words possible.)

The point to keep in mind is this: some of the best and most readable writing is that which uses the simplest, most direct words. Writers of intelligence documents need not prove that their vocabulary is greater than the average reader's. Even if that proof is conclusively established, an average reader will be so turned off by the writing that he or she will never finish the document. If you have to go to the dictionary or thesaurus for the meaning of a word, anticipate that your reader may have to do the same thing. Give that reader the benefit of a doubt. Use short words.

And what about your sentences? How short is short? What constitutes a long sentence? (Some might say 20 years to life.) Generally, however, a sentence of 20–30 words ("experts" disagree) is long enough. But the important principle is this: vary the length of your sentences. Too many short sentences will make your work sound choppy and irregular. At the other extreme, a succession of 20- or 30-word sentences will tire your readers and cause their train of thought to derail.

A number of word-processing software programs can help you determine the strength or weakness of your writing in the use of long words and sentences. Beware, though, the ones that don't allow you to input your own vocabulary. Your writing may be judged weak because of too many "uncommon words." If the subject of your paper is terrorism in Europe, you may find that the uncommon words list includes such terms as "terrorist," "terrorism," and "Europe."

Be Active, Not Passive

The normal order for the English language is the active voice: subject—verb—object, in that order. When you turn that order around and put the object before the subject, it generally tends to weaken the writing, and it leaves your reader with a question of "whodunit?" Look at the following examples:

"Economic aspects need to be considered when assessing the military capabilities of a nation." Of course they do but by whom? The writer could have anticipated his readers' question and written, "Intelligence analysts must consider economics when assessing a nation's military capabilities."

"As a result of the increasing number of protests, the need for timely and accurate sociological and political intelligence was recognized." Again the reader asks, "By whom?" The example is a little wordy, too. Compare this rewrite: "Because of increasing protests, officials recognized the need for timely and accurate sociological and political intelligence."

The passive voice, per se, is not *wrong*. It is simply to be discouraged when you're looking for a strong, positive writing style. If the object is more important than your subject, or if you simply want to emphasize the object rather than the subject, use the passive voice: "The motorized rifle regiment was sighted by the observer in OP Alpha." That's passive voice, but it emphasizes the important part of that sentence—the potential threat—rather than the observer at an observation post (OP) who did the sighting. Note the difference when that sentence is recast in the active voice: "The observer in OP Alpha sighted the motorized rifle regiment." Ho, hum.

Another acceptable use for the passive voice is when the subject or "doer" of the action is unknown: "The enemy soldiers were sighted at 2200 hours." It might be awkward to turn that sentence into active voice: "An unknown outpost sighted the enemy soldiers at 2200 hours." Clearly, the important event in that sentence is the sighting of the enemy, and the fact that the sighter was unknown is immaterial to your reader.

It's important, though, that you avoid using the passive voice as a "cover-up" for the unknown: "A friendly aircraft was fired upon last night near the border." Your reader wants to know, immediately, by whom? If you don't know the answer to that obvious question, then anticipate its asking and rephrase the sentence: "Unidentified antiaircraft artillery or surface-to-air missiles fired at a friendly aircraft last night near the border."

You haven't answered the question, but you have told the reader—positively!—that you don't have the answer.

You will also encounter the passive voice frequently in academic writing: "The importance of widgits to the North Korean economy will be described in this chapter." Passive voice does something for the writer of scholarly treatises: it precludes the need for using the first person ("I will describe . . .").

Other than the few examples cited above, it's wise for you to stick to the active voice. Your reader will find that your writing is stronger and makes a more positive statement.

Be Precise

I discussed the importance of precision back in chapter 2 under the heading "Correctness." But it bears repeating here. One of the hallmarks of a well-written intelligence product is the author's use of precise language. Even a precisely stated "I don't know" is more convincing than a fuzzily worded attempt at "talking around" the problem.

Some words are almost guaranteed to be imprecise because they are subject to interpretation by various readers. As you read the following words, try to form a mental image of their precise meanings: many; a few; several; quite; rather; a number of; very. Got the picture? Obviously, those are words to be avoided in your intelligence writing. Yet, every one of them has been used repeatedly in student papers.

Mark Twain suggested that, when you want to use the word "very" in your writing, you substitute "damn" instead. Twain surmised that an editor would delete the word, and your writing would be better for it.

Precision carries over into word usage and the way you put your sentences together, as well. Be sure that you have exactly the right word for the situation or event you are trying to describe. Then be certain that your sentences are woven together in such a way that they convey exactly the meaning you have in mind. Examine sentences for context and clarity. Try to decide whether they will make sense to the average reader who doesn't have your background and experience. The syntax of your sentences—the way words are strung together to form a meaningful thought—is a major factor in determining the precise meaning of what you are trying to say.

The following examples of imprecise writing led me to believe that the authors didn't care much about precision, either in choice of words or in syntax.

"One of the basic tenants for cooperation among terrorist groups is that they have a similar ideological basis." (What must the landlord think of these terrorist tenants? The precise word choice would have been "tenet"—a basic truth or principle.)

"In the 1970's nationalistic, autonomous terrorist groups plagued various European countries such as the Baader-Meinhof Gang." (The country of Baader-Meinhof? Is that anywhere near Wo-ist-der-Bahnhof? To be more precise, the writer should have said "terrorist groups such as the Baader-Meinhof Gang.")

"What these ties and cooperative efforts do not mean is that there has been no evidence for the formation of a single international terrorist organization." (It's not clear that there is no sense to that sentence. Always be suspicious of a sentence that has a double negative in it. Two wrongs may never make a right, but two negatives make a positive. In a roundabout, wordy kind of way, this sentence actually says: "These ties and cooperative efforts are evidence of a single international terrorist organization." But that is not what the author intended because the rest of the paper argued against any such terrorist organization. What's a reader to believe?)

I've used more illustrations for the idea of precision than any other tenant—er, tenet—so far in this book. I hope that you can appreciate the importance of this principle in your writing of intelligence papers.

Prune the Deadwood

Be your own most ruthless critic in pruning deadwood from your writing. Don't think of words only as combinations of letters to fill white space on a page or dark space on a monitor. Think of words as the tools of your profession—the only means you have of communicating to an audience the important work you're doing. You don't have time to waste in writing papers—neither do your readers have the time to devote to excess words and phrases in your writing.

Always allot a portion of your time to proofreading and editing your paper. Even under the pressure of a tight deadline, you can program *some* time for that purpose. Devote at least one proofing to looking for redundancies and other excess baggage. Check for the wordiness that often results from such usages.

"There's still too much to learn to allow myself to become too narrowly specialized." (That student's writing was too, too much. The repetitive "too" and "to" combination is irritating to the reader. The student might have said, "I still have much to learn before I pursue a narrow specialty.")

"Provide the needed revenues necessary to reduce the budget deficit." (The reader gets the point that the revenues are both needed and necessary. Is that really necessary? Drop one or the other, and the sense is better.)

"The classes presented to us were helpful. I thought they were helpful." (I always appreciate a student saying nice things, but that was overdoing it.)

The deadwood in the examples above is obvious. The excess stuff in your own writing won't be nearly so plain to you. It will take hard work, perseverance, and a lot of practice before you'll be able to prune the deadwood adequately. But it will be worth every minute of the time you spend because of the immense satisfaction you'll gain from the polished, professional finished product.

Ending on a Positive Note

I've spent many pages now telling you about some of the taboos of intelligence writing. Now that I'm nearing the end of this section on polishing your writing, it might be fitting to end on a positive note—just like intelligence writing should do.

Too often we read "Gloom and Doom" in intelligence writing. It leads us to believe that someone who studies and writes intelligence for a living must be terribly depressed! While there certainly are instances of depression in the intelligence community, like any other profession, we need to ensure that our writing doesn't carry an attitude of negativism or pessimism. (You're probably thinking, "That's easy for *you* to say! But I have to write papers about imminent hostilities or a new bomb that can destroy half of civilization. Do I end my paper by saying, 'Have a nice day!'?")

There is a time and place for all kinds of attitudes, and a paper of the nature just described certainly would not lend itself to a humorous or light treatment. But that's not what I have in mind. Look over your paper and review your thesis or main idea. Say, for example, your paper has the title "The Fizzle Fighter: An Idea Whose Time Has Come." Even from the title a reader can determine that your thesis is a positive one: you believe that the Fizzle is a state-of-the-art piece of equipment, or at least that its design is suited for its intended purpose.

With that idea in mind, your reader would not expect the paper to end by concluding that the Fizzle is unsuited to its primary mission or that it is an antiquated platform. Your writing should convey the positive outlook implied in your title.

A final example will illustrate this point and conclude this section. A graduate student wrote a four-page paper on the importance of biographic intelligence to his profession. He ended that paper like this:

> As such, biographics has proven repeatedly that it is a crucial tool in the war against terrorism. It often provides valuable information regarding terrorists' motivations and possible international connections, and thus aids counterterrorist analysts, but can only very rarely be used as a predictive tool by the antiterrorist professionals who must guard against terrorist attacks.

In just those few lines at the end of the paper, that student had negated his entire thesis on the importance of biographic intelligence. Read now how I recommended that this paragraph be rephrased for a more positive impact:

> Although biographic intelligence can rarely be used as a predictive tool by antiterrorist professionals, it has proven repeatedly

that it is a crucial tool in the war against terrorism. It often provides valuable information about terrorists' motivations and possible international connections, and thus aids counterterrorist analysis.

As the saying goes, "Think Positive." You *can* write with intelligence. And you *can* make a significant contribution to a worthy profession and to all the consumers of intelligence who will depend upon your writing for information.

Peer Review: A Means toward Revision

For those of you who envision yourselves tucked away in a cubicle laboriously churning out page after page of written text, and especially for you extraverts who dread such solitary confinement, I recommend a peer writing group. If you doubt the benefits of such interaction, let me speak pedagogically for a moment about collaborative learning. Learning must be more than the static retrieval of information from a teacher's head or a book and its transmission to paper. Dynamic learning occurs when we interact with others: when we discover, create, think up, and communicate our knowledge with others. Dynamic learning happens in a peer writing group.

Benefits of a Peer Writing Group

Certainly the peer group is a vehicle for trying out already formulated ideas, but it can also benefit the writer who has not yet begun to draft the paper. By engaging in a brainstorming session, the group lays before the potential writer an array of possible topics or approaches to a topic. From there, the group can assist the writer by making connections or by raising questions that the future paper may need to answer.

Since studies confirm that groups are more effective at solving problems than individuals, the peer group members can function as troubleshooters for any stage of the writing. One member of the group, for example, may know just the book

Revision: Polishing Your Writing / 199

needed to round out a writer's argument. Another member may have a more effective scheme for organizing the paper's argument.

Furthermore, exposure to individual viewpoints helps all of us look at the issues from a number of different angles: What is the opinion of the female in your group about women in combat? How does that devout Catholic sitting next to you view the sanctuary afforded Manuel Noriega by the Papal Nunciature in Panama?

Reacting to an In-Draft Text

From the Writer's Point of View

Before I discuss ways in which a peer group can respond constructively to an in-draft text, let me talk to the writer of that text. We all have "glitches" in our writing style, and getting rid of them is a life's work. Writing a lot, receiving feedback on that writing, and engaging in active, serious revision (which is *not* just editing out misspellings and errors in grammar) are the best ways to refine the writing. We also must realize that the ideal of a perfected text is a myth. Every text is reworkable, ultimately incomplete. Even the finished course paper may later be transformed into a thesis, revised for publication as an article, or used as a chapter for a future dissertation or book. What I am emphasizing is that nothing is engraved in stone. If you have a paper that you feel is perfect or that you no longer want to rework, that is not the text to submit to the group. You will not be receptive to the constructive criticism that, I promise you, some will offer. Expecting warm fuzzies and instead getting suggestions for revision only makes you, the writer, defensive.

From the Reviewers' Point of View

As a reviewer, how can you offer constructive criticism without damaging the writer's ego? Donald Murray, a writer and composition instructor, says we should not "put content" into a writer's work but rather "draw out what is already there."[2]

Thus, do not start with what is wrong with the text. Begin by pointing out the text's strengths. Encourage what is already there. Since writing is a matter of making choices, the peer readers can, by sharing their varied perceptions of the text, help writers flesh out their arguments, support them better, rethink their organizational scheme, and improve the writing's clarity.

Don't waste energy and time repairing the text (circling misspellings or pointing out punctuation problems) or quibbling over matters of word choice or phrasing that simply pit your taste against the writer's. The key is not to evaluate the text (that is the supervisor or professor's responsibility) but rather to help the writer improve it. *Respond* to the text; put questions to the writer about substance, structure, and style.

Guidelines for Forming a Group

The following guidelines may be helpful to those interested in forming a group as well as those presently in one:

1. Groups can range from two to seven people. Ideally, the group should have five people. Group members might come from your classes, your advisory track, or your office.
2. The most effective groups have members with a variety of backgrounds, skills, and viewpoints. If forming a group on your own, try to mix sexes, ability levels, leadership qualities, and personality types. If you are already a part of a group and it is not functioning effectively, perhaps the necessary variety is missing. Faculty members or managers can assist you in scrambling the eggs, so to speak.
3. Meet regularly, not sporadically. Make every Wednesday your group's day for a brown-bag lunch. Or meet early once or twice a week for morning coffee. Granted, a 40-minute lunch or 30-minute kaffee klatsch is not a lot of time, but if you dispense with the idle chitchat about professors, courses, or co-workers, much can be accomplished. (It is even possible that your group's lunch or coffee together may be one aspect of your week that you really look forward to.)

4. Try to give every member equal time. You may want to devote the whole time to a different member each week or break the session in half to accommodate two members. Just remember that it is terribly frustrating never to have your work discussed, just as it is nerve-racking to always be "on deck."

Your professor or supervisor might be willing to meet with your group, at your request. You might find that helpful to get you started in the first few meetings, and then continue on your own.

Review of Content

Most people view revision as a time to do a spell-check, the time to get all the commas in the right places. Revision is much more than that. It is the time when the writer reenvisions the entire text and "cleans house." Remember that, while you may be the only one who has to live with a cluttered house, your reader has to live with your writing.

Your first concern during the revision stage should be to examine the content of your writing. After all, if the paper lacks a focus, if the content doesn't convincingly and logically support the thesis, does it really matter that every word is spelled correctly and every sentence punctuated properly?

Both the "Three *R*" Method of Revision and "The Hierarchy of Reviewing and Editing Concerns" that follow give priority to content revision. They cover ways you can make your content focused, organized, cohesive, and logical.[3]

"Three R" Method of Revision

Reread

After a period away from the completed draft (at least a day), reread it carefully. Share it with another pair of eyes. A constructive, critical reading by one or more readers will help you achieve objectivity.

- Read first to see what the draft actually says (as opposed to what you were trying to say); see if you can outline the structure.
- Consider the draft from another reader's perspective.
- Identify (and list) specific problems and shortcomings: misplaced material; vague or abstract passages; and the need to acknowledge counterarguments.

Reenvision

- Reconsider your original purpose.
- Review your materials and gather additional information. Reread research notes to uncover counterarguments.
- List possible solutions to any problems: misplaced material (restructure entire body?); vague or abstract passages (add specifics, examples); and the need to acknowledge counterarguments (look up in research notes).

Rewrite

Rewrite the draft in light of what the rereading and reenvisioning revealed. Your revisions may be minor or major, focus on one small part of the draft, or reconstruct the entire essay. Move from "global" to "local" revisions—revisions that improve overall clarity and correctness.

- Make major revisions.
- Make sentence-level revisions, and edit to correct errors.

The Hierarchy of Reviewing and Editing Concerns

Organization: Thesis, sequence of ideas, opening paragraphs, abstracts, introductions, arrangement.

Missing Data: Contextless information, gaps in chronology, unnamed or partially named objects.

Logic: Badly arranged information, implausible evidence, gaps.

Paragraphing: Sequence, subordination, topic sentences; coherence.

Sentence Combining: Flow, rhythm, subordination, sequence.

Sentence Structure: Construction—impacted syntax, insufficient syntax, clause sequences; parallelism; syntax—agreement, ambiguous agent.

Diction: Word choice—erroneous or inexact term, jargon, or lack of jargon.

Style: A command- or agency-specific error, presentation error, or inconsistency.

Usage: A way of using words that the general reader does not accept.

Grammar: Error.

Proofreading: Typos, spacing, punctuation, indents.

Thesis and Overview Statements

To help readers find their way, especially through lengthy and difficult works, writers provide two kinds of orienting information: thesis statements to declare the main point and overview statements to identify the thesis and preview a text's plan.

Thesis Statements

Readers naturally look for the point of the paper. They need a context in which to understand the many diverse details and ideas they encounter as they read. If the writer does not supply a thesis, readers will construct one themselves, or they will try to.

Most readers look for the main idea early in the paper. Some expect papers to open with the thesis, and they need such statements to orient them. Although a thesis can go anywhere in the paper, I suggest that you place it up front to give readers a sense of control over the subject, enabling them to anticipate the content and more easily understand the relationship between its various ideas and details.

Below are some sample thesis statements written by students in a graduate degree program. The writers have clearly identified their purposes, and their readers will know what to expect as they read:

> Thesis 1: The end result of the U.S. effort in Vietnam was a tactical victory and a strategic defeat.

> Thesis 2: Although the invasion of Panama on 20 December 1989, known as Operation Just Cause, successfully protected the short-term U.S. interests, it failed to achieve long-term stability in Panama.

> Thesis 3: Amazon Basin development has had, and will continue to have, significant international impact and, particularly, an impact on the relations between the U.S. and Brazil.

Overview Statements

Overview statements are special kinds of thesis statements that not only identify the main idea but also give an overview of the way the thesis will be developed. Although the above thesis statements do forecast what is to come (we know, for example, that thesis 1 will discuss the tactical and strategic aspects of U.S. effort in Vietnam), we do not know what specific aspects will be covered. Thesis 2 does not identify the short-term U.S. interests for us either. The sample thesis below much more specifically prepares the reader for the main parts of the paper:

> Overview statement: Operation Just Cause was a military success and achieved its objectives of protecting U.S. citizens in Panama, apprehending Noriega, restoring democracy, and safeguarding the canal.

Paragraphing to Group Related Ideas and Details

Paragraphing signals to readers where one idea begins and ends; it groups sentences that focus on one topic together—or at least it should. Keep your paragraphs at a manageable length, manageable for you and for the reader. Note how difficult it is to digest the content of the following paragraph from a student's paper:

Today, the Aral Sea is quickly becoming a wasted, briny lake. The sea has shrunk from 68,000 km to 41,000 km because of the use of almost all of the water from the Amu Darya and Syr Darya rivers for the irrigation of cotton and other crops. With the rising water level decreasing at 1 meter per year and salinity rising to over 27 grams per liter, the shrinking of the sea has killed all the fish. Consequently, the fishing industry died on the Aral in 1983. Fishing villages that used to thrive with activity on the banks of the sea are now oasis towns in the middle of the desert. They survive on the canning of fish brought in by railroad from the Baltic. Visitors to the sea today find rusted members of the fishing fleet beached on sand dunes. The environment of the area also is endangered. Noticeable changes such as shorter, hotter summers and longer, colder winters are already taking their toll on the land and people. The growing season for cotton, the largest regional crop, has shrunk by 10 days, causing some areas to change to other crops. Huge dust storms, now averaging 9–10 per year, leave millions of tons of salt scattered over a large area around the lake, increasing the salinity of the soil. This affects the crops that can be grown in the region, since the sodium chloride and other salts that are blown by the wind are toxic to many plants. Another danger to the area is the excessive pesticide and herbicide usage noted in the Aral basin. Agricultural effluents such as defoliants, insecticides, chemical fertilizers, industrial waste and raw sewage have flowed into the rivers and the Aral, poisoning them. Since the people of the area use the water directly from irrigation ditches and rivers for domestic purposes, many now suffer from a variety of illnesses, including liver disorders, typhoid, and cancer of the throat. One Soviet visitor noted in a recent trip along the Syr Darya river: "When we tried to boil [water for] tea . . . the water curdled on the fire like sour milk. The flakes of sediment drove thirst away instantly." These problems have led the Soviet government to declare the sea and the surrounding region an ecological catastrophe.

Topic Sentence Placement

Readers are most attentive at two points in a paragraph—the beginning and the end. Therefore, you should position your topic sentence in one of those two places. Generally, you will put the topic sentence at the beginning, to orient the reader, and use the last sentence to either reemphasize the paragraph's main point or to transition into the next paragraph or section.

Wording of Topic Sentences

Because a new paragraph signals a shift in focus, the writer must clearly reorient the reader with the topic sentence. If this new paragraph is developing a topic already introduced, that needs to be clear. If the paragraph is moving on to another topic, the writer must inform the reader how this new topic follows from or fits with what has already been discussed.

Topic Sentences that Announce the Topic

Here are some topic sentences from the Aral Sea paper mentioned above. Note how each one clearly announces the topic of the paragraph.

- To fix the problems associated with the former regimes, the Gorbachev government has assigned more money for environmental controls and activities.
- The perishing of the Aral has been especially hard on the three million people who live in the region.
- Several Soviet officials and environmental scientists have provided general prescriptions on how to fix environmental policy.
- Western analysts who look at ecological questions are quite critical of the historical environmental policies of the USSR.

Topic Sentences that Forecast Subtopics

Besides announcing the topic, some topic sentences give readers an overview of subtopics that will be developed. Note how the following student accomplishes this: "Gorbachev's New Political Thinking included four basic themes that bore directly on Moscow's foreign policy: security, interdependence, the Third World, and socialist relations."

Topic Sentences that Make a Transition

Not all topic sentences point forward. Some also refer back to ideas in the previous paragraph and connect the two.

If there are any rules to follow for paragraphing, they are these:

- Paragraphs must be focused.
- Paragraphs must be unified.
- Paragraphs must be coherent.

What this is simply saying is that the sentences in the paragraph must be meaningfully and clearly related to one another. Note how in the paragraph that follows the writer has failed to follow the universal rules:

> Quantitative analysis could be the direction in which the future of intelligence is heading. Intelligence analysts quantify enemy order of battle, domestic and economic issues, and population data, as well as other tangible data. It is incumbent upon analysts to investigate their intuitive feelings or hunches.

Even though all these sentences relate to analysis and two of them mention a specific type of analysis—quantitative—there is no unity. There is no single idea unifying the sentences, nor do the sentences "stick together" or cohere. The reader feels disoriented.

Cohesive Devices

In addition to thesis and overview statements, paragraphing, and topic sentences, writers use cohesive devices to orient the reader. Writers can add cohesion to their texts by using pronouns, repeating words or using synonyms for those words, repeating a sentence structure, or using collocation.

Pronoun Reference

Using a pronoun to refer back to a noun that has preceded it glues a paragraph together. The noun to which the pronoun refers is called the antecedent. Note how this works in the following paragraph (italics are mine):

> Castro's ambitions to be a player in the international arena could never be realized as long as *he* remained simply the leader of a small Latin American country in the shadow of the U.S. hegemon. An alliance with the Soviet Union provided *him* with the means to pursue *his* revolutionary and personal ambitions. *It* immediately thrust *him* into the international spotlight and provided *him* with a protector to ensure *his* regime against a hostile U.S. while freeing *him* to radicalize Cuban society and foreign policy.

This cohesion device, however, works only if the pronoun's antecedent is clear. Note what happens in the paragraph below (italics are mine):

> Spurred by domestic conditions and growing international competition, Gorbachev implemented New Political Thinking to create a stable environment in which the Soviet Union could restructure its faltering economy. Cuba's special relationship with the Soviet Union made *it* particularly vulnerable to fluctuations as a result of the changes taking place there.

Did you read the italicized *it* as a reference to the Soviet Union? You were correct in doing so because the rules of grammar tell us that the pronoun refers back to the noun closest to it.

I sense, though, that the writer really meant that Cuba was vulnerable to fluctuations in the Soviet Union.

Word Repetition

To avoid confusion, especially if a pronoun might confuse the reader as in the Cuba paragraph above, the writer might choose to repeat a word or phrase. Note how the overlapping of words and phrases links the two paragraphs below together (italics are mine):

> The national counternarcotics effort, publicly acclaimed as the "War on Drugs," includes three basic elements: supply reduction, *demand reduction*, and profits reduction. Currently, the national strategy focuses primarily on the interdiction of two of these elements—the inbound supply of illegal drugs and the outbound flow of illegal profits. *The third element, demand reduction*, remains relegated to an existing conglomerate of well-intentioned but uncoordinated organizations, both public and private. *Demand reduction* lacks an overarching strategy, without which it cannot be effective.
>
> A possible source of guidance for dealing more effectively with *this third component* of the counternarcotics effort comes from the volume of knowledge developed from examination and study of insurgency and counterinsurgency operations. Indeed, counterinsurgency strategy has application in the development of a counternarcotics effort that will fully integrate *demand reduction* into the overall U.S. national drug-control policy.

Sentence-Structure Repetition

Writers also can repeat the same sentence structure to achieve connection. Although repetition of sentence structure should be used sparingly, it does function as a powerful stylistic device, as below:

> We shall not flag or fail, we shall go on to the end. We shall fight in France, we shall fight on the seas and oceans, we shall

fight with great confidence and growing strength in the air, we shall defend our island, whatever the cost may be; we shall fight on the beaches, . . . we shall fight in the fields and in the streets, . . . we shall never surrender. —Winston Churchill

Collocation

Collocation occurs when words that relate to a certain topic occur together. This occurs naturally for most writers. Note the network established in the following lists (read down the columns):

computer	economic indicators	Desert Storm
data	GNP	U.S.-led coalition
mainframe	inflation	SCUD missiles
input	trade	Republican Guard
software	balance of payment	rapid deployment

Transitions

Transitions are bridges. They connect sentence to sentence and paragraph to paragraph in the paper. Not only do transitions connect, but they also indicate how the two items are related. Read the following two sentences. Without transitions, the sentences have several possible meanings:

The child eats dirt and plaster. He has a condition known as pica.

Without looking at the right answer at the end of this discussion of transitions, write on a separate sheet of paper what you think the writer is trying to say.

Never place the burden of interpretation on the reader. You can risk misinterpretations or a frustrated, angry reader who may decide your paper is not worth reading.

What Transitions Can Do

Transitions can be divided into three basic groups, depending on the relationships they identify: logical, temporal, and spatial. The job of the writer is first to identify how the sentences are related and then to select the appropriate word that will signal that relationship.

Logical Relationships

Does the child eat dirt and plaster *because* he has pica? Does the condition pica *cause* strange eating habits? Or does the child have two conditions—a disease called pica *and* a craving for nonfoods? Without transitions, we do not know how the two sentences are logically related. We can only guess.

Note how the following student uses the transitions *on the other hand* and *however* to introduce opposing points of view:

> International attention has been centered on the environmental effects of the Polonoroeste program and the BR-364 highway. The *Calha Norte* Project, *on the other hand*, promises to cause more environmental problems in a shorter period of time than the previous Amazon Basin developmental programs ever did. The Project has so far been considered a strictly military program; *however*, under the terms of the national security doctrine still in effect in Brazil, this new program is another step in the drive to develop the Amazon Basin economically.

Temporal Relationships

In addition to showing logical relationships, transitions can signal a progression in time or sequence as the following student demonstrates (italics are mine):

> Hitler and German intelligence underestimated Soviet capabilities. Overconfident with the successes of the preliminary operations, Hitler thought the Red Army was nearing collapse. As a result, he diverted one army to Leningrad, two divisions to the West, and two divisions to Army Group Center. *As the offensive continued*, Hitler would not accept that the Soviet forces were large and becoming increasingly professional while German forces were steadily weakening. *In the end*, German objectives exceeded their means.

Spatial Relationships

Spatial transitions orient readers to objects in a scene. This relationship is demonstrated in the following seminar paper (italics are mine):

> The location of the traveling lock is quite different in the Soviet tank. On Western tanks, the tie down is *on* the engine compartment roof. For traveling, the turret is rotated *to the rear,* and the gun is locked in position. On the T-55 the tie bar comes *down* from the turret roof and is attached to a lug *on the top of* the breech mechanism. This method was retained since it has the advantage of allowing the crew to prepare the tank for combat without leaving the vehicle.

Sending the Right Signal

Using the wrong transition can confuse the reader and distort meaning. Those of you who wrote "*Because* the child eats dirt and plaster, he has a condition known as pica," sent the wrong meaning to your readers. So did those who said, "The child eats dirt and plaster. *In addition,* he has a condition known as pica." Instead, you should indicate that pica causes strange eating habits: "The child has pica; *therefore,* he eats dirt and plaster."

Don't be like the Scarecrow in *The Wizard of Oz.* When Dorothy asks you "Which way to Oz?" point in the right direction and in only one direction. Using transitions along with the other methods of cueing the reader will help you keep your readers on track.

Transitions Showing Logical Relations

To introduce an additional item: first, second, next, then, furthermore, moreover, in addition, finally, last, besides, as well as, and.

To introduce an illustration: for instance, for example, that is, namely, specifically, in particular.

To introduce a cause or result: consequently, as a result, hence, accordingly, thus, so, therefore, then, because, since, for.

To introduce a conclusion or summary: in conclusion, finally, in short, to sum up, all in all, clearly, evidently, altogether, of course.

To introduce a restatement: that is, in other words, in simpler terms, to put it differently.

To introduce an opposing point: but, however, yet, nevertheless, on the contrary, on the other hand, in contrast, conversely, still.

To introduce a concession to an opposing view: certainly, of course, granted, it is true, to be sure.

To resume the original line of reasoning after a concession: nonetheless, all the same, even though, still, nevertheless.

Transitions Showing Temporal Relations

To indicate frequency: frequently, hourly, often, occasionally, now and then, again and again.

To indicate a particular time: then, at that time, in those days, last Sunday, next September, in 2009, at the beginning of fall, at 9 a.m., in the morning, three days ago.

To indicate duration: during, briefly, for a long time, minute by minute, for many years.

To indicate the beginning: at first, in the beginning, before then, in the preceding months.

To indicate the end: eventually, finally, at last, in the end, subsequently, later, afterward.

Transitions Showing Spatial Relations

To indicate closeness: close to, near, next, alongside, adjacent to, facing, here.

To indicate distance: in the distance, beyond, away, far, on the far side, there.

To indicate direction: up, down, forward, backward, sideways, along, across, right, left, front, back, at an angle, above, below, inside, outside.

What about Grammar-Checkers?

If you use a computer, you'll find many software programs to help you take a more objective look at your writing. These programs are not without their problems, though, so treat them only as adjuncts, to give you one more set of "eyes" in the revision process. Note that grammar-checkers are not always spell-checkers. Be sure that your word-processing software has a good spell-check program, too. Again, though, don't rely too heavily on these programs for spelling. They might highlight the word and ask if you're sure it's correct, but they will not recognize the difference between *affect* and *effect* or between *principal* and *principle*. If you accidentally type *form* when you meant to type *from*, the computer spell-checker will think that's just fine.

Software programs to help in the writing process are not new, but they are getting better. They work on the principles of artificial intelligence. The grammar-checkers can be a big help in your writing, but they do not always recognize the nuances of style, and they may occasionally mislead you. For example, some style guides recognize the use of abbreviations like NATO and UK without the periods, and some style checkers may flag those as a problem.

How, then, might you use a computer program to help with your writing? Software has advantages in being fast and, usually, thorough in checking sentence structure (word length, sentence length) and passive voice. Those areas alone, if corrected in most intelligence papers, would improve them greatly. Remember to treat these programs as adjuncts to your writing, and consider each recommended change on its own merit. The human factor should always enter into any decision to revise your writing.

To illustrate that point, below are sentences from this book that were called to my attention as needing correction. Pay particular attention to the suggested corrections. They are all *wrong*.

My sentence: But they were not all reporting the same facts nor offering similar interpretations of those facts. *Suggested correction*: But they were not all neither reporting the same facts nor offering similar interpretations of those facts.

My sentence: Next, read interpretations of his ideas that include the experts and cover the span of history up to the present. *Suggested correction*: Next, read interpretations of his ideas that includes the experts and cover the span of history up to the present.

My sentence: [H]e answered the question he had raised in the title. *Suggested correction*: [H]e answered the question he had risen in the title.

My sentence: Words and phrases are in use today that were unknown to our grandparents. *Suggested correction*: Words and phrases are in use today that was unknown to our grandparents. *Another suggestion, also wrong*: Words and phrases are in uses today that were unknown to our grandparents.

Readability Indexes

Readability indexes, built into most computer software programs now, are popular because they seem to reduce to a simple formula the complex art of writing. Some businesses like them because of their apparent mathematical exactness. Keep in mind, though, that however useful readability indexes are, writing is not a science. Good writing can never be measured by a mathematical formula. Yes, these formulas can help you improve clarity and conciseness, but used incorrectly they can result in short, choppy sentences and overly simple words—dull writing.

Commonly Asked Questions about Revision

When Does Revision Occur?

Revision can occur throughout the writing process. Finding a mechanical error may lead a writer to reexamine a passage for other errors. Reading a paper aloud and stumbling across a sentence may cause a writer to rethink what he or she is really trying to say. Revision, therefore, is not something we do only at the end of the whole writing process.

What Kinds of Revisions Are Possible?

Some revisions make the text more readable. In fact, the end product of all revision should be to make the writing say what it has to say clearly and gracefully. Some writers, however, can revise to make the text less readable. The writer who slavishly conforms to the advice of his or her grammar-checking program may move from a readable style to one that resembles a child's primer. Finally, it is possible to revise and make no meaningful changes to the draft.

Some changes will affect the whole draft—sweeping organization overhauls, a shift in focus, and changes in audience. Other revisions will be made at the sentence level—defining words, editing for conciseness, correcting errors.

Do Good Writers Always Revise Extensively?

Some writers like James Michener, who labeled himself "one of the world's greatest revisers," revised extensively. James Joyce tinkered with *Finnegan's Wake* for 17 years just trying to get the words right. Other great writers, like Robert Frost, dashed off poems in a few hours. Also, we cannot say conclusively that bad writers make only minor corrections. What one has to conclude is that individual writers revise in different ways and seldom revise the same way each time.

For Examining Your Own Writing Process

1. How do you typically go about preparing for a writing assignment? Describe the steps you take, including rereading the assignment, asking questions about it, talking to instructors or friends, jotting down ideas, gathering information, and so on. How far in advance of the due date do you usually begin working on the assignment?
2. When and where do your best ideas often come to you?
3. Where do you usually do your writing? Describe this place. Is it a good place to write? Why, or why not?
4. What materials do you typically use when writing? Pen or pencil and notepad? Computer?
5. Describe your typical drafting process. Do you finish a draft in one sitting, or do you prefer to take breaks? How many drafts do you usually go through before the final one? Why?
6. If you "get stuck" while writing, what do you usually do to get moving again?
7. How do you typically go about revising, and what does your revising include? What are the things you think about most as you revise?
8. What would you say is most efficient and effective about your writing process?
9. What is least efficient and effective about your writing process?
10. What specific steps could you take to improve your writing process?

Exercises in Revision

Exercise 1: Thesis and Overview Statements

Thesis Statement

Readers naturally look for the point of the paper. They need a context in which to understand the many diverse details and ideas they encounter as they read. If the writer does not supply a thesis, readers will construct one themselves, or they will try to. Review the section on thesis statements earlier in this chapter. Then, on a separate sheet of paper, consider a topic you are working on, and write your thesis statement.

Overview Statements

Overview statements are special kinds of thesis statements that not only identify the main idea but also give an overview of the way the thesis will be developed. Review the earlier section on overview statements, then write your own overview statement.

Exercise 2: Paragraphing to Group Related Ideas and Details

Exercise in Paragraphing

Paragraphing signals to readers where one idea begins and ends; it groups sentences that focus on one topic together—or at least it should. Keep your paragraphs at a manageable length—manageable for you and for the reader. Note how difficult it is to digest the content of the following paragraph, taken from the student paper example on paragraphing earlier in this chapter. How would you break this massive paragraph into smaller paragraphs? Put a paragraph symbol (¶) immediately before the opening sentence of each paragraph.

> Today, the Aral Sea is quickly becoming a wasted, briny lake. The sea has shrunk from 68,000 km to 41,000 km because of the use of almost all of the water from the Amu Darya and Syr Darya rivers for the irrigation of cotton and other crops. With the rising water level decreasing at 1 meter per year and salinity rising to over 27 grams per liter, the shrinking of the sea has killed all the fish. Consequently, the fishing industry died on the Aral in 1983. Fishing villages that used to thrive with activity on the banks of the sea are now oasis towns in the middle of the desert. They survive on the canning of fish brought in by railroad from the Baltic. Visitors to the sea today find

rusted members of the fishing fleet beached on sand dunes. The environment of the area also is endangered. Noticeable changes such as shorter, hotter summers and longer, colder winters are already taking their toll on the land and people. The growing season for cotton, the largest regional crop, has shrunk by 10 days, causing some areas to change to other crops. Huge dust storms, now averaging 9–10 per year, leave millions of tons of salt scattered over a large area around the lake, increasing the salinity of the soil. This affects the crops that can be grown in the region, since the sodium chloride and other salts that are blown by the wind are toxic to many plants. Another danger to the area is the excessive pesticide and herbicide usage noted in the Aral basin. Agricultural effluents such as defoliants, insecticides, chemical fertilizers, industrial waste and raw sewage have flowed into the rivers and the Aral, poisoning them. Since the people of the area use the water directly from irrigation ditches and rivers for domestic purposes, many now suffer from a variety of illnesses, including liver disorders, typhoid, and cancer of the throat. One Soviet visitor noted in a recent trip along the Syr Darya river: "When we tried to boil [water for] tea . . . the water curdled on the fire like sour milk. The flakes of sediment drove thirst away instantly." These problems have led the Soviet government to declare the sea and the surrounding region an ecological catastrophe.

Exercise in Cohesive Devices

Review the earlier section on cohesive devices. Then do the following exercise. Underline the network of words that form a *collocation chain* in the following paragraph from a student's paper:

The growth in the scope of the international money market has been paralleled by an increase in volatility and an incredible decrease in maturities, again made possible by worldwide electronic information and communications. Back in the early 1960s, in the staid and stable world at the beginning of this financial revolution, bonds were mostly issued with 25–40 year maturities. Today, any bond with a maturity greater than 12 months is considered "long," and such "long-term" instruments are necessarily hedged and traded with a wide variety of new futures and options contracts on currencies and interest rates. Similarly, "overnight" loans between banks and corporations are no longer limited to adjacent institutions on Wall Street, but are routine transactions between Tokyo, Frankfurt, London, and New York.

Exercise in Transitions

Go back to the Aral Sea passage again and underline any logical, temporal, and spatial transitions.

Exercise 3: Review of Mechanics

In addition to "global" or content revisions, you also must be concerned with "local" revisions, revisions that improve overall clarity and correctness. Many software programs are available to help you edit your writing; the pros and cons of these are discussed earlier. Most writers use a good manual to help them proofread their writing. This book contains sections on punctuation, agreement, parallelism, wordiness, and other mechanical concerns. I cannot hope to offer a comprehensive review of mechanics, nor do I need to reiterate what is readily available elsewhere. Instead, I offer a refresher course, if you will, in some of the bugaboos that frequently plague student writing.

Exercises in Proper Usage

Usage rules are not forced on the general population by stodgy old English professors; those rules evolve from the way the language is used by the people and simply give us guidelines to codify existing usage. Mark Twain said, "The difference between the right word and the almost right word is the difference between lightning and the lightning bug."
1. *Its/it's.* Explain the difference in meaning between these two sentences:
    a. A wise dog knows its master.
    b. A wise dog knows it's master.

2. *Affect/effect*. Choose the correct word in each sentence.
   a. Glasnost had an enormous (affect)(effect) on Europe.
   b. The (affect)(effect) of the bombing remains unknown.
   c. Turbulent conditions in Latin America may (affect)(effect) the arms control talks.
   d. Our unit was not (affected)(effected) by the budget cuts.
   e. Although U.S. relations with Egypt have been strained over the years, the Persian Gulf crisis (affected)(effected) a new friendship.
3. *Principal/principle*. Choose the correct word.
   a. Our (principal)(principle) aim is to help intelligence professionals write better.
   b. Brutal repression of the demonstrators clearly violated the (principal)(principle) of free speech.
   c. Your (principal)(principle) earns more interest here.
   d. High school (principals)(principles) are not well paid.
4. *Alot/a lot*. Choose the correct answer.
   a. Alot of Iraqi soldiers are deserting.
   b. A lot of Iraqi soldiers are deserting.
5. *Cite/site/sight*. Choose the correct word.
   a. She (sited)(cited)(sighted) the dictionary as her source.
   b. He (sited)(cited)(sighted) the sergeant for bravery.
   c. We visited the (site)(cite)(sight) of the battle.
   d. The construction crew (sited)(cited)(sighted) the building at the same location it had been before the explosion.
   e. As he neared enemy territory, the tank driver (sited)(cited)(sighted) an obstacle in the road ahead. His (site)(cite)(sight) was excellent at night.
6. *Imply/infer*. Choose the correct word.
   a. I (implied)(inferred) a mistaken conclusion from his estimate.
   b. He (implied)(inferred) in his article that there may be a coup d'etat.
7. Choose the correct usage in each set.
   a. The data (is)(are) incomplete.
   b. The (medium)(media) often show bias in their reports.

c. That was a (phenomenon)(phenomena) we did not anticipate.
d. On what (criterion)(criteria) should we base our analysis?
e. Each of the regiments (are)(is) moving back to (their)(its) garrison.

Exercise in Spelling

Because most word processors have spell-checkers, most computer-generated writing is free of misspellings. Those computers don't do you much good, though, when you are taking an essay examination in class or completing an application form by hand. The following is a practice quiz on words intelligence professionals use daily.

Choose the correct spelling from the pairs below.

1. independant independent
2. colocate collocate
3. guerilla guerrilla
4. judgement judgment
5. accommodate accomodate
6. alleged alledged
7. defense defence
8. separate seperate
9. ommitted omitted
10. threshhold threshold
11. occured occurred
12. harrass harass
13. seize sieze
14. evidence evidance
15. apparant apparent
16. theater theatre
17. allegience allegiance
18. accessible accessable
19. rapprochement rapproachment
20. transhipment transshipment
21. adviser advisor
22. supercede supersede
23. recieve receive
24. potato potatoe

Exercises in Composition

Composition makes the language intelligible among English-speaking peoples. These are the conventions of sentence and paragraph design. Other considerations of sentence and paragraph composition include the following: use active voice instead of passive; use concrete, specific language; and avoid wordiness.

1. *Passive and active voice.* First, determine whether the sentence is passive or active voice. If it is passive, change it to active voice. You might have to supply the subject if it is missing from a sentence in the passive voice.
   a. The village was attacked by the rebels.
   b. We were uncertain of the outcome of the battle.
   c. The mission was canceled because of bad weather in the target area.
   d. Economic aspects need to be considered when assessing the military capabilities of a nation.
   e. It is recommended that we analyze the situation.
   f. In Lieutenant Johnson's research, it was learned that the enemy's tank battalions were being increased in size.
2. *Concrete language.* Rewrite the following sentences with more precise, specific language. Use your imagination to supply missing information.
   a. An interval of unfavorable weather caused problems for the operation.
   b. Several tanks, armored personnel carriers, self-propelled artillery pieces, etc., took part in the attack.
3. *Wordiness.* Prune the wordiness from the following sentences.
   a. A realization by European terrorist groups has taken place, that not only will their survivability improve, but that their impact on Western society can be greatly enhanced by unification and mutual cooperation among each other. (36 words)
   b. Even though Russian was the officially recognized language of the USSR and was taught throughout the Former Soviet Union, for many Soviet citizens, Russian was a second language. (28 words)

Exercises in Proper Form

Issues of *form* usually differ among style manuals or office correspondence manuals. For example, you will find various conventions for the forms of quotations, headings and subheadings, margins, and numerals. You should be familiar with the requirements of your school, command, or agency.

At many academic institutions, the form and format for student research papers, seminar papers, and theses are spelled out in a prescribed style manual. One of the most widely used is Kate L. Turabian's *A Manual for Writers of Research Papers, Theses, and Dissertations*, 7th ed. (Chicago: University of Chicago Press, 2007). Another excellent publication is *The Chicago Manual of Style*, 15th ed. (Chicago: University of Chicago Press, 2003). Many government employees use the *United States Government Printing Office Style Manual* (Washington, D.C.: Government Printing Office [GPO], 2003). That manual is often called simply the "GPO Style Manual."

Abbreviations and Acronyms   What do the following abbreviations and acronyms mean? When is it appropriate to use them?

a. *i.e.* = for example or that is?   e. START
b. *e.g.* = for example or that is?   f. INF
c. *ibid./op. cit./et al.*   g. SOTA
d. *etc.*   h. NOFORN

Proofreading Exercises   The job is never over until the paperwork is done, and one of the last elements of the paperwork is proofreading. Many state-of-the-art computer programs can help you with this chore, but in the final "proof" there is no substitute for the human eye. Ask a friend, your spouse, or your classmate to proofread your work if you feel you have missed something.

Following are two exercises in proofreading that contain some of the most common errors I have seen in student papers. I discussed most of these errors earlier. See how many you can find, then compare your proofing with the answers at the end of this chapter. Remember that you are simply *proofreading* here—looking for *errors*—and *not* editing for style or content.

Proofreading Exercise 1 There is many reasons why a student should learn to write correctly. Evidence of poor writing is apparant in many papers submitted to the college faculty. In our judgement, a principle reason for learning to write correct papers are the professionallism inherant in clear, concise writing. Your ability to produce a coherant paper may ultimatly effect your career.

Profreading is one technique that will help to insure correctness in your writing. One affect of proofreading is to prevent common errors from occuring. Irregardless of your writing experience, you will benefit from the proceedure of carefully proofreading your writing.

Proofreading Exercise 2 Media reports site numerous examples of an alledged international conspiracy among terrorist organizaions. Their are many possible reasons for terrorists groups to ban together, including the following: their mutual desire to destabalize a Government, or to disrupt an Alliance such as Nato; shared goals in an independance movement; or one groups willingness to accomodate the seperatist philosophy of another group.

A principle effect of a terrorist conspiracy might be it's devastating consequences in terms of International Alliances. The occurence of the Achille Lauro hijacking, for example, proved that a handfull of terrorists could affect a governments stability and have ominous repercussions on international relations. If an alliance of terrorist organizations had been involved in that incidant, it's outcome may have been even more serious.

Answers to the Exercises in Chapter 6

Exercise 1: Thesis and Overview Statements

Answers to this exercise will vary, depending upon the subject you're writing about. Concentrate here on focusing the topic and narrowing its scope. Also remember to ask yourself whether your topic is of interest to the intelligence community or whether it has implications for U.S. national security. If the answer to either of those questions is "no," then you may need to rethink your thesis and overview statements or realign their focus.

Exercise 2: Paragraphing to Group Related Ideas and Details

Exercise in Paragraphing

Note where the paragraph symbols (¶) have been placed in the Aral Sea paragraph below.

Today, the Aral Sea is quickly becoming a wasted, briny lake. The sea has shrunk from 68,000 km to 41,000 km because of the use of almost all of the water from the Amu Darya and Syr Darya rivers for the irrigation of cotton and other crops. With the rising water level decreasing at 1 meter per year and salinity rising to over 27 grams per liter, the shrinking of the sea has killed all the fish. Consequently, the fishing industry died on the Aral in 1983. Fishing villages that used to thrive with activity on the banks of the sea are now oasis towns in the middle of the desert. They survive on the canning of fish brought in by railroad from the Baltic. Visitors to the sea today find rusted members of the fishing fleet beached on sand dunes. ¶ The environment of the area also is endangered. Noticeable changes such as shorter, hotter summers and longer, colder winters are already taking their toll on the land and people. The growing season for cotton, the largest regional crop, has shrunk by 10 days, causing some areas to change to other crops. Huge dust storms, now averaging 9–10 per year, leave millions of tons of salt scattered over a large area around the lake, increasing the salinity of the soil. This affects the crops that can be grown in the region, since the sodium chloride and other salts that are blown by the wind are toxic to many plants. ¶ Another danger to the area is the excessive pesticide and herbicide usage noted in the Aral basin. Agricultural effluents such as defoliants, insecticides, chemical fertilizers, industrial waste and raw sewage have flowed into the rivers and the Aral, poisoning them. Since the people of the area use the wa-

ter directly from irrigation ditches and rivers for domestic purposes, many now suffer from a variety of illnesses, including
liver disorders, typhoid, and cancer of the throat. ¶ One Soviet
visitor noted in a recent trip along the Syr Darya River: "When
we tried to boil [water for] tea . . . the water curdled on the fire
like sour milk. The flakes of sediment drove thirst away instantly." These problems have led the Soviet government to declare the sea and the surrounding region an ecological
catastrophe.

Exercise in Cohesive Devices

*Words that form a collocation chain are italicized in the following
paragraph:*

The growth in the scope of the *international money market* has
been paralleled by an increase in volatility and an incredible
decrease in *maturities*, again made possible by worldwide electronic information and communications. Back in the early
1960s, in the staid and stable world at the beginning of this *financial revolution*, *bonds* were mostly issued with *25–40 year maturities*. Today, any *bond* with a *maturity* greater than 12 months
is considered "long," and such *"long-term" instruments* are necessarily hedged and traded with a wide variety of new *futures*
and *options contracts* on *currencies* and *interest rates*. Similarly,
"overnight" *loans* between *banks* and corporations are no
longer limited to adjacent institutions on *Wall Street*, but are
routine *transactions* between Tokyo, Frankfurt, London, and
New York.

Exercise in Transitions

*Words that show logical, temporal, and spatial transitions are ital-
icized below.*

Today, the Aral Sea is quickly becoming a wasted, briny lake. The
sea has shrunk from 68,000 km to 41,000 km *because* of the use of
almost all of the water from the Amu Darya and Syr Darya rivers
for the irrigation of cotton and other crops. *With* the rising water
level decreasing at 1 meter per year and salinity rising to over 27

grams per liter, the shrinking of the sea has killed all the fish. *Consequently*, the fishing industry died on the Aral in 1983. Fishing villages that used to thrive with activity on the banks of the sea are now oasis towns in the middle of the desert. They survive on the canning of fish brought in by railroad from the Baltic. Visitors to the sea *today* find rusted members of the fishing fleet beached on sand dunes.

The environment of the area *also* is endangered. Noticeable changes such as shorter, hotter summers and longer, colder winters are already taking their toll on the land and people. The growing season for cotton, the largest regional crop, has shrunk by 10 days, causing some areas to change to other crops. Huge dust storms, now averaging 9–10 per year, leave millions of tons of salt scattered over a large area around the lake, increasing the salinity of the soil. This affects the crops that can be grown in the region, *since* the sodium chloride and other salts that are blown by the wind are toxic to many plants.

Another danger to the area is the excessive pesticide and herbicide usage noted in the Aral basin. Agricultural effluents such as defoliants, insecticides, chemical fertilizers, industrial waste and raw sewage have flowed into the rivers and the Aral, poisoning them. *Since* the people of the area use the water directly from irrigation ditches and rivers for domestic purposes, many now suffer from a variety of illnesses, including liver disorders, typhoid, and cancer of the throat. . . ." *[no others]*

Exercise 3: Review of Mechanics

Exercises in Proper Usage

1. *Its/it's. Its* is the possessive pronoun; *it's always* means either *it is* (as in "*It's* raining") or *it has* (as in "*It's* been raining this morning").
   a. A wise dog knows its master. (This dog recognizes that the owner is the boss.)
   b. A wise dog knows it's master. (This smart-aleck mutt thinks that *it* is the master.)
2. *Affect/effect. Affect* is a verb, meaning to influence, change, or have an impact on something. (Good writing *affects* my

promotions.) *Effect* is usually a noun and means "the result." (The *effect* of *good* writing is clear.) When *effect* is used as a verb, it means "to cause, to bring about." (The coup *effected* a bloodless change of government.)

a. Glasnost had an enormous *effect* on Europe.
b. The *effect* of the bombing remains unknown.
c. Turbulent conditions in Latin America may *affect* the arms control talks.
d. Our unit was not *affected* by the budget cuts.
e. Although U.S. relations with Egypt have been strained over the years, the Persian Gulf crisis *effected* a new friendship.

3. *Principal/principle.* Both words are nouns, but *principal* may also be an adjective. *Principle* is always a noun.

a. Our *principal* aim is to help intelligence professionals write better.
b. Brutal repression of the demonstrators clearly violated the *principle* of free speech.
c. Your *principal* earns more interest here.
d. High school *principals* are not well paid.

4. *Alot/a lot.* Alot is not a word. There is a word *allot*, meaning "to distribute, or to assign shares or portions," but that is usually not what the writer of "alot" has in mind. Most of the time a better sentence will result by rewriting to avoid the use of "a lot"; even though it is grammatically correct, it is imprecise. The correct answer for this exercise was as follows:

b. *A lot* of Iraqi soldiers are deserting.

5. *Cite/site/sight.* Cite is a verb, meaning to quote, mention, or commend, as in a *citation*. Site, as a noun, means a place. Used as a verb, it means to locate something on a site. *Sight* may be either a verb or a noun, and means the act or fact of seeing.

a. She *cited* the dictionary as her source.
b. He *cited* the sergeant for bravery.
c. We visited the *site* of the battle.
d. The construction crew *sited* the building at the same location it had been before the explosion.

    e. As he neared enemy territory, the tank driver *sighted* an obstacle in the road ahead. His *sight* was excellent at night.

6. *Imply/infer.* The writer or speaker *implies* when stating something indirectly. The reader or listener *infers* when drawing a conclusion or making a deduction based upon what he or she has read or heard.

    a. I *inferred* a mistaken conclusion from his estimate.

    b. He *implied* in his article that there may be a coup d'etat.

7. These sentences dealt with singular and plural forms.

    a. The data *are* incomplete. (Before you start howling, note that it is becoming increasingly common to see the plural form "data" being used with a singular verb like "is," especially in the world of computers. Strict rules of usage, however, call for the plural verb.)

    b. The *media* often show bias in their reports. (The most frequent violators of this usage are—you guessed it—the media themselves. Radio is a medium. So is television. Radio and television are media.)

    c. That was a *phenomenon* we did not anticipate. (One event is a phenomenon; two or more are phenomena.)

    d. On what *criteria* should we base our analysis? (Note that "criterion" would also be correct in this sentence if we were basing our analysis on only one factor. More likely, though, as good analysts we are looking at many criteria. In addition, the plural form would call for the use of "which" instead of "what.")

    e. Each of the regiments *is* moving back to *its* garrison.

Exercise in Spelling

The correct spelling is *italicized* in each pair below. (See the notes immediately following the list of words for further explanations.)

1. independant *independent* 13. *seize* sieze
2. colocate *collocate* 14. *evidence* evidance
3. guerilla *guerrilla* 15. apparant *apparent*
4. judgement *judgment* 16. *theater* theatre

5. *accommodate* accomodate
6. *alleged* alledged
7. *defense* defence

8. *separate* seperate

9. ommitted *omitted*
10. threshhold *threshold*
11. occured *occurred*
12. harrass *harass*
Notes:

17. allegience *allegiance*
18. *accessible* accessable
19. *rapprochement* rapproachment
20. transhipment *transshipment*
21. *adviser* advisor
22. supercede *supersede*
23. recieve *receive*
24. *potato* potatoe

2. Some dictionaries allow spelling it either "colocate" or "collocate."
3. Some spell-checkers won't catch the misspelling with the single *r* ("guerilla").
4. The spelling with the first "e" ("judgement") is considered chiefly British, like "defence" (number 7) and "theatre" (number 16).
7. See note 4, above.
16. See note 4, above.
21. Some dictionaries allow either spelling. Consult the style manual used by your school or organization.

Exercises in Composition

1. *Passive and active voice.* (Your answers may vary slightly.)

Voice tells whether the subject is doing the action (*he questions us*) or being acted upon (*he is questioned*). When the subject is acting, the verb is in the active voice; when the subject is being acted upon, the verb is in the passive voice. The passive voice is formed, as is this sentence, by using the appropriate form of the verb *to be* followed by the past participle of the main verb. Intelligence writers use the active voice as much as possible because it makes prose more *active*, more lively. To say that "the situation was reviewed" (passive voice) does not give the sense of action or immediacy that "Joan reviewed the situation" (active voice) does. The most problematic use of the passive voice occurs when writers seek to avoid responsibility for what they have written. A university president who announces that "it is recommended that fees be raised substantially" skirts a number of pressing questions: recommended by whom? raised by whom?

a. The rebels attacked the village.
b. We were uncertain of the outcome of the battle. (This sentence is already in the active voice but is past tense. Don't be confused by the past tense form of the verb *to be*. Look for the past participle of the verb, too. In this case, "uncertain" is an adjective, not a verb.)
c. Wing headquarters canceled the mission because of bad weather in the target area.
d. Consider economic aspects when assessing a nation's military capabilities. (Or, Analysts must consider. . . .)
e. We must analyze the situation.
f. Lieutenant Johnson learned that the enemy was increasing its tank battalions in size.

2. *Concrete language.* (Answers will vary.) Precise choice of words is more important in intelligence writing than in most other kinds of writing. William Strunk and E. B. White say, "Prefer the specific to the general, the definite to the vague, the concrete to the abstract."[4]

a. Heavy rains and gale-force winds slowed the attack.
b. Tanks, armored personnel carriers, and self-propelled artillery pieces took part in the attack.

3. *Wordiness.* (Answers will vary.)

a. European terrorists realize that both their survivability and their impact on Western society can be enhanced greatly by unification and cooperation. (21 words)
b. Even though Russian was the official language and was taught throughout the Former Soviet Union, it was a second language for many Soviets. (23 words)

Exercises in Proper Form

Abbreviations and Acronyms   In formal writing, use abbreviations and acronyms sparingly and with caution. Many writers misunderstand abbreviations such as the ones in a–c below, and that in turn confuses the reader. When you use abbreviations like those, don't forget the periods. If you must use an acronym, spell it out first, followed by the acronym in parentheses. Note also how the acronyms below (START, INF, SOTA, and NOFORN) are formed differently. "START" takes the first two letters of its first word ("STrategic"); "INF" doesn't even include every word ("range") in its acronym; "SOTA," which can mean several things depending on what you're talking about, has an acronym ("SIGINT") within an acronym; and "NOFORN" is a hodgepodge. That's why people often forget what acronyms mean, and it can be embarrassing if you use one and are unable to answer when someone asks, "What's that mean?"

a. *i.e.* is the Latin abbreviation for *id est*, meaning "that is." It is often confused with *e.g.*

b. *e.g.*, the Latin abbreviation for *exempli gratia*, means "for example."

c. *ibid.* is the abbreviation for the Latin *ibidem*. It means "in the same place" and is dearly beloved among scholars. Modern style manuals, however, are replacing *ibid.* (as well as *op. cit.* and *et al.*) with an English-language equivalent. Writers often forget that *ibid.* is an abbreviation, and they omit the period. The term *op. cit.*, like *ibid.*, is falling into disuse in modern writing. It means *opere citato*, "in the work cited." Finally, *et al.* is another Latin term meaning "and others." Note that *et* is a complete word, but *al.* is the abbreviation for *alia*. Why try to remember all this when you can simply use "and others"?

d. *etc.* is another of those ancient Latin phrases, *et cetera*, meaning "and so forth." Do not use this vague term in intelligence writing because it signals your readers that you are leaving it up to them to complete whatever list you ended with that phrase: "The new battlefield formation is known to have tanks, self-propelled artillery, etc." A more precise way of writing that sentence would be, "The new battlefield formation is known to have weapon systems such as tanks and self-propelled artillery."

e. START = *ST*rategic *A*rms *R*eduction *T*alks.

f. INF = *I*ntermediate-range *N*uclear *F*orces.

g. SOTA = *SIG*INT (*SIG*nals *INT*elligence—an acronym within an acronym!) *O*perational *T*asking *A*uthority, *or* *S*pecial *O*perations *T*eam *A*lfa (a U.S. Army Special Operations Forces unit). It might also mean *S*tate *o*f *t*he *A*rt or, if you see the notation in the margin of your returned paper, *S*ame *O*ld *T*ired *A*rgument.

h. NOFORN = *NO*t Releasable to *FOR*eign *N*ationals.

Proofreading Exercises Remember that these exercises called for you to *proofread, not* to *edit*. You were merely looking for errors here, *not* trying to revise the style (although it could certainly stand some improvement).

Proofreading Exercise 1 There *are* [subject-verb agreement; the true subject of the sentence is the word *reasons*, not the expletive *there*. It requires the plural verb *are*] many reasons why a student should learn to write correctly. Evidence [spelling] of poor writing is apparent [spelling] in many papers submitted [spelling] to the college faculty. In our ju*dgm*ent [preferred usage in American English is without the first *e*], a princi*pal* [usage error; *principal* is the adjective] reason for learning to write correct papers *is* [subject-verb agreement; *reason* is the subject, not *papers*] the professiona*l*ism [spelling] inherent [spelling] in clear, concise writing. Your ability to produce a coherent [spelling] paper may ultimately [spelling] *a*ffect [usage error; the verb form *affect* is needed here, meaning "have an impact on"] your career.

Proofreading [spelling] is one technique that will help to ensure [preferred spelling; *insure* means to insure life, health, or property] correctness in your writing. One *e*ffect [usage error; here you need the noun *effect*, meaning "result"] of proofreading is to prevent common errors from occurring [spelling]. *Regardless* [there is no such word as *irregardless*] of your writing experience, you will benefit from the procedure [spelling] of carefully proofreading your writing.

Proofreading Exercise 2 Media reports cite [to mention is to *cite*; *site* is a location] numerous examples of an alleged [spelling] international conspiracy among terrorist organizations [spelling].

The*re* [spelling] are many possible reasons for terroris*t* [singular, not plural or possessive] groups to ban*d* [usage error; *ban* means to prohibit] together, including the following: their mutual desire to destab*i*lize [spelling] a *g*overnment [capitalize the word only when writing about a specific one, for example, *U.S. Government*], or to disrupt an *a*lliance [again, capitalize only when being specific, as in *Alliance for Progress*] such as *NATO* [acronyms are all uppercase]; shared goals in an independe*n*ce [spelling] movement; or one grou*p's* [possessive, not plural] willingness to acco*mm*odate [spelling] the sep*a*ratist [spelling] philosophy of another group.

A princi*pal* [usage error; the adjective form is *principal*] effect of a terrorist conspiracy might be *its* [possessive form is *its*, *not* the contraction *it's*] devastating consequences in terms of *i*nternational *a*lliances [neither word should be capitalized when writing in general terms]. The occu*rr*ence [spelling] of the *Achille Lauro* [ships' names are italicized or underlined] hijacking, for example, proved that a handfu*l* [spelling] of terrorists could affect a governmen*t's* [possessive, not plural] stability and have ominous repercussions on international relations. If an alliance of terrorist organizations had been involved in that incid*e*nt [spelling], *its* [possessive again, not the contraction] outcome may have been even more serious.

Notes

1. These and the other statistics quoted in this paragraph are found in David Wallechinsky and Irving Wallace, *The People's Almanac #2* (New York: Bantam Books, 1978), 685.

2. Donald Murray, "The Listening Eye: Reflections on the Writing Conference," *College English* 41 (1979): 13–18.

3. Materials in this section are based on a "Workshop on Reviewing Analytical Papers," conducted at the Joint Military Intelligence College, Washington, D.C., on March 27, 1989, by Frans Bax, course director for Office of Training and Education, Intelligence Training Division, Central Intelligence Agency.

4. William Strunk Jr. and E. B. White, *The Elements of Style*, 4th ed. (New York: Allyn & Bacon, 1999), 21.

7

Writing and Reviewing Analytical Papers

Summary

Most writing in the intelligence profession boils down to the ability to *analyze* as you write, so that you reach *conclusions* about your subject. Be prepared to review your own paper or someone else's paper using the basic guidelines for analytical writing.

- Intelligence writing may describe, explain, or estimate. To be "analytical," a paper must identify significant facts for interpretation; and it must focus on conclusions, be relevant to its intended audience, concentrate on essentials, and avoid prescribing policy.
- One model for reviewing an analytical paper calls for discovery, judgment, and deciding what action to take.
- Many constraints impinge upon the review process, including time, the reviewer and writer's experience, expectations, and attitude.
- Styles of review include holistic (the whole thing), top down, and bottom up.
- As you review an analytical paper, keep a checklist of the guidelines in front of you. Use the "Four Sweeps" strategy to review a paper: read for clarity, persuasiveness, packaging, and the writing itself.

When you write an intelligence paper, keep your focus on writing *analytically* throughout the process.

The Types of Intelligence Writing

Intelligence professionals need to recognize their style of writing to satisfy customers' needs. If a commander asks his intelligence officer for an assessment of what will happen in the next 24 hours, he's not interested in a wrap-up of the *past* 24 hours or an explanation of why something else happened. For this discussion of the analytical writing process, then, it may be helpful to set the stage by looking at the three most common types of intelligence writing: descriptive, explanatory, and estimative.

Descriptive: Using the Senses

As the name implies, this type of intelligence writing describes something in sensory terms—size, shape, composition, and color, for example. It is by far the most commonly encountered writing style in the intelligence community. Orders of battle, country studies, and basic imagery reports are examples of descriptive intelligence writing.

Explanatory: Here's How—or Why—It's Done

This type of writing explains how something works, why it performs the way it does, or why something happened. In scientific and technical intelligence (S&TI), writers often explain how a piece of foreign equipment or a sophisticated system works. Thesis writers usually explain events that relate to their thesis, placing those events into a meaningful context.

Estimative: Looking Ahead

Estimates look toward the future and make forecasts or predictions, suggesting the implications for U.S. national security.

National intelligence estimates and other future-oriented products of the intelligence community are primarily estimative. The final chapters of many master's theses also focus on conclusions and implications for the future, an estimative writing style.

What *Is* an Analytical Paper?

It's easy to think of an analytical paper as one that analyzes something; but that explanation is too simplistic. In my classes I ask students the question that headlines this subsection. I get a wide variety of answers, most of which contain elements of truth. To get at the core of what constitutes an analytical paper, let's first define the term *analysis*.

"Analysis" is defined by Joint Chiefs of Staff Joint Publication 1-02 as follows: "In intelligence usage, a step in the processing phase of the intelligence cycle in which information is subjected to review in order to identify significant facts for subsequent interpretation."[1]

Intelligence analysts and students review huge volumes of information during the course of a normal business day. It's important to note the part of the definition that calls for "*identify[ing] significant facts for subsequent interpretation.*" It is that interpretation that separates the analytical scholar from the amateur. It's relatively simple to look at something and describe or define what is going on. But when you begin to take the event apart and interpret its *meaning*, you are beginning to think in terms of an analytical paper.

Some of the features that characterize an analytical paper include its *focus* (on conclusions as well as the future); its *relevance* to consumers, most of whom are policy makers or decision makers; and its *concentration on essentials* only, with meaningful characterizations and avoiding policy prescription.

Focus

When you write an analytical paper, keep in mind that its ultimate focus should be on its conclusions, which are oriented toward the future. That is not to say that the paper cannot have a section—perhaps one chapter of a thesis, for example—containing some historical background. Such background is often necessary to establish a context for the problem or issue at hand. The amount of history included must be the result of audience consideration. Think about how much your audience already knows about the topic and how much they need to know in order to understand what you are now writing. But keep the focus of the writing on the future.

Relevance

It is possible to produce a descriptive paper without doing any analytical writing; but the utility of that work to a consumer will probably be diminished unless the work is relevant to some problem or issue faced by that consumer. Our users are grappling with real-world problems every day, whether their mission is peacekeeping, humanitarian operations, planning, or simply pushing papers across a desk. Be sure that you understand the mission of your users so that you can ensure the relevance—and thereby the utility—of your writing.

Concentration on Essentials

One way to be sure that you maintain your focus on essential issues in your writing is to keep those issues in front of you all the time. The *"bottom line up front"* concept is one way to do that. You know, for example, that the thrust of your paper concerns an impending threat to U.S. forces performing peacekeeping operations in Panaragua. You then begin your paper with a sentence that defines your best assessment of the nature of the threat and its imminence. Concentrate on the essential information and conclusions that relate to that threat. You can always follow up later with a more detailed discussion of the problem; but for now, you want to meaningfully characterize a threat to U.S. forces.

Avoiding Policy Prescription

Remember this caution concerning your analytical paper and its conclusions: As a member of the intelligence community, it is not your job to recommend policy to commanders, decision makers, and policy makers; and it is certainly beyond the scope of your mission to prescribe policy. That is often a difficult distinction for intelligence professionals to make. You have performed an enormous amount of work on a topic and may well be the most knowledgeable member of your command or agency concerning that topic. The temptation is great to take your assessment just one more step and to tell the consumer what you think he or she should *do* about the problem or issue at hand. *Don't.*

Perhaps an example will make this point clearer. By studying current imagery, you have uncovered a likely ambush site along the highway U.S. forces will travel into Panaragua City tomorrow. You write, "Latest imagery suggests a high probability that the battalion's convoy will be ambushed along Camino Real as they enter DeSoto Canyon tomorrow. The U.S. forces should instead take Highway 1 on the north rim of the canyon."

Those two sentences may sound innocent enough. In the first sentence you have indeed put the bottom line up front, warning of the impending danger. To your credit, you have also shown that you are aware of the U.S. forces' operations. But then you took it that extra step, telling the commander what he "*should*" do. You'll find many commanders resent being told by their intelligence officer what operational decision they should make.

Don't misunderstand and think that you should make no suggestions. On the contrary, when you learn of the threat on Camino Real, your most logical course of action is to determine other possible avenues of approach to the objective. If Highway 1 is the only other trafficable road to Panaragua City, then you say that as your follow-on to the threat: "Considering the potential threat on Camino Real, we have searched for alternative approaches. The only other road with bridges capable of supporting our battalion's armored vehicles is Highway 1." Now you have given the commander an analytical perspective as an intelligence professional, and he can decide whether to fight it out on Camino Real or divert his attention to Highway 1.

A Model Process for Reviewing an Analytical Paper

Now that you've written your analytical paper, it's important that you know a viable procedure for reviewing it. This process goes beyond the simple aspects of proofreading and editing discussed in chapter 6. It starts with the realization that most written work can stand improvement, whether it is yours, mine, or someone else's. In this section I will cover a process you can use to review your own writing or a colleague's. The four steps in this process are discovery, judgment, action, and motion. The procedures you use will differ slightly, depending upon whether you are reading your own work or someone else's.

Discovery: Your Writing

To "discover" your own writing style, you must do a lot of reading, both of your own material and of other writing in the genre. You'll contribute to the accuracy of the piece by doing thorough research and conducting a dialogue with others knowledgeable about the subject. It is often helpful to carry on a silent dialogue with yourself about your subject. Ask yourself what questions someone might have if they were reading what you've written. Then answer those questions as best you can. It may require that you gather more information, even when you're facing a tight deadline and longing for closure; but the final product will be better for it.

Another important consideration in discovering your own writing process is allowing the writing to "cool down" after you have written. In your own writing, your eye will not see things that are there, or they will convince you that something *is* there when it is not. One helpful remedy for this eye problem is to set the writing aside for a while before you begin the review. Then when you approach the task again, treat it as though you had never seen the writing before.

Discovery: Someone Else's Writing

When you review someone else's written work, you should try to find something positive to say about the writing up front so as not to discourage the writer. Some of the best writers say that they were most influenced early in life by a teacher or a peer who pointed out the strengths of their writing. If there are numerous grammatical errors or misspellings, you'll find yourself jumping ahead in the review process and moving right into judgment, where you'll decide that the writer needs to go "back to the drawing board." But often you can find considerable substance and worthwhile content even in a paper that is a bumpy read because of grammatical problems.

It is also important at the outset of any review process to establish firmly the ground rules under which you'll be working. When someone asks you to review a paper, they typically will say something like this: "Will you take a look at this for me?" Three different people will no doubt have three different definitions of the phrase "take a look." Does the writer want you to proofread for errors? To edit for style? To check for accuracy in content? Often you may be reluctant to ask for fear that the answer may be, "All of the above." But depending upon what the writer wants you to do, a different process is involved in proofreading, editing, or reviewing content. I'll discuss those processes later in this chapter. So it behooves you to nail down exactly what someone wants you to do when they ask you to "take a look" at their writing.

In all cases of reviewing someone else's writing, you have to consider the time available. If Jerry gives you his 10-page paper at 2 p.m. and expects it back by 2:30 the same day, you can do little more than a cursory review, perhaps for organization and clarity. But if you have several days before the writer wants it back, then you can provide a far more valuable service. To illustrate a viable review process, let's take Jerry's 10-page paper and give ourselves portions of three working days to review it.

As soon as possible after you receive the paper, read it all the way through without making any marks on it. That may be exceptionally difficult if you—like me—are troubled by mechanical errors that you want to fix. Get an idea of the content, the organization, and the flow of the paper start to finish. Ensure that the bottom line is up front and that there are substantiated conclusions at the end. There should also be a focus on the future throughout, but especially in the conclusions. You may want to make a few notes during this phase, just to remind yourself of any potential problem areas or to highlight main points being made by the writer.

Next, set the paper aside for some time—10 minutes, an hour, or even overnight. Approach it again with a fresh perspective, this time looking more deeply for grammatical correctness, clarity of thought in the sentences and paragraphs, conciseness of words and phrases, and coherence of the paper as a whole. If anything is unclear or incomplete, or if you find assessments that appear to have no basis in logic, then you may need to go back to the writer and ask questions.

A cursory reading of a peer or classmate's paper might take only a few minutes; but a thorough review that includes both editing and proofreading, taking into account all the elements I addressed above, will probably take from 5 to 10 minutes *per page*. So if someone has asked you to "take a look at" his 10-page paper, you can anticipate spending between one and two hours on it.

Judgment: Your Writing

Start every review process by telling yourself that your paper *can* be improved. Most writers tend to be dissatisfied with the first draft of anything they have done; so it's permissible to keep company with those who judge their work worthy of improvement. One of the most frustrating things you may ever face is to realize that you've been working like a dog for days or weeks, only to find out that you're chasing the wrong car. That is, perhaps you've gotten off track or lost the focus you had earlier in the paper.

It is often better to scrap a bad idea and start over than to try to patch it together like a quilt. For example, if you believe as you approach page 12 of a 20-page paper that you have wandered completely off the topic, then you might need to start the paper again from the last point you made that still related to the main idea. That's a tough pill to swallow when you're facing a deadline; but in the long run you may spend more time trying to repair a badly damaged paper than you would restarting it from your original prewriting. Of course you will still be able to salvage considerable amounts of material; but you'll have to do a great deal of rewriting.

An example might put this into perspective for you. In 1986 I set out to write my first book—a textbook to accompany the courses that I taught at a degree-granting U.S. Government institution. Since I taught both writing and briefing, I designed the book to have separate "parts" on each subject. Part 3 of the textbook would be called "Briefing with Intelligence." I outlined the five or six chapters that would constitute that section of the book, then I set about the task of writing.

My point of view was that of a young lieutenant who had just been ordered to give a big briefing to a general officer a week or so in the future. As I wrote chapters 1, 2, and 3, I realized that the point of view just didn't seem to be working. I tried to convince myself that it would be better to rewrite those chapters from a different perspective, perhaps a more objective third-person account. But I didn't listen to my own advice and proceeded over the next few days to write more than 60 pages from the young lieutenant's point of view. It was only after I had finished that section, put it aside for a few days, and returned to read it again that I realized how badly written it was! It was frustrating and time consuming, but I rewrote the entire briefing section— almost 60 pages—from scratch. In the long run, I believe my students and other users of that book were better off for it.

My point is this: the earlier in the writing process that you are able to judge the overall quality and acceptability of your writing project, the better off you are likely to be. That does not mean that you should stop and reread every sentence or every paragraph and judge its acceptability on the spot. On the contrary, you are likely to stymie the flow of your creative juices if you try to do it that way. Rather, make your judgment calls at acceptable intervals during the progress of your writing. There will be "natural breaks" created by the end of a business day or school day, a major section of a paper or chapter of a thesis, a staff meeting, or a lecture you're required to attend. Use those breaks to review your paper for acceptability, potential, and quality.

Judgment: Someone Else's Writing

As I mentioned earlier, you may be tempted on occasions to leap from your preliminary review of someone's writing (the discovery phase) right into the judgment stage. We're all human beings, and as such we have innate intelligence that demands our placing things in context. So when we read something that assaults our senses—whether from its mechanical flaws or its substance—we render a hasty judgment.

Although it's a difficult task, you should try to give the writer the benefit of a thorough review of the paper. Look at the original requirement from the boss or from the professor. How many pages were assigned? On what subject? What were the specific instructions concerning format, content, and conclusions? If the paper is totally off the mark in all these requirements, then you may have the unenviable chore of telling the writer to start all over again. Usually, though, the corrections should be less severe than that, and you can give the writer some good news along with the bad.

Action and Motion: Your Writing or Someone Else's

The processes that deal with action to be taken on the paper and where it goes from here are similar for both your own writing and someone else's. This is the point in the review process where you must consider what changes are to be made to the work. If you still have questions—of yourself or of the author—ask them now and get an answer before you proceed. Accept suggestions from your superiors, your peers, or your classmates, or give them in a constructive manner to the person whose work you are reviewing.

Then decide where the paper goes from here. It may need to go back for more research, coordination, or a thorough rework; or it may be ready to go forward to the boss or to the professor. The final decision might not be yours; but if it is, then at least try to ensure that this is the best work you can do.

Constraints on Review

It's easy for me to write all these words about reviewing your work or someone else's, but when the rubber meets the road—or the red ink meets the paper—everyone faces constraints that hinder review. Among these constraints are time, experience, expectations, and attitude. You run out of time as the deadline nears; you're asked to review a paper and you learn that you have no experience in that subject; too much is expected of you; or your attitude needs adjusting.

Time: Always Flying

Probably the number one constraint we all face in our daily lives is time. You have a deadline to meet, and it always seems to arrive before you expected it. All of your professors might have assigned you a paper to do, and all are due on the last day of class—the same day as the final exam.

The best solution for this problem would be to come up with more time. But we are unfortunately restricted to 24 hours per day. So the "next best" idea is to make the best of the time you have. Most time management experts agree that we all waste time every day, and there are ways to waste less of it. That process almost always involves planning. I covered some of this earlier, but it merits review here.

Starting with the day the work is due, plan backward. *Write down your anticipated milestones.* You know that you want to allow time to have your paper reviewed, so build that time into your schedule. There will no doubt be peers or classmates asking you to review their papers as well. Plan a few hours for that contingency.

It is important for you in the review process to consider the amount of time already invested in the writing. If it is a 10-page term paper, and you have a week or two before it is due, you might be inclined to do serious rewriting, or to recommend rewriting to a colleague. But if it is a thesis or a study that you have been working on for six months, any major problems could result in required adjustments to your schedule. You might not receive that degree on time, or the publication window could be missed.

You can count on the inevitable slips in the schedule here and there. Nonetheless, when you review your plan regularly and see that dates are beginning to slip, you can adjust accordingly, before you are forced to pull an all-nighter just before the deadline.

Reviewer and Writer's Experience: It Comes with Time

Whether you are the writer or the reviewer of a piece of writing, the experience you have had in that field will have a direct bearing on your review. If you have never read an intelligence product or written an intelligence paper, then the genre itself may give you problems. Remember where to look for that bottom line. Remember also that there should be conclusions reached in an analytical paper and that the focus should be on the future.

Students often feel overwhelmed with the task of writing four, five, or more papers every quarter. Yet after the first quarter's work they have gained considerable experience in the type of writing expected of them, and the onerous chore becomes less intimidating.

The only way to gain experience, of course, is to do something. When you are asked to write a paper, try to focus it on a topic in which you have experience. The old admonition to "write what you know about" is more than a caution; it's darned good advice. By the same token, it is always helpful to have experience in the area a colleague is writing about, so that you can give substantive advice. Because that will rarely be the case, though, you may need to go back to the discovery phase of review and ask questions or have a dialogue with the writer.

You can still be of great help to someone and provide them loads of advice even if you know *nothing* about the subject. Consider, for example, the hundreds of papers I reviewed every year. I had substantive expertise in perhaps 30 percent of those papers, and most of that experience was based on my reading rather than any personal knowledge. Yet I could help the writers of all those papers by conducting a basic "sanity check": I read for clarity of thought and expression, and for basic organization. Of course I checked for grammatical errors as well. Help in those areas, even without the substantive expertise, can go a long way toward improving someone's writing.

Expectations: Great or Otherwise

It's always helpful when you are writing something, or when you are reviewing someone else's writing, to know what is expected of you. In reviewing your own work, your expectations may be more clearly defined; but when others ask you to review what they have written, they should clearly define the level of proofreading or editing they expect of you. If they do not, then *ask*.

By the same token, of course, you should clearly define your terms when you ask someone else to review your work. If you are concerned about the paper making sense, then ask a disinterested person to read it only for clarity. If the paper seems disjointed to you, then seek a check for organization. And if you're worried about grammar and mechanics, then ask for a thorough proofreading. It's possible that if you ask for "all of the above," you'll either get nothing at all or you'll get a cursory scan of the work that will satisfy no one. Expect everything, and you'll probably get nothing.

Attitude Check

More often than we like to admit, our attitude has a lot to do with our performance. It comes into play as well when we are writing and reviewing intelligence papers. If you genuinely dislike writing, and you hate to edit someone else's writing, then this entire process will be agonizing to you. But if you realize that writing is the cornerstone of the intelligence profession—the means by which we disseminate what we know—then perhaps you can compel a little attitude adjustment and make the job easier for yourself and your colleagues.

When you are reviewing someone else's work, try to remain as detached and objective as possible. Give the writer a chance, even if the writing carries a politically liberal slant that is the polar opposite of your more conservative philosophy (or vice versa). At least read the viewpoints and critique the writing for form, clarity, and grammar if not for content.

The time of day may have a great deal to do with your attitude. I have always tended to be a "morning person," rising before the sun and getting to work in the dark. Some of my best writing and reviewing of others' papers are done before noon. By 3 p.m., though, I'm brain-dead. Don't tell me at 3 p.m. that you must have a paper reviewed by close of business the same day. I simply burn out by that time as far as proofreading and editing skills are concerned. Whenever you can set your own agenda for writing and reviewing, accommodating your preferences for time of day, you will do wonders for your attitude.

Just like the process of writing, the review process also is well served by choosing the right place for it. The crowded, noisy cafeteria is not the place to give the final once-over to your overdue paper. For best results, find a quiet spot where you are less likely to be interrupted—down by the lake, out on the quad. Do whatever it takes to minimize distractions and facilitate the process of review.

Styles of Review

There are as many styles of review as there are styles of writing. No one method is right or wrong, although one style might be more suited to the particular task of review you have in mind. You may find it helpful to understand the different review styles so that you can apply the one most suitable. Generally, those styles are holistic, top down, and bottom up.

Holistic

A holistic style is characterized by looking at the whole paper. It is often an outgrowth of experience and intuition, where the substance of the paper is important. It is also a style well suited to reviewing for clarity and organization. The holistic reviewer tries to get the flavor of the whole paper rather than its individual parts. In attempting this style of review, avoid having a pen or pencil in your hand.

↓ Top Down ↓

A top-down review moves from generalities to particulars— much like the deductive approach to writing that I discussed in chapter 5. It is an approach that you might try when you are looking for topic sentences with supporting facts and figures.

↑ Bottom Up ↑

As you might expect, bottom-up review is the opposite of top-down review. It is characterized by a move from particulars to generalities, like the inductive approach. The bottom-up review, often associated with copyediting, is the one you should use when you are looking for grammatical problems or mechanical errors.

Review Guidelines:
14 Points for Better Analytical Writing

As you write an intelligence analysis paper, consider the following questions. If you address each question and do what it suggests, your paper should be on the mark. The questions also serve as a quick checklist when you review or edit someone else's paper.

1. Does the paper have only one major focus (bottom line or major judgment)? (It should have only one.)
2. Is the focus clearly stated, rather than implied, at the beginning of the paper? (It needs to be.)
3. Do the key judgments, or the summary, contain the major judgments of the paper? (They should.)
4. Are the key judgments written to catch the reader's attention? (They need to be.)
5. What is the significance of the focus for the United States? (There must be some significance.)
6. Is the significance clearly stated? (It should be.)
7. Does all information in the paper relate directly to the focus? (It must relate directly.)
8. Is there information that is interesting or unique but not directly related to the focus? (If so, take it out.)
9. Is like information together? (It must be together.)
10. Is there repetitive or contradictory information? (This must be fixed.)
11. Are all judgments clearly supported by evidence? (They must be.)
12. Are there missed opportunities for making judgments, generalizations, or good topic sentences? (Push to make them.)
13. How can the writing be made more straightforward, concise, and precise? (Think simple.)
14. Does the paper end abruptly? (It shouldn't.)

A "Four Sweeps" Strategy for Reviewing Papers

When you review a paper for *clarity*, you look for focus, the message being conveyed, and the paper's organization. Likewise, you look for certain discrete elements when you read for *persua-*

siveness, when you check the product's *packaging,* and when you edit or proofread the *writing.* The "four sweeps" that follow will help you zero in on what you're looking for.[2]

Sweep 1: Clarity

1. *Focus*
   - Does the paper have *only one principal focus?*
   - Is the focus *an intelligence question* relevant to policy officials?
   - Is the paper's focus *consistent* throughout? In the title, table of contents, introduction, outlook, and key judgments?
   - Does the *introduction* or the *scope note* place the paper's *focus* in the context of the "big picture" or of previous research? Does it indicate why the paper is being done now? Are significant *intelligence gaps* identified?
2. *Message*
   - Does the paper deliver a clear bottom line or message?
   - Does it provide judgments about the future, or does it remain largely descriptive or past oriented?
   - Is the message stated clearly and consistently throughout? In the key judgments, outlook, implications, and title?
3. *Organization*
   - Does the body of the paper develop the message in a *logical order* that is apparent to the reader?
   - Do section *headings* and subheadings *move the analysis forward* and deliver a clear message?
   - Do *all* major sections *relate to* the paper's *focus?*
   - Are any *sections* or section headings *contradictory,* explicitly or implicitly?
   - Should sections be *added* or *deleted?* Put in a *different order?*

   Is the *length* of the paper *appropriate:* overall, among individual sections, text versus graphics?

254 / Chapter 7

Sweep 2: Persuasiveness

1. *Argumentation*
   - Is the paper *sufficiently analytical* (versus descriptive)?
   - Will the intended audience find *useful insights* in it, or does it seem simplistic, obvious, or deliver "old news"?
   - Is the analysis *consistent*, or are there dramatic shifts in tone or emphasis?
   - Is the paper *convincing*? Have you questioned the soundness of the major judgments?
   - Are the major judgments backed by *sufficient evidence* and *sourcing*? Is the paper overly dependent on any one source or type of sourcing?
   - Does the paper *distinguish* between *facts, reporting,* and *beliefs*?
   - Is the *level of detail appropriate* for the intended audience? Too much background or historical information? More evidence than needed to prove the point?
   - Are *key issues* left *unaddressed* or raised but not answered?
   - Is a *methodological explanation* needed?
2. *Topic Sentences*
   - Can the reader *follow the analysis by scanning* the topic sentences?
   - Does each topic sentence *highlight the key point* of each paragraph? Does the paragraph support the topic sentence?
   - Are some topic sentences *too descriptive*? Do some simply present one piece of evidence that does not highlight the point of the paragraph?
3. *Outlook*
   - Is the outlook section *forward looking*? Does it take the analysis as far as reasonably possible?
   - Does *outlook follow from* information presented in the *main body*, or does it come out of the blue?
   - Are forward-looking judgments presented *consistently* throughout the paper?
   - Do these judgments *make sense*?

- Are *assumptions* underlying the judgments *stated*?
- Are intelligence *gaps acknowledged* and conclusions tempered accordingly?
- Are *alternative scenarios presented*, including any with a low probability but high impact on U.S. interests? Are the reasons for the most likely scenario *clear* and *persuasive*?
- Are the *alternative scenarios* really *plausible*? Are the circumstances under which they become more likely set forth? Is there an *indicators list*?

4. *Implications*
   - Are there *different implications* for the *region*, for *U.S. friends* or *key adversaries, for the United States*?
   - Are implications *stated consistently* in the text and key judgments? Are implications presented prematurely in the body of the paper?
   - Can implications be *strengthened* or made more precise? Are some so general as to be obvious, or worse yet, *meaningless*?
   - Do *different implications flow* from alternative future developments?
   - Are there *opportunities* or *vulnerabilities* for the United States?
   - Are any implications stated in a *policy prescriptive* fashion? Do any sound like *special pleading* for command, agency, or institutional interests in certain operations, collection efforts, or other peculiar concerns?

5. *Key Judgments*
   - Do key judgments *stand alone* for the busy policy maker?
   - Do they focus on *major, forward-looking judgments* of the paper, including the implications for the United States?
   - Do key judgments try to *summarize too much* of the paper? Do they follow unnecessarily the outline of the paper?
   - Are they *consistent* with the stated focus and message found in the other parts of the paper?

- Do the key judgments present or emphasize *analysis or pieces of evidence* that were *not in the paper*?
- Are key judgments *concise* (four to seven paragraphs), *snappy* in style, and *understandable*? Or are sentences too long, transitions abrupt?

Sweep 3: Packaging

1. *Assembly*
   - Is the paper *properly formatted* and *mechanically correct* to enhance its rapid review and processing?
   - Is there a *title page*? *Table of contents*, if needed? Does the table of contents include appendixes and list of graphics?
   - Are text *pages numbered*? Are front-end pages in Roman numerals?
   - Are *graphics, photos, in-text boxes* ("sidebars") *attached* at the end of the paper?
   - Are *references* made *in the text* to the appropriate location of maps, photos, graphics, or in-text boxes? Are these the *right locations* to break the reader's eyes away from the text?
2. *In-Text Boxes, Appendixes, Annexes*
   - *Can the flow* of the text and the clarity of focus and message *be improved* by putting historical, tutorial, or highly technical material in one of the supporting sections?
   - Do all the in-text boxes *belong there*, or in the back of the paper? If they belong up front, are they as *short* as possible? (Each in-text box will break the reader's eyes away from the body of the paper.)
   - Are there *too many* or *too few* in-text boxes?
   - Is *all the material* in annexes or appendixes *worth publishing*?
3. *Graphics, Tables*
   - Does information in *graphics contradict* or diverge from statements made in the *text*?
   - *Can* a sequence of *graphics or tables provide analysis* in place of text?

- Are the graphics *accurate* and *up to date*?
- Are graphics *properly located* and *referred to* in the text?
- Are all the graphics or tables *necessary*?

4. *Pictures, Maps*
   - Are there *too few* or *too many*?
   - Does each picture or map *support the paper's focus* or message?
   - Are *captions* for pictures *informative and consistent* with the text? Can pieces of analysis receive emphasis in a photo and caption?
   - *Can maps* of obvious or well-known geography *be enhanced* with new information or graphics displayed on them?

Sweep 4: Writing

1. *Style*
   - Is the writing style *too academic*?
   - Is the style *clear, crisp,* and *straightforward*?
2. *Transitions*
   - Is there transitional language that *moves the reader smoothly* from one section of the paper to the next?
   - Does each major section need an *introduction* or *summary paragraph*?
3. *Paragraphs*
   - Does each paragraph have a *topic sentence*?
   - Are some paragraphs *too long*? (four to six sentences is most effective.)
   - Is the *length* of the paragraphs *varied enough* to ease the reader's burden or to provide emphasis? (Short paragraphs are more visible on the page and attract reader attention.)
   - Should any paragraphs be *combined*? *Split*?
4. *Sentences*
   - Are sentences *short* and *straightforward*? (Reader comprehension rises if at least 50 percent of sentences are simple: subject, verb, object.)

- Is the *active voice* used? If passive voice is used, is there a valid reason? (If the object is more important than the subject, or if the subject is unknown, the passive voice may be necessary.)
- Check grammar, usage, lost or unclear antecedents, unparallel construction, and punctuation.

5. *Words*
   - Are *vigorous, exact nouns and verbs* used rather than bland, general ones?
   - Can you *substitute simpler words* for complex ones, *single words* for several words, without violating the preceding guideline?
   - Are some *words used too often*?
   - *Minimize* use of *abbreviations. Avoid clichés.*
   - *Minimize* the use of *jargon* or unfamiliar *acronyms*. Is a *glossary* needed?
   - Check *spelling* and *capitalization.*

Exercises in Writing and Reviewing Analytical Papers

Exercise 1: The Types of Intelligence Writing

1. *Descriptive*: As the name implies, this type of intelligence writing describes something in sensory terms—size, shape, composition, and color, for example.
2. *Explanatory*: This type of writing provides an explanation of how something works, why it performs the way it does, or why something happened.
3. *Estimative*: Estimates look toward the future and make forecasts or predictions, suggesting the implications for U.S. national security.

With those definitions in mind, answer the following questions:

1. Into what category do you think most intelligence writing falls?

2. Name a type of intelligence product that you think might fit into each category:
   a. Descriptive:
   b. Explanatory:
   c. Estimative:
3. Where would analytical papers fit?

Exercise 2: Reviewing an Analytical Paper

List on a separate sheet of paper some of the features you think might characterize an "analytical" paper.

Questions for Discussion in Class

1. When you review someone else's paper, what is the *first* thing you do?
2. When you review *your own* paper, what is the *first* thing you do?
3. Briefly describe your review process for a 10-page paper if you are given
   a. ten minutes.
   b. two hours.
   c. ten days.

Exercise 3: Some Analytical Papers for Your Review

Review Number 1: Iran-Contra—Hearing Is Believing

We asked students to write an essay on the question, "What impact do you think the Iran-Contra hearings will have on the National Security Council?" We asked it in September 1987, while the hearings and the 1988 election campaign were in full swing. Here is one student's response, exactly as submitted.

As a intelligence professional I don't like any intelligence matters to be reviewed by the world on the evening news, because the intelligence process is on trail. The National Security Council is not an intelligence organization and should not be runing covert intelligence operations. They should be keeping the president informed of National Security matters of vital interest to the Country. They don't have the time, charter, or money to be developing seperate intelligence organizational and operational channels in other nations.

The congress, press, public, and the intelligence community must believe that the President is in charge of his National Security Council. Key operations (covert or overt) that require oversight (by law) by the U.S. congress in a timely manner, cannot be taken lightly by staff members of the National Security Council. Because of the Iran-Contragate hearings the congress will demand reform in the NSC. Heads have rolled and new people have been appointed and still the NSC is in operation today. I don't think the president or the congress will consider the elemination of the NSC because of the nature of its mission. The NSC's budget will be reviewed very carefully in the future when dealing with special covert activities. We have a large experienced Intelligence Community that is in the business of solving these types of problems. The future of the NSC will probably continue to reflect the presidents use of the organization. If he continues its use on a daily basis and respects the solutions and actions that are generated by the NSC, then the impact will be to a lesser degree. However, if the congress and the public make the NSC an issue during the election year, then we could see a reduction of staff and mission. This is not in the best interest of the country. Only time will tell.

Questions for Discussion

1. Did you look first to see *how long* the essay is?
2. Did you pick up a pen or pencil before you started reading?
3. Using the "Model Process for Reviewing an Analytical Paper" discussed earlier, describe the processes you used in reviewing this essay.
4. Considering the way you approached this exercise, can you identify your *style* of review—holistic, top down, or bottom up?
5. Where is the *theme* of this essay first stated?

Review Number 2: A "Treasury" of Information

This extract introduced a student paper entitled "U.S. Treasury Department Intelligence Capabilities: A Brief Description of Major Subordinate Operating Bureaus, Organizations and Functions." The paper was to have been no longer than 15 pages.

> This research paper will focus on the Treasury Department and its intelligence capabilities. I will briefly discuss the history of the Treasury Department and its relationship with the Intelligence Community.
>
> The Treasury Department maintains staff cognizance and responsibilities for various bureaus and offices which possess a unique intelligence capability. For the uniqueness of these bureaus and the U.S. Customs service; I selected the following agencies in a effort to provide a better understanding about how they function:
>
> 1. The U.S. Department of the Treasury.
> 2. Bureau of Alcohol, Tobacco, and Firearms.
> 3. Internal Revenue Service.
> 4. U.S. Secret Service.
> 5. U.S. Customs Service.
> 6. The evolution of the role of the U.S. Treasury Department.
> 7. The role of the Treasury Department in the National Foreign Intelligence Community.
>
> I will address several of these issues in the following discussion of the Treasury Department and its subordinate operating bureaus and their Intelligence capability. First, I will identify their various responsibilities and relationship to the Treasury Department. Second, I will offer an assessment of the Treasury Departments future of effort. Finally, I will provide an assessment of where the organization is and offer an analysis of where the organization is headed.
>
> Background
>
> U.S. Department of the Treasury (DOT), is an executive department of the U.S. Government, charged with the management of the nations financial actions. The Treasury Department

was established on the September 1, 1789, by an act of Congress. Currently the Secretary of the Treasury is charged with numerous duties to include sub-agencies responsible for guarding the President, enforcement of laws in such areas concerning counterfeiting, illegal imports, and tax evasion.

The Secretary of the Treasury is appointed by the President, and is aided by various operating bureaus subordinate to the Treasury Department. The Secretary of the Treasury serves as the Principal adviser to the President on fiscal matters.

Questions for Discussion
1. Could the student have reasonably expected adequate coverage of this topic in 15 pages?
2. What was the *fundamental* problem with this paper's intent?

Review Number 3: Conference in Canberra

This paper was a draft submitted by a young intelligence analyst in a national agency. Minor changes were made for security reasons.

A conference on U.S. and European naval activity in the Southern Hemisphere will be held this winter in Canberra. The agenda will be similar to that convened last spring in Montevideo. According to a usually reliable source in Paris, a Libyan hit team will be sent to attack delegates from countries inimical to Libyan interests and to its policy aims. Based on this report and other information, we believe they will be armed with [a] shoulder fired missile launcher. The weapon's range would allow it to be fired from beyond the security perimeter set up around the meeting facilities. The team will likely target our embassy also and that of London and France. Libyan failure to successfully attack delegates to the Montevideo conference was because of its lack of this weapon, which they had tried to acquire.

The targeting of U.S., British and French interests is planned because Qhaddafi regards these countries as the principle impediments to him achieving the radical anti-shipping aims, which are the subject of the conference. Such action might weaken other West European resolve to retaliate for Libyan terrorism in their countries. They will likely continue trying to convince the U.S. to improve relations. U.S. objections to Soviet representation however, block Chinese efforts to attend, because the other countries will not accept one without the other. Prime Minister Thatcher has announced she will not stand in the way of Moscow taking part in deliberations affecting Soviet interests.

In our view, based on actions last spring, Qadhafi believes that our likely reprisals will not go beyond one or more surgical strikes on Libya. The Libyan claim that its forces downed U.S. planes there could give Qadhafi a pretext to avoid further escalation.

Questions for Discussion
1. What is the *theme* of this paper?
2. Where is that theme first stated?

Review Number 4: A Wordy, Wordy Introduction

The following extract was the first page of a student's seminar paper on civil-military relations in Pakistan. Review and discuss the piece. Where might words be cut?

Introduction

Since achieving independence in 1947, Pakistan has gone through several phases of civil-military relations. It is not possible to place a specific reason why the military has been able to retain its power in civil government and control both domestic and foreign policy. It is more likely a combination of factors, which creates the optimal situation for military intervention into civil government. Therefore, Pakistan has become an ideal country to study civil-military relations. The readings that were provided over the last two months exposed several theories that can be applied to Pakistan's civil-military relations. However, these authors and their theories do not provide the total explanation of Pakistan's situation, but provide a firm foundation that explains why the military is able to dominate government activity. It is the purpose of this paper to

provide a clear explanation of the military dominance in Pakistan civil-military relations with the aid of these theories. The
format that will be taken to obtain this explanation will be laid
out in four sections. First, a brief history is appropriate in order
"to set the stage," causes and effects of the military's role in
government are the second and third sections, and the fourth
is the conclusion, that will assess the civil-military relations in
Pakistan.

A Brief History of Pakistan's Civil-Military Administrations

It is necessary to give a brief history of Pakistan between independence and the present. These years produced four key
governments that set the stage for the current civil-military
government. It is important to recognize these governments in
order to show the evolution that resulted in a military domi-
nated government. Even though the military continuously had
power within the government during this time period; the degree of power was different according to whom the leaders
were. These leaders are factors, which produced change, and
ultimately created the right influences for a dominating military regime.

Review Number 5: Humint in the Old Testament

This final example is the introduction to a graduate research
paper. It was to have dealt analytically with the subject of human
intelligence (Humint) in biblical history. See if you think this paper can be called "analytical." If so, why? If not, why not?

The collection of information, either by legal or illegal means,
through the use of human sources, whether about one's friends
or enemies, has long been an accepted practice. This collection
activity, referred to as human intelligence (Humint), is as old as
recorded history. Hence this study which examines the single
source of our most ancient written history, the Old Testament.

It must be understood and accepted at the outset that many
of the references and/or indications of Humint activities described in this paper may be in error due to the possibility of
mistakes in the various translations or interpretations of the
source. Never-the-less, the study will examine the incidents

where it appears that Humint activities have been recorded or referenced, and will attempt to analyze the utility, accuracy and effect of the collected intelligence within it's particular circumstances.

There will be no attempt to treat the source as other than an academic text. References to persons, places, or being described therein will be treated as factual. Other sources, commentaries, opinions, topical guides, indexes, etc., will be utilized to further make, clarify or substantiate a point, as required.

The earliest recorded event of Humint exploitation occurs in the Garden of Eden. Here a serpent tempted Eve to eat of the tree of knowledge of good and evil, saying it would make her as the gods, knowing good and evil, and that it was desirable to make one wise. Where did the serpent get this information? The record is mute on that point. This may be one of those times when the source can accurately be described as unknown. The serpent's information, from whomever or wherever it was obtained, was accurate, and it surely changed the course of events for Adam and Eve, if not the entire world, as they were cast out of the Garden of Eden to become members of the human race in the lone and dreary world of weeds and sweat and intelligence gathering and analysis.

Answers to the Exercises in Chapter 7

Exercise 1: The Types of Intelligence Writing

1. Despite our best efforts, most intelligence writing still seems to be *descriptive*.
2. a. *Descriptive*: Orders of battle or country studies.
   b. *Explanatory*: Scientific and technical (S&T) intelligence studies and reports.
   c. *Estimative*: National intelligence estimates, defense intelligence estimates.
3. Analytical papers really cover the gamut of intelligence writing. They are often based on historical (mostly descriptive) writing, but their *focus* is—or should be— *estimative*.

Exercise 2: Reviewing an Analytical Paper

An analytical paper has many characteristics, but perhaps the most important are those listed below.

1. An analytical paper is *oriented toward conclusions, not just a summary.*
2. It is *focused on the future, not the past.*
3. The paper contains *essentials and evidence.*
4. An analytical paper is *relevant to policy makers and decision makers.*

Questions for Discussion in Class

1. Put your pen or pencil down, and read through the entire paper once. Get a feeling for its organization, style, and content.
2. In reviewing your own paper, let it sit for a while before you try to review it.
3. The review process differs geometrically with the amount of time you have to do the review. If you're limited to only a few minutes, *skim* the paper looking for major problems. You really don't have time to do anything else. If you have two hours for a 10-page paper, that gives you more than 10 minutes per page. Use the review processes I wrote about earlier. If you have as many as 10 days to review a paper, chances are you'll still spend about the same amount of time as if you had two hours. But it helps if you do your holistic review at one sitting, then return for a second look later (later in the day or even days later).

Exercise 3: Some Analytical Papers for Your Review

Review Number 1: Iran-Contra—Hearing Is Believing

1. When you are assigned a limited time to accomplish a task, always determine first the scope of your task. You immediately should have turned ahead to see the length of the essay you were charged to read.

2. The simple act of having a pen or pencil in your hand will often cause you to begin marking any errors you see. That in turn may cause you to miss the forest because you're too busy pruning the trees.

3. Chances are you began an immediate "discovery" process by reading the essay. It probably didn't take long for you to reach a "judgment" on the quality of this essay. You certainly could have had many suggestions for the author, and you would probably send the paper back for reworking.

4. If you read quickly through the whole paper, you employed a *holistic* style. That's a good one when you want a quick flavor of what the paper is *about* and how well it is organized. A look at "the big picture"—again reading the whole paper but with more attention to content—would be characterized as a *top-down* style, which is often effective in looking at coherence or in answering the question, "Does this paper answer the question?" If you began by marking typos and other errors, you were reading with a *bottom-up* style, an approach usually associated with proofreading.

5. The first hint of the real *theme* of this essay—the sentence that addresses the question asked and should have been the first sentence in the piece—is in the sentence beginning, "Because of the Iran-Contragate hearings. . . ." Notice, too, the classic noncommittal ending: "Only time will tell."

Review Number 2: A "Treasury" of Information

1. Considering the scope of information promised by this student in his introduction, he had absolutely no hope of covering the topic adequately in 15 pages (probably not even in *1,500* pages!).

2. The *fundamental* problem with this paper's approach was its *focus*. The student ignored everything we had said about prewriting and moved straight into the first draft.

Review Number 3: Conference in Canberra

1. The *theme* of this article is a possible terrorist threat against delegates to a forthcoming conference.
2. Violating a cardinal rule of intelligence writing—bottom line up front—this writer waited until the *third sentence* to state the theme.

Review Number 4: A Wordy, Wordy Introduction

My edited version of this paper appears below. It reduces the original 317 words to 142—a 55 percent saving of the reader's time. Compare this version to the original:

Introduction

Since its independence in 1947, Pakistan has seen several civil-military governments. The military's power and its control of both domestic and foreign policy create the optimal situation for military intervention in civil government. Therefore, Pakistan has become an ideal case study in civil-military relations. While the theories do not provide a total explanation, they do illustrate why the military dominates government activity in Pakistan. History sets the stage for military dominance in Pakistan.

A Brief History of Pakistan's Civil-Military Administrations

The years between independence and the present produced four governments that set the stage for the current civil-military regime and reflected the evolution toward military domination. Even though the military continuously held power since 1947, the degree of power differed according to the leaders. These leaders produced changes that ultimately created the right environment for a dominating military regime.

Review Number 5: Humint in the Old Testament

This student and I shared a good laugh when we talked about his paper. He had unintentionally injected a great deal of *humor* (*not* Humint!) into the piece. He agreed when I explained to him that to begin in the Garden of Eden was "a stretch," since there were only two humans on Earth at the time. So if anything, he was writing not about Humint, but *Serpint*, since the snake was the culprit. There's little of any analytical value in this piece, but it provides one of the classic lines of any paper I've ever read: "[T]hey were cast out of the Garden of Eden to become members of the human race in the lone and dreary world of weeds and sweat and intelligence gathering and analysis." So it was written; so it shall be.

Notes

1. Department of Defense, Joint Chiefs of Staff, Joint Pub 1-02, *Department of Defense Dictionary of Military and Associated Terms* (Washington, D.C.: Government Printing Office, December 1, 1989), under the word "analysis."

2. For the information contained in this section, I am indebted to Martin Petersen. His article, "Managing/Teaching New Analysts," appeared in the Fall 1986 issue of the unclassified *Studies in Intelligence*. It was reprinted with his permission in one of my earlier books, *Wordshops*. For information in the remainder of the chapter, I express my thanks to Frans Bax of the Central Intelligence Agency, who conducted the earlier-cited "Workshop on Reviewing Analytical Papers" at the Joint Military Intelligence College in 1989.

8

Supplemental Exercises

Exercise 1: Writing a Thesis Statement

Writing with intelligence begins with an idea—a central topic, narrowly focused, with the key point up front in the writing. That key point is the topic sentence of the first paragraph. It also may be called a key judgment (especially in an analytical paper or an estimate), an executive summary, or a thesis statement. This first exercise uses a printed advertisement as an example of how a thesis statement is developed. Then in exercise 2 you'll take the next step and, using one of the eight components of intelligence, you'll write a well-developed paragraph.

Assignment

Find an advertisement in a magazine or newspaper that catches your eye, either because it makes you want to buy or use the product or service, or because it made you decide that you will *never* buy or use it. Study the ad carefully for a few minutes, and then answer the following questions.

1. Identify the purpose and the audience.
   Purpose: Why do you think the advertiser wrote the ad the way it is written? (The *obvious* answer is to sell the

product; go beyond that, and apply some critical thinking.)

Audience: For whom do you believe the ad was written—specifically?

2. Gather information. Don't worry about relevance. Collect as much as possible about the ad. Use brainstorming techniques.

3. Group the pieces of information and determine their relationships. Look at the information you have collected and see if it can be arranged into categories or groups (for example, photos, ad copy, information, data, detractors, or statistics).

4. Write an assertion for each category. What is *said* in the ad about each category or group of information? What is *not* said? What do you think each assertion *means*?

5. Determine an organizing idea. What central idea causes all the assertions to come together and convey a meaning to the reader?

Exercise 2: Writing a Paragraph

Assignment

Write a well-developed paragraph on the subject "The Importance of [one of the eight components of strategic intelligence] in ____." (Your instructor will help you "fill in the blanks.") Assume that the paragraph is the first one in a longer document intended to convince an audience of the crucial importance of this component; so the content of your argument in persuading the audience will be important. Your audience is a group of midlevel intelligence professionals who are aware of the components but who need to be convinced of the importance of the one you choose.

Other Guidance

Remember to narrow your topic to a manageable focus. Use one or more of the prewriting devices covered in chapter 4 (freewriting, outline, or mind map) to help focus your topic. Write four to six well-focused sentences on the topic. Be sure you have a topic sentence. The components of strategic intelligence are listed below. This assignment should take you no more than 30 minutes.

Components of Strategic Intelligence ("BEST MAPS")

Biographic	Military Geographic
Economic	Armed Forces
Sociological	Political
Transportation and Telecommunications	Scientific and Technical

Writing Evaluation Sheet: The Paragraph

The sentence is the basic element of all writing, but the paragraph is the first place where sentences come together to form the cohesive idea that you want to convey to your reader. To help you evaluate a paragraph—your own or a peer's—use the following checklist. *Circle grammatical and spelling errors in your paragraph, but do not correct them.*

- What are you trying to say in your paragraph? What is your *main idea*? Is that main idea contained in the *topic sentence*?
- Who might be interested in reading this paragraph? Is it fitted to its intended audience?
- Are key terms defined? What does the writer assume the reader already knows?
- Are the sentences clear and readable?
- What sentences (if any) confuse you or especially appeal to you? Why?
- Does the paragraph flow smoothly from point to point? If not, where does coherence break down?
- Are words used correctly?
- Which words struck you or stood out or resonated?

- What do you like *most* and *least* about the paragraph?
- Summarize the thesis or argument contained in the paragraph.
- After reading this as an introduction, where would you expect the longer piece to go? Can you offer helpful suggestions to improve the paragraph?

Exercise 3: Writing a Summary

Often in your work, you will need to condense and rephrase source material and then to embed this summarized information or opinion into the structure of your paper. It is never appropriate to string together numerous lengthy quotations from your sources. Therefore, you will need to identify, select, and recast the main ideas from your research materials. For this exercise, select an article from a newspaper or newsmagazine. The piece should be 1,000–2,000 words long.

The mentality you need for the summary is that you are a mirror to the original material, reflecting its content accurately *without injecting your own thoughts or feelings.*

1. It is always a good idea to read a chapter or article completely and carefully before attempting to summarize it. Sometimes a writer delays stating the main point until late in the essay. You cannot see how all the parts fit together until you have read the whole piece.
2. Reread the article, underlining key words and phrases (usually nouns, verbs, and adjectives).
3. Look away from the original and, on scratch paper, write one grammatically complete sentence in your own words that restates the main point of the article.
4. Repeat this process for each paragraph. Obviously some flexibility is necessary here: some paragraphs may require two sentences while others may be summarized with one sentence.

5. Do not use "according to this article" or "the author states" since you are not a commentator upon the material.
6. Make a rough count of the total number of words. You normally reduce the original to one-quarter its length. If you are far below the word limit, check the article to see what points you have omitted. If you are above the limit, check your sentences for wordiness, repetition, or unnecessary details.
7. Generally speaking, your sentences should reflect the arrangement of the original material. However, you may do some rearranging to avoid organizational problems in your summary. For example, if the thesis of the article occurs in your third sentence, you may move that sentence to the beginning of your summary to organize it more effectively.
8. Decide whether your summary needs paragraphing. Generally, one paragraph is sufficient, but if the article deals with two (or more) distinctly different aspects of a topic, you will need two (or more) paragraphs.
9. Now join your ideas together by providing transition. Some methods include using conjunctive adverbs (*however, in addition, for example,* and so on), substituting a pronoun for a noun to avoid unnecessary repetition (the exam . . . it), or joining sentences with conjunctions (*and, or, but, although, because*).
10. Reread your summary, checking for good organization and accurate content. Then proofread it for spelling and mechanical errors.

A good summary of an essay has three qualities:

Brevity: Condense the piece to about one-fourth its original length.
Completeness: A summary should contain
1. the central idea of the essay;
2. the relationship between its main points; and

3. the author's attitude (objective? sarcastic? condemning?), if this is important.

Objectivity: Your opinion of what the author is saying has no place in a summary, whether you agree, disagree, or champion the essay's meaning. Just say what the author says without editorializing.

A summary must be *in your own words*. Do not quote from the original unless a few of the words are essential to the meaning.

Exercise 4: Getting the Bottom Line Up Front

1. One important consideration of intelligence writing is that the main idea or central assertion of the paper be up front in the writing. Why?
2. What is the main difference between key judgments and an executive summary?
3. Following is the first paragraph of a 10-page paper. Read the paragraph and be prepared to discuss in class whether you think it contains key judgments or an executive summary. If so, why? If not, why not?

> The purpose of this paper is to evaluate the conflict between Panaragua and Nicador. The study will trace the roots of the confrontation and will examine possible causes leading up to the most recent dispute. I will use a "levels of analysis" approach, concentrating on national and regional issues. I will also compare and contrast the situation in each country and attempt to reach conclusions about the confrontation. Finally, I will attempt to forecast the prospects for both countries in the years ahead.

4. Following is the first paragraph from another 10-page paper. Read it and be prepared to discuss in class whether it contains key judgments or an executive summary. If so, why? If not, why not?

Panaragua and Nicador declared a cease-fire on 12 October, and negotiations have begun. Nevertheless, the two countries continue to squabble over the 10-mile-wide strip of land that separates them. Both nations have claimed the disputed territory since 1892, when a treaty split Panaraguador into two separate countries. Wars have erupted frequently since then. The latest year-long battle shows the failure by both sides to achieve any progress. Prospects for solving the border dispute are dim, and renewed fighting is likely in the months ahead. United States mining, agricultural, and petrochemical interests in Panaragua are at risk of seizure or destruction if another conflict occurs.

Guidelines for the Preparation of Key Judgments

Lengthy intelligence papers—generally those more than five pages—are read by few people. Instead, most people read only the key judgments. Thus, those judgments must convey accurately and succinctly the analytically based findings of the paper.

Key judgments do not merely summarize the paper but also convey what the analyst would say (or should say) to a high-level user if given only two minutes in which to convey the findings. Therefore, key judgments do not explain the sources of information used in the paper, persons consulted during its preparation, the methodologies employed, or any other information not related directly to the author's findings.

As a rule of thumb, the key judgments should not exceed 10 percent of the length of the paper. Key judgments generally come in one of two formats.

One Format

The opening paragraph sets the scene by explaining the topic of the paper and conveying a sense of its importance. It should be four to six sentences long.

- The first bullet is the most important judgment.
- Then follows the second most important judgment.

- Continue with clear, concise judgments until all important points have been covered.
- The language of the key judgments should parallel that used in the text so that someone reading the full text will not wonder how the key judgments link to the paper.

An Alternative Format

A series of short, pithy paragraphs convey the essence of the conclusions reached in the paper.

Generally the key judgments parallel the structure of the paper. That is, the first key judgment is drawn from the beginning of the paper and the last from the end.

All important points made in the paper should be reflected in the key judgments.

Exercise 5: Types of Intelligence Writing—Descriptive, Explanatory, and Estimative

Description

Descriptive writing tells about something in sensory terms—size, shape, composition, color, or capacity, for example. It relies primarily upon adjectives and nouns to convey its meaning. Description often provides an effective means of appealing to emotions. Look at the two sentences below, and decide what descriptive elements each contains.

1. The new Russian tank is larger than the Abrams tank, with more armament and greater range.
2. The new production model of the Russian T-94 tank is 50 percent larger than the U.S. M1 Abrams tank. The T-94 also has twice as many weapons on board and three times the range of its U.S. counterpart.
   - How might the above items be made more descriptive?

Explanation

Explanatory writing tells how something works, why it performs the way it does, or why something happened. In explaining a *process*, chronological order is often of particular value, taking the process step-by-step for the benefit of the reader.

- Look at the example below and determine whether you could accomplish the specified task, given the information provided.

Opening a can of beer: Grip the can firmly in your left hand. With your right hand, pop the top. Enjoy yourself.

- Assume that your reader has never opened a can of beer. (Obviously not a college student!) Rewrite the instructions above to ensure that the reader could accomplish the task.

Estimation

Estimative writing looks toward the future and makes forecasts or predictions, suggesting the implications for U.S. national security.

Look again at the sample paragraph from the key judgments exercise, reprinted below. What portions are estimative? Why?

Panaragua and Nicador declared a cease-fire on 12 October, and negotiations have begun. Nevertheless, the two countries continue to squabble over the 10-mile-wide strip of land that separates them. Both nations have claimed the disputed territory since 1892, when a treaty split Panaraguador into two separate countries. Wars have erupted frequently since then. The latest year-long battle shows the failure by both sides to achieve any progress. Prospects for solving the border dispute are dim, and renewed fighting is likely in the months ahead. United States mining, agricultural, and petrochemical interests in Panaragua are at risk of seizure or destruction if another conflict occurs.

Exercise 6: Avoiding Passive Voice and Wordiness

Passive Voice

Look for the passive voice and wordiness in the following sentences. Rewrite them in the active voice, supplying your own subject when none is stated. If you think the sentence is better left in the passive voice, explain why.

1. John was called by the division chief in order to answer questions about the IG visit.
2. The job was finished by Sue in sufficient time for an extra incentive bonus to be awarded by her office.
3. No explanation of why she was fired by Ken was given by Barbie.
4. Don't worry; the paperwork will be finished when you return from the trip.
5. Roger Rabbit was accused of murder.
6. When Joe's boss arrived Tuesday morning, the job had been finished as he promised.
7. George W. Bush was elected president in 2004.
8. Social Security benefits have been slashed.
9. The test was designed to challenge even the most skilled mathematician.
10. Obviously, mistakes were made.
11. The interview was conducted by Joe, a skilled questioner.
12. To evaluate recent movies about dinosaurs, the history of the animals must be read.
13. The Pentagon said the contract had been canceled.
14. All costs need to be considered when a contract is being worked on.
15. Egypt Air's flight data recorder was found on November 14, 1999.
16. This set of exercises is finished!

Eliminating Wordiness

Rewrite these sentences to eliminate wordiness. Be sure to retain the meaning.

1. There is a distinct possibility that we could finally determine that the SDI laser system is a somewhat less feasible alternative than we think of it now, and we would thus be enabled to enter into other research programs as the United States seeks to develop defensive systems in the nuclear arena that are more cost effective.

2. It has been shown that the government was really searching for a way that was painless in a political sense to reduce the deficit of the federal budget. To do this Congress enacted the Balanced Budget and Emergency Deficit Control Act of 1985. This act is better known as Gramm-Rudman-Hollings (GRH). The president signed this bill.

3. The goal of GRH was to achieve a budget at the federal level that was very balanced. Under this law there are lower and lower ceilings on deficit spending in each fiscal year. The budget that is agreed upon and approved by Congress and the president must be within $10 million of the target that is specified by the Balanced Budget and Emergency Deficit Control Act. When this target is not reached and met, there are cuts in spending that the Congress and the president must begin across the board.

4. There are many basic similarities between the film version of George Bernard Shaw's *Pygmalion* and Lerner and Loewe's *My Fair Lady*. For one thing, Eliza is a flower seller in both the film and the play who is uneducated and really talks with a Cockney accent.

5. There is another similar scene that is included in both works when Eliza really practices her vowels that she can't say by reciting "The Rain in Spain." The film and the musical play also have exactly the same concluding end, with Eliza returning to the flat of Henry Higgins.

6. The movie version, which relies heavily on the Broadway musical produced earlier, kept two of the first and foremost important actors, in my opinion—Rex Harrison and Stanley Holloway. However, it's certainly true that this ending is very different than the ending of Shaw's play, which has Eliza going off to marry Freddy and Professor

Higgins laughing in a sarcastic way about the future prospects of this marriage.

7. Due to the fact that Eliza is both something Higgins creates and a person who fights back, I believe that her conflict with him is basically an indication that she likes him a lot. Basically, the play appearing on Broadway portrays in a comedic way how love can cross class lines, but this can happen only at the point where the professor learns some humility and Eliza realizes that she is a human being who is entitled to respect from him.

8. A realization by terrorist groups in Europe has taken place, that not only will their survivability improve, but also that their impact on Western society can be greatly enhanced by unification and mutual cooperation among each other.

9. There were also indications subtle in nature of an advance forward, such as handwritten documents and testimony of captured enemy, which were collected by military intelligence personnel.

10. It is a matter of grave importance to the health of any writer who has a history of problems with a lack of conciseness that he or she immediately begins a program of very careful proofreading in order to whittle away the excess baggage from his or her writing.

Exercise 7: Reviewing Writing— Your Own and Others'

There are many helpful guides to reviewing writing. I am including several in this exercise for your use both in class and out of class. I hope these guides will be helpful when you begin reviewing writing on your own or as a member of a peer group.

Self-Evaluation Sheet

To help you, your professor, or your peers evaluate your writing, explain where you are in the writing process by answering the following questions. Be as specific as possible, but keep your answers brief. Be prepared to discuss your answers in class.

1. What are you trying to say in your paper? What is your main idea?
2. Who might be interested in reading your paper upon its completion?
3. What do you like *best* about your paper?
4. What do you like *least* about your paper?
5. What would you work on if you had two more weeks to spend on your paper?

Questions for Peer Response Exercise 1

1. What is the paper about? Underline a sentence that contains the thesis statement or main idea.
2. Paraphrase the author's paper in one or two sentences.
3. What do you like best about the paper?
4. What sentences (if any) confuse you?
5. What sentences (if any) especially appeal to you?
6. Circle grammatical and spelling errors, but *do not correct them.*
7. Are key terms clearly defined? What does the writer assume the reader already knows?
8. Does the paper flow smoothly from point to point? If not, where does coherence break down?
9. What questions do you still have after reading the paper?
10. What helpful suggestions can you offer the writer to improve the paper?

Questions for Peer Response Exercise 2

Criterion-Based Responses

1. *Quality of Content*
   a. Is the basic idea supported by logic or valid argument?
   b. Is it supported by evidence and examples?
   c. Is the piece fitted to its intended audience?

2. *Organization*
   a. Is the whole thing unified?
   b. Are the parts arranged in a coherent, logical sequence?
   c. Is there a beginning, a middle, and an end?
3. *Language*
   a. Are the sentences clear and readable?
   b. Are the words used correctly?
   c. Is it succinct enough for its audience and purpose?
4. *Mechanics and Usage*: Are there mistakes in grammar, usage, spelling, or punctuation?

Reader-Based Responses

1. *Moment by Moment Report*
   a. Which words struck you or stuck out or resonated?
   b. After reading the introduction, where do you expect the piece to go?
   c. What kind of person does the writer seem to be in the beginning?
   d. Did anything surprise you in this piece?
   e. What didn't you understand?
   f. What kind of person does the writer seem like at the end of the piece?
   g. What pleased you about the piece? What displeased you?
   h. Did your feelings change as you read the piece? How?
2. *Summary Responses*
   a. Summarize the writer's thesis or argument.
   b. Tell what you *wish* the piece had said.

Peer Review of a Thesis Proposal

Formats for thesis proposals vary among institutions. The format that follows, however, is conducive not only to the review of most proposals but also, perhaps with slight modification, to major papers of all kinds—at the graduate or undergraduate level—and especially to papers oriented toward an intelligence-related subject.

Topic and Research Question Refinement

1. Is the topic *specific* and of *interest to the intelligence community*?
2. Does the topic have *one principal focus*?
3. Does the topic lend itself to an *analytical approach*?
4. Is the topic *supportable in the literature*?
5. Is the research question *all encompassing*, and does it *avoid a yes or no* answer?

Review of Related Literature

1. Does this section evaluate a *body of relevant work* on the topic?
2. Are *important sources omitted*?
3. Is the literature *evaluated* and *not* merely *enumerated*?

Hypothesis and Key Questions

1. Does the proposed hypothesis contain an *issue* or *problem* of *intelligence interest*?
2. Is the issue or problem *too broad* to be covered adequately?
3. Does the issue or problem provide a *focal point* for the paper?
4. Are the key questions *relevant* to the hypothesis?

Research Design and the Strategies

1. Is the description of research methods to be used *clear* and *complete*?
2. Are there *clearly enunciated* and *separate collection* and *analytical strategies*?
3. Can the writer *expect to accomplish the research* based on this design?
4. Do methods and strategies *slavishly follow the format*, with no apparent thought to the individual requirements of this thesis?

Contents and Milestones

1. Are probable *chapter titles* and *major subheadings* stated, in outline form, as the contents?
2. Do the proposed contents cover the subject *thoroughly* and *conform to the key questions*?
3. Are milestones stated in terms of *target deadlines*?
4. Are the milestones *realistic,* allowing sufficient time for *committee review* and *multiple drafts*?

Preliminary Bibliography

1. Does the preliminary bibliography *begin on a separate page*?
2. Does the writer appear to have considered a *relevant body of literature*?
3. Can you recommend *other sources of information* for the writer (for example, books, periodicals, or subject-matter experts to be interviewed)?

Exercise 8: Peer Review of Student Writing

The three readings that follow are designed for in-class reading and discussion. Consider dividing the class into three groups, each focused on one of the readings and answering the following questions: (1) Is the writing analytical? If so, why? If not, why not? (2) What are the most serious problems with the writing? (3) What suggestions might you offer the writer to improve his or her writing? It is also helpful if the entire class reads all three pieces, with each group then focusing on the one assigned to it.

Reading 1 for Peer Review Exercises

Students were asked to read unclassified excerpts from *Soviet Military Power, Understanding Soviet Naval Developments,* and *Jane's Fighting Ships*. Then they were to write a short paper on how viewpoints toward Soviet aircraft carrier developments had changed and to explain why early analysis had gaps or inaccuracies. Students were to focus on their personal view of what might have influenced naval analysts who were monitoring Soviet aircraft carriers during the 1980s. Here is one student's response exactly as it was turned in.

Football, Farrah Fawcett, and Fortune-Telling
[not the student's title]

How many times have you heard it? Maybe a hundred? The biggest football game of the season is on the line. Three distinguished football commentators are describing in great detail all the reasons the next play must be either a long pass to the wide receiver, or a draw play up the middle. The quarterback calls signals, the play starts to develop. What is it? A screen play good for 22 yards and a touchdown.

Then it happens. One of the announcers says those immortal words, "Well guys, that's why we're up here and the coach is down there."

Welcome to the wonderful world of intelligence analysis, a world often filled with people trying to forecast. These people know that forecasting is very difficult, especially if it's about the future. Don't believe me? Consider the plight of the poor souls trying to divine answers to how the Soviets will build ships the Soviets themselves have never built.

First, the analysts *knew* one basic truth: The moment you forecast you're gonna be wrong; you just don't know when and in which direction. Unflinchingly accepting their fate, they endeavored to find answer to tough questions. How well did they do?

Over the course of the next several years, they blew estimates on just about everything: the propulsion system, flight deck, launch and recovery systems, and the airplanes involved, among others. They blew just about every decision at least once, or so it seemed. Why? Because the heard instinct among forecasters makes sheep look like independent thinkers. They tried to integrate what they observed with ways the good guys would and could solve the problems the Soviets confronted. Also, they tried to do to much; they gave hard projections. Wrong!

When presenting a forecast: give them a number or give them a date, but never both. Economists state the GNP growth projections to the nearest tenth of a percentage point to prove they have a sense of humor. The intelligence analysts on this project kept at it to buy time. They slowly made and corrected errors to eventually come up with an accurate picture of Soviet solutions to unique Soviet problems. They helped the entire Naval community understand what was out there long before anyone else could have.

And finally, these brave analysts relearned and redemonstrated that he who lives by the crystal ball soon learns to eat ground glass. But in the end, they were successful. They had an accurate depiction, and because of them, so did everyone else. When you consider that an economist is a guy who would marry Farrah Fawcett for her money, intelligence analysts look pretty good.

Reading 2 for Peer Review Exercises

This paper was written by a graduate student. Her assignment was to write a 750-word paper on factors that inhibit objectivity in intelligence analysis, including any relevant biographic information.

Objective Analysis: Forced Self-Realization
[student's title for the paper]

Two factors which do not come easily nor willingly to mind, that reduce my ability to conduct objective analysis and posit solutions are; my inability to take the time to select the most important variables as opposed to those less substantial when gathering information for my analysis. As well as, me subconsciously setting milestones that are met before proceeding one way or the other with analysis and ultimately arriving at a solution.

Being from a family where I am surrounded by all brothers, a dominant father and a mother who urged me to be independent, there was no chance of me being anything less than the extroverted, decision-minded, analytical in nature person that I am. Coupled with my upbringing I have spent the past 11 years of my life in the Army. The initial five years was in an all-male, infantry unit and the last six in an echelon above corps unit where I was, for a majority of that time, the only female officer. I emerged from those environments with a definite tendency to be strong-willed and decision oriented.

Having recently taken the Myers-Briggs Type Indicator (MBTI) test it has confirmed that I am, at least on that particular day I was, an ESTJ as well as on a previous occasion in 1988 when I first took the MBTI. I bring up this point so that you can reflect to the qualities of an ESTJ and begin to assimilate that the problems I do face with objective analysis are personality driven and somewhat inherent in my upbringing, as well as, in my occupational background.

My first problem that I encounter when doing analysis, my inability to select the most important variables as opposed to those less substantial when gathering information probably stems from what the MBTI indicates as my personality types tendency to jump to conclusions. I invariably will gather information that is the first received, but not always the most relevant, to begin digesting for my analytical consumption. Due to being driven to get requirements done on time or merely because ESTJ's like to observe quick results I will spend a minimum amount of time thinking about what information I may need to draw a conclusion and a largely disproportionate amount of time collecting the information.

A remedy is to reverse the amount of time spent collecting the information and spend a considerable more amount of time examining the relevance and importance of particular variables and factors before pursuing the collection of information that really carries no critical bearing on the analysis. I need to insure that one of my conscious goals is to seek a better quality of sources.

The second factor involved in inhibiting my objective analysis is the fact that I subconsciously set milestones that have to be met prior to proceeding one way or the other with analysis. What I call the "if, then" syndrome fits my style of analysis. I look at what I consider the facts bearing on the situation and I begin to form a conclusion. However, in my mind I begin to set gates that can open or close by the addition or exclusion of information. When I receive a new piece of information, I examine it and determine "if" this is the case "then" I go this direction with my analysis. Example, I have been looking at

Corvettes and decide that I may want to purchase one. I shop at different dealerships and determine that one in particular will give me my best options. I intensely study the facts about the car and determine what price I would purchase the car for. My decision to buy the car will hinge on if milestones, that I have set, are met by the dealer. Number one, if they will give me the price I want for a trade in, number two, if they offer a selling price that I agree reasonable and number three, if I can obtain the financing that I feel suits me. If any of these gates close as a result of the dealer not accepting my terms then I will not purchase the car, however, if he does and gates remain open, I will continue to negotiate until I have purchased the car. Ultimately all or nothing, usually a compromise is not a factor.

Again, reflecting to the MBTI, ESTJs are not always receptive to new advice or additional information. More or less firmly embedding in our minds what it is we want and what direction we want to go. Rarely being receptive to newly injected information. The solution could be painstakingly slow. To become in the long run more open-minded and flexible to different opinions, options and ideas. I'm only 30 I guess it can be done. [798 words]

Reading 3 for Peer Review Exercises

This paper was written by a graduate student. His assignment was to write a paper on factors that inhibit objectivity in intelligence analysis, including any relevant biographic information.

Analysis Perceptions and Techniques
[student's title for the paper]

Various factors influence analysis from the controllable to the uncontrollable. Two important factors include analysis technique and perception of events, these are not all inclusive factors yet they do impact the analysis process.

Many Factors and situations influence analysis techniques. Training and background knowledge are subsets of analysis. Training has a high impact on the thought process. Its factors include the impact of the instructors viewpoint, the biases of the institution, and course material prospective. In some cases instructors impose ideas and methods that they find useful. Presenting various methods and allowing the student the option of choosing the style that is helpful to them. From public recognition to academic isolation emphasize both the benefits and negatives accompanying conformity. Background knowledge is also a critical element. It runs the gamut from studying history to keeping up with current events. This knowledge can also include such items as personal experience and reading other professionals analytical works and adapting those methods to ones own style. Pouring water in a glass until its volume reaches 50%. How this is interpreted by an individual is a good example of perception of events. Some would say the glass is half full others would say half empty. Perception of events is a wide topic. Sometimes it is crucial in the analysis process. It is intertwined with techniques of training and background knowledge. Perception of events has a more personal touch. This includes personal point of view, personal interest, open-mindedness to name a few. Ones point of view is very important to analysis. The need for keeping an impartial attitude can be critical. Personal interest can sometimes cause misconceptions and mistakes. It plays an important part in background knowledge. For example its hard to form a good analysis on the prudence of a national day-care program if one does not have children. However, the analysis may change if one plans on having children in the future. Personal interest can skew analysis. Analyzing material that one finds interesting is easier. It takes more energy and is usually harder to analyze and organize tedious material into a useful format. Having a closed mind can also be detrimental to analysis. Close-mindedness stops the crucial need for testing and examining other sources. To only use one source for reference without looking for others is a good example of this fault.

Finding ways to deal with and correct wrong analytical techniques and misperception of events can be challenging. One solution is to identify what the problem is to see if it is worth the effort to change. Some would say being critical of everything, is a good approach. However, this can be as detrimental as helpful. One can spend all available time being critical instead of trying to analyze. Increasing ones knowledge base in the area in question also helps. Reading other analytical works on the subject in question can give insights not thought of and start the creative process down different avenues. Keeping an open-mind is critical to seeing all aspects of the problem. Seeking new and different sources of information can increase background knowledge and open the mind. Training should not end when "schools out." Training should increase the desire to seek different methods and test those already known for usefulness. Open-mindedness again comes into play, Institutional biases and instructors influence should be viewed as only one path. Testing personal perception and viewpoints for usefulness in the job at hand will reveal hidden biases. Sometimes these biases can be helpful in determining what course of action will suit the situation.

Objective analysis is very elusive. Rarely can one claim true objectivity. As analysis professionals we must actively embrace our strengths and shortcomings in our ability to analyze. This ability will grow as training, personal drive, and exposure to analytical methods increase. For the good of our nation it is our duty to strive toward better analytical skills. [655 words]

Answers to the Exercises in Chapter 8

Exercises 1, 2, and 3: Writing a Thesis Statement, Writing a Paragraph, and Writing a Summary

These exercises are designed for in-class or homework assignments. They have no single answer but will be based on topics to be assigned during class.

Exercise 4: Getting the Bottom Line Up Front

1. Audience consideration is one of the first principles to consider when you write. Our audience consists primarily of decision makers, policy makers, operators, commanders, and others who don't really care about all our fancy analysis and methodologies. They want the bottom line. That's why it needs to be *up front*.

2. *Key judgments* tend to be associated with an analytical paper or an estimate. They are an encapsulation of the main points made in the analysis and conclusions of the paper. An executive summary may simply summarize a piece of descriptive or explanatory writing. While it certainly can contain judgments, it is more descriptive than evaluative.
3. This paragraph tells the reader a lot about what the writer will tell him later. But it doesn't contain one single analytical judgment or element of assessment. It is "packing material."
4. The rewritten paragraph contains both judgments and summary. There are many different ways the paragraph could be written; for example, the last sentence could be placed first to show the immediate threat to U.S. interests. Analytical words are contained throughout, such as "squabble," "frequently," "battle shows," "Prospects . . . dim," and "likely." Note the focus on conclusions and on implications for the United States. That focus is the heart of analytical intelligence writing.

Exercise 5: Types of Intelligence Writing—Descriptive, Explanatory, and Estimative

Description

Even though number 2 has more description in it than the first sentence, there is still considerable vagueness and lack of detail. For example, a reader would have to know the dimensions of the U.S. Abrams tank in order to determine the size of the T-94. Also, we are not sure what the writer means by "larger." That vague word could mean height, width, overall dimensions, or weight. Then we need to know how many weapons the Abrams tank has before we know how many constitute "twice as many"; and we are uncertain whether the writer means the "range" of the vehicle or the armament.

294 / Chapter 8

Explanation

Although most of us already know how to open a can of beer or soda, we might have trouble doing so for the first time if these were the only explanations given for how to do it. When you "grip the can," for example, you might place the palm of your hand over the top of the can, restricting access to the pop top; or you might even grip it upside down. The point here is that explanation needs to be clear and as complete as possible. You might say that it needs to be made "idiot-proof."

Estimation

Remember that an estimate is forward looking, projecting some assessment for the future. Although this paragraph has a number of judgments and analytical assessments, the *estimative* portion begins with the sentence, "Prospects for solving the border dispute are dim. . . ."

Exercise 6: Avoiding Passive Voice and Wordiness

Following are some possible answers to the exercises. Your answers may differ.

1. The division chief asked John to answer questions about the IG visit.
2. Sue finished the job in time for an office incentive award.
3. Barbie gave no explanation why Ken fired her.
4. Don't worry; I'll finish the paperwork before you return from the trip.
5. The district attorney accused Roger Rabbit of murder.
6. When his boss arrived Tuesday morning, Joe had finished the job as promised.
7. The people elected George W. Bush president in 2004. (Note that this rewrite sounds awkward. This sentence is one instance where the passive voice is acceptable because emphasis should be on the person elected, not those doing the electing.)
8. Congress has slashed Social Security benefits.

9. MathWorld designed the test to challenge even the most skilled mathematician. (Again, this sentence is probably better left in the passive voice because we want to emphasize the test, not the company that designed it.)
10. Obviously, I made mistakes. (One does not hear this sentence often in Washington. When a former White House official said, "Obviously, mistakes were made," one columnist called it the "past exonerative.")
11. Joe, a skilled questioner, conducted the interview.
12. To evaluate recent dinosaur movies, read the animals' history.
13. The Pentagon canceled the contract.
14. Consider all costs when you work on a contract.
15. Egypt Air found the flight data recorder on November 14, 1999.
16. We have finished this set of exercises!

Following are suggested rewrites for the wordy sentences. Your answers may differ.

1. We might determine that the SDI laser system is infeasible, thus enabling us to initiate other research programs as we develop more cost-effective nuclear defense systems.
2. Searching for a painless political solution to reduce the federal budget deficit, Congress enacted the Balanced Budget and Emergency Deficit Control Act of 1985, better known as Gramm-Rudman-Hollings (GRH), which the president signed.
3. A balanced budget was the goal of GRH, which required lower ceilings on deficit spending each fiscal year. The budget agreed upon by Congress and the president must be within $10 million of the target specified by the law. When this target is not met, across-the-board spending cuts begin.
4. The film version of George Bernard Shaw's *Pygmalion* and Lerner and Loewe's *My Fair Lady* are similar in many ways. For example, the uneducated Eliza, who

talks with a Cockney accent, sells flowers in both the film and the play.

5. Another similarity is Eliza's practicing her vowels by reciting "The Rain in Spain." The film and the play also have the same conclusion, when Eliza returns to Henry Higgins's flat.

6. The movie kept two of the most important actors—Rex Harrison and Stanley Holloway. However, the movie's ending differs from the play, which has Eliza marrying Freddy and Professor Higgins laughing sarcastically about the prospects of this marriage.

7. Because Eliza is both Higgins's creation and a person who fights back, her conflict with him indicates that she cares for him. Basically, the Broadway play portrays comedically how love can cross class lines, but only after the professor learns humility and Eliza realizes that she is a human being entitled to his respect.

8. European terrorists realize that they can greatly enhance both their survivability and their impact on Western society by unification and cooperation.

9. Military intelligence personnel also collected subtle indications of an advance, such as handwritten documents and testimony of captured enemy.

10. Any writer with a history of wordiness should proofread carefully.

Exercise 7: Reviewing Writing—Your Own and Others'

This exercise has no set answers. The various questions, checklists, and peer review exercises are intended for your use in class and at home, while reviewing papers you have written or when looking over the work of a classmate or a peer.

Exercise 8: Peer Review of Student Writing

The readings are intended for in-class peer review exercises with guidance from the instructor. This type of writing was certainly atypical among my graduate students, but these exercises offer a humorous look at some carelessly written assignments. The primary intent of the exercises is to enable students to critically dissect someone else's writing and then to be reminded that they can apply that same level of critique to their own writing. Students should scrupulously avoid the items that troubled them in these essays. The comments on each piece are based on my own remarks when I read the original, as well as years of accumulated student responses.

Reading 1 for Peer Review Exercises

It's okay to use a metaphor in intelligence writing, but this student drifted among sets of metaphors, from football to fortune-telling to Farrah Fawcett. Perhaps if he had followed through on the football metaphor—without overdoing it—the essay would have been better. It is *not* an analytical piece because it fulfills none of the requirements mentioned earlier about analytical writing. The author even contradicts himself, saying early that "the moment you forecast you're gonna be wrong"; then in the end, he points out that the analysis was "successful." Not once in the entire paper is the term "aircraft carrier" used, although that was the assigned subject. The paper is interesting but unfocused; it is humorous but not analytical; and it contains a classic line for intelligence analysts to remember when they tackle estimative intelligence: "Forecasting is very difficult, especially when it's about the future."

Reading 2 for Peer Review Exercises

This essay might be considered analytical—*psycho*analytical. The student writes in a complete stream of consciousness, recounting her childhood, her family, life as a female in the army, her ESTJ MBTI (which she assumes her reader understands), and buying a car. The essay is disjointed, and it doesn't answer the question. It needs *focus*.

Reading 3 for Peer Review Exercises

I was encouraged at first when I read the first two sentences in this essay and learned that the student would focus on two "factors": "analysis technique" and "perception of events." Although I didn't fully understand where he was headed with the topic, I read on . . . and on . . . and on. The second paragraph, for example, contains 356 words in 30 sentences! Readers lose their way en route to whatever point was to have been made. Keep it short; keep it simple; and focus on answering the question at hand.

II

BRIEFING
WITH INTELLIGENCE

9

Why Brief?

Summary

The intelligence briefing is one of the most frequently used means of communicating intelligence. Whether it is an organizational briefing, a special presentation, a recurring briefing, or a nonrecurring briefing, it is a useful way to convey a lot of information in a short time, face-to-face with an audience. The success of an intelligence briefing depends upon the ability of the briefer to follow a few basic principles.

Getting the Word Out

Earlier in this book I pointed out the need for intelligence professionals to be able to write well. It comes with the territory. All the collection of information and production of intelligence do no one any good unless the resulting product is communicated to someone in a timely and appropriate form. The written word is one of the most frequently used forms. The other is the intelligence briefing.

The Learning Process

From the time we are infants, we learn things from words. All our senses come to bear in the learning process. We touch a stove and learn not to do that stupid thing again; the word "hot!" takes on a new and very personal meaning. We smell something cooking on the stove and learn that chow time is soon to come. We taste the strained baby food and learn that we'd rather be eating steak with the rest of the family.

The two senses that teach us the most, however, are sight and hearing. All around us we see people, places, and things, and we ask who, where, and what they are. We respond to oral clues in our environment. Our parents say "No!" and we quickly get the picture (at least until we are teenagers, and then that word seems to be forgotten). Much of the learning process in our schools is based on aural (heard) and visual (seen) stimuli.

But what about retention? Many of us read and write and see and hear, and then forget completely what we have learned in the process. Did you ever find one of your old papers from high school or college and reread it after a number of years had intervened? It probably seemed like it could have been written by someone else. Our human brain is remarkably inefficient at retaining knowledge. The grey matter in those lobes is seldom used to capacity.

Of that which we *do* retain, much of it is a combination of what we have seen *and* heard at the same time. And what is an intelligence briefing? It is really just a combination of the spoken word and carefully constructed visual stimuli, designed specifically to impart information to a listener or viewer, with the hope that the recipient will retain the information long enough to act on it. We have a better chance that our briefing recipient will retain what he or she has heard because both the senses of sight and hearing are brought to bear.

Why brief? Because we have information that we have collected, massaged, evaluated, analyzed, and turned into intelligence. We want to share that intelligence with someone who can *do* something about it—a planner, a decision maker, a force developer, or a commander. And the best way to do that with some assurance that our audience will remember is by giving a briefing.

Types of Briefings

There are many types of briefings, and different commands, agencies, or headquarters have their own policies for how they are to be conducted. It is not my intent in this book to provide an iron template that governs the conduct of every briefing you will ever encounter. Instead, I plan to introduce some of the basic principles common to most briefings, with the hope that you can apply these principles to almost *any* situation you encounter that calls for an oral presentation.

Briefings might be characterized by their content (threat; organization, mission, and functions; imagery); by their type (information; decision; staff; mission); by their currency (current intelligence; background; estimative); or by other means peculiar to a given headquarters.

Generally, though, intelligence briefings cannot be categorized readily. There are as many types of intelligence briefings as there are organizations. The style, format, and content of these briefings are driven not by intelligence people but rather by commanders, decision makers, operators, planners, chiefs, directors, and others whose specific needs for intelligence are fulfilled by periodic briefings. In the following pages I will address four of the most common types of intelligence briefings: organization, mission, and functions; specialty; recurring; and nonrecurring. The first two are topic oriented, and the last two are frequency oriented. The same principles, though, apply to all.

The Organization, Mission, and Functions Briefing

This presentation focuses on a command or agency and is informative or explanatory in nature. It usually centers on a diagrammatic representation of the organization (a line-and-block

chart or "wiring diagram"), and it explains the roles and functions of various components of the organization. It is generally a
short briefing—10 to 20 minutes—and it may often be conducted
informally, even at deskside, by an analyst who explains his or
her role in the organization.

The Specialty Briefing

The specialty briefing is common in the intelligence community. It may concern only a single subject and offer comprehensive coverage of that subject (an imagery briefing, or a scientific
and technical briefing about a particular piece of equipment);
or it may cover a subject as broad as an intelligence discipline
(Sigint [signals intelligence] operations in the theater, or a
Humint [human intelligence] Plan). Specialty briefings vary
widely in their length and mode of presentation. They may be ad
hoc, responding to a single request for information, or recurring,
based on a standing requirement for updates on a given subject.

The Recurring Briefing

Many commands and agencies offer recurring briefings that
are not specifically organizational or mission oriented but rather
deal with the perceived threat to their command or theater, with
products and services being offered, or with a specific subject of
intelligence interest to that headquarters. While either of the previously discussed types of briefings might be considered recurring, this category is a broader one, encompassing more topics
than either the organizational or the specialty briefing. A daily
briefing prepared for the chairman of the Joint Chiefs of Staff is
a recurring briefing. The information differs every day, but the
briefing occurs daily.

Recurring briefings may, however, contain the same information each time but be given to different audiences. A military
command's threat briefing is an example. Visitors to a major military headquarters may receive a briefing on that command's organization, mission, and functions, followed by a specialty

briefing in their area of interest, and capped off by a recurring command briefing about the enemy threat to that command.

Many recurring briefings are "canned" or "off-the-shelf" presentations, meaning they are prepared in advance and ready to be offered with little or no advance notice. Often they are presented by the same individual(s) as part of his or her normal duties. The recurring briefing may have a "base time" of 20–30 minutes but is generally adaptable to different audiences by adding or removing visual aids and script.

The Nonrecurring Briefing

Often the most time-consuming type of presentation, the nonrecurring briefing may respond to a single requirement for information, and then never be given again. On the other hand, if it is well received by the audience, it may suddenly become a recurring briefing. This type of briefing will vary widely in its length, formality, and method of presentation.

"All of the Above" or "None of the Above"?

Rest assured of one certainty: if you serve in the profession of intelligence, you *will* be called upon to brief from time to time. You might never be a professional briefer, but you will spend a considerable amount of time writing, preparing, and presenting briefings.

Perhaps the most frequent requirement placed upon intelligence professionals is for informal deskside briefings. Those may deal strictly with the organization, mission, and functions, or they might be more specific informational briefings about a specialty area. It's a good idea to have an off-the-shelf briefing about your role in the organization, including any particular subject areas of current interest to someone who might drop by. Depending upon the visual aids immediately available to you, two or three overhead transparencies, PowerPoint or 35 mm slides, a computer program, butcher paper flip-charts, or copies of slides in a three-ring binder can help you cover a lot of ground.

Regardless of the type of briefing you are called upon to give, certain principles can help you prepare and present a fast-moving, hard-hitting, interesting briefing. I'll discuss those principles in the next chapter.

10

The ABCs of a
Good Intelligence Briefing

Summary

The elements of a good briefing are as simple as *ABC*: *A*ccuracy, *B*revity, and *C*larity. Ensure accuracy by doing careful research and analysis. Be as brief as you can under the circumstances imposed upon you by your supervisors. Be clear in speech and in the words you use—plain, simple, easy-to-understand words, in short, hard-hitting sentences.

Easy as ABC

> The brain starts working the moment you are born and never stops until you stand up to speak in public.
>
> —Anonymous

You've no doubt sat through a briefing where the briefer's mind seemed to shift into neutral and never change gears. It's agonizing for an audience to be subjected to some of the inane presentations that are dubbed "intelligence briefings." With only a little foresight and preparation, however, virtually anyone can give a well-organized, clear, concise briefing.

What exactly is an intelligence briefing? One definition says that it is a concise, factual presentation meant to inform. Each of these three major elements of the definition—conciseness, fact, and information—will be covered in detail later in this chapter.

The components of a good intelligence briefing are as easy to remember as ABC: Accuracy, Brevity, and Clarity. None of these elements can be sacrificed or shortchanged without destroying the basic purpose of the briefing: to clearly and concisely impart factual information to a recipient or an audience with some reason for hearing it.

Be Accurate

> Get your facts first, and then you can distort them as much as you please.
>
> —Mark Twain

You might have given the same briefing 100 times to 1,000 different recipients, and you are convinced that you know the information cold. Then in the 101st presentation, you "ad lib" some information for General Newsance, with no assurance that your information is correct because there hasn't been time for your fellow analysts to evaluate the data thoroughly. As it turns out, your information was incorrect. Five years later, you run into General Newsance in the Officer's Club. Guess what one piece of information he has retained from your entire briefing?

It is incumbent upon intelligence professionals to be as accurate as possible in the assessments and estimates that form the basis for intelligence briefings. We can never be absolutely certain that our information is correct unless we have highly reliable sources verified by unimpeachable sources. We can, however, make our best effort to ensure that whatever information we have is well researched, documented wherever possible, and cross-checked with other sources.

Analysts often feel bound to their desks and filing cabinets when it comes to research and analysis; but there's no need to be confined to the sources within an arm's reach of the desk. The work is never complete until it's been checked with as many other commands and agencies as possible. For example, if you work air order of battle for a particular geographic region, you should consult frequently with your fellow analysts at other commands and agencies who have the same area of interest. Talk also to other air order-of-battle analysts, even though they may not have your same geographic area of interest. Exchanges of analytical methodology often help solve long-standing problems.

No one has invented a "magic formula" to ensure accuracy. The best way to assure yourself that your briefing will be as accurate as possible is to *do your homework*: thorough research and exhaustive analysis. The basic principles of research and analysis that I discussed earlier in this book apply as well to the early stages of briefing preparation. Most briefings, after all, start out—and often finish—as written products.

Be Brief

It goes without saying that a briefing should be brief. But if you've ever sat through a 5-minute briefing that's been "crammed" into 30 minutes, then you know that's not always the case. The English historian Northcote Parkinson is noted for his "Parkinson's Law": "Work expands so as to fill the time available for its completion." He might have said the same thing about briefings because far too often they expand to fill the time allotted to them.

The basic principle to remember in ensuring brevity is this: tailor the *time* to the *briefing, not* the briefing to the time. Of course, that's not always an easy thing to do, especially when the boss calls and says, "I want you to prepare a 30-minute briefing for General Lektrik who'll be here next Tuesday morning." But there is a technique you might be able to use in getting the time tailored to the briefing. It involves the use of an outline.

> Speeches cannot be made long enough for the speakers, nor short enough for the hearers.
>
> —Herbert V. Prochnow

Outlining to Trim the Time

The outline you prepare for a briefing is no different than one you might have done for a written product on the same subject. Think first about the major topics you want to cover in your briefing. (Those topics might have been provided to you already by your considerate boss, who may not have wanted you to waste your time on such trivial thoughts.) Write the major headings and topics down, organize them, and decide what you want to say under each of them.

Once you've developed your outline into a satisfactory design for the briefing, decide how much time you'll need to cover those topics. If it comes to less than the 30-minute requirement the boss laid on you, go back up the chain, show him the outline, and explain that you can cover the ground in less than 30 minutes. It is then incumbent upon the management to determine whether they want additional information to "pad" the briefing and fill time, or whether the extra time might be spent doing something more productive.

Allotting the Time

Often you will find that the "30-minute briefing" specification is an arbitrary one. The chain of command may know that they have a high-ranking visitor coming in, and they "parcel out" his time among the staff. The intelligence staff may get a total of one hour with the visitor. The senior intelligence officer, then, breaks that time down according to his perception of the visitor's interests. No one, though, wants to waste the VIP's time and leave a sour taste in his mouth about his visit to the headquarters. So if you suggest an alternative to a long, padded briefing, it may be to everyone's advantage. And the resulting 20-minute presentation may ultimately be more interesting and well received because of its brevity.

Be Clear

The principle of clarity is one of the basic ones I stressed earlier in this book. It is even more important in briefing. If you slip up in your writing and something is unclear, the reader can always go back a sentence, a paragraph, or a page, and try to "catch up." The recipient of a briefing doesn't have that luxury. Some senior people will stop you during the briefing and ask you to clarify something that they didn't understand; but you'll probably find that most of your recipients will politely allow the moment to pass, and the point will be lost. Worse, if your audience misses a point of information, they may sit thinking about it for a minute or so. The next thing they know, you're deeper into the briefing, and you have lost their attention completely.

You can make some preparations ahead of time to help ensure clarity in your briefing. These preparations include adequate planning, use of the principles of good writing, and careful selection or preparation of visual aids. I'll discuss all these items in the following chapters.

11

The ABCs of a
Good Intelligence Briefer

Summary

You can be a good briefer, too, by remembering another simple ABC: *Appearance, Bearing,* and *Cognizance.* First impressions count, so be sure you present a sharp appearance to your audience. Keep your poise and bearing throughout the briefing. And be fully aware—cognizant—of your briefing subject and the environment in which you will brief.

The Other Half: The Briefer

The words and graphics are only half the formula for a good intelligence briefing. The other critical element of that equation is the *briefer.* Recipients' overall appraisal of a briefing will be shaped by a combination of what they have heard and seen, plus the way it was presented. The ABCs of a good briefer are *Appearance, Bearing,* and *Cognizance.*

Appearance: First Impressions Count

Many briefings will begin with the briefer already in place behind a lectern and the intended recipient escorted into the

room. Others may require the briefer to move to the platform—
for example, as one of a number of presenters. Regardless of the
method employed, the first impression the audience will receive
of the briefer will set the stage for the presentation to follow.

If there is any hint of disarray or untidiness in personal appearance or clothing; if there seems to be an air of disorganiza-
tion; or if there is any aspect of confusion in the environment, the
audience will immediately become an unfriendly one. Their attitude will change from "I'm here to learn something" to "*Show*
me that you can tell me something I don't already know."

It takes only a few minutes to ensure that your audience will
at least give you the benefit of a doubt when you first take the
lectern. On the day of the briefing, be sure that you wear a clean,
well-pressed, fresh uniform or, if you are a civilian, a neat and
conservative suit or dress. Check yourself out in advance. Ideally, use a full-length mirror and examine your clothing from
head to toe. Be sure everything that buttons, zips, snaps, or fas-
tens is buttoned, zipped, snapped, and fastened.

Greet your audience with a pleasant smile. It may not always
be appropriate to offer a verbal greeting, but at least acknowledge their presence with a cheerful gesture like a smile. (As the
old saying goes, it might make your audience wonder what
you're up to!)

Bearing: Keeping a Stiff Upper Torso

Among the synonyms for the word "bearing" are carriage,
manner, demeanor, air, mien, presence, and poise. All these
words relate specifically to the way you conduct yourself during
a briefing. Novice briefers probably have more problems with
their bearing than with any other aspect of a briefing. Even "old-
timers" who have briefed for years occasionally feel the twinge
of nervousness, the butterflies in the stomach, the trembling
knees that can detract from their bearing.

It's easy to spill out a few platitudes about how not to be
nervous; but the only way you will ever learn poise and bearing
is through the experience of briefings. There are, however, a few

hints that may help you avoid some of the most common pitfalls briefers fall into.

What, Me Worry?

Probably the single biggest detractor from a briefer's poise is unnecessary movement behind the lectern. Shuffling the feet, "fidgeting" with the hands, and shifting the weight from foot to foot in a rocking motion are common distractions. It's difficult for an audience to pay attention to a briefer whose rocking motion back and forth gives the impression of being at sea. Most of these motions are nervous reactions to the situation. Our hands feel like swim fins at the ends of our arms, and we feel like we have to keep the blood circulating in our legs and feet or we'll pass out.

People who have briefed or done public speaking for years have developed a number of techniques to deal with these problems. First, if you're a caffeine addict, avoid drinking your usual dose of coffee or cola for four to six hours prior to the briefing. (Go ahead, *moan!*) Caffeine is a stimulant that is a great waker-upper in the morning but is also a great nerve-racking experience when you're under pressure. Try decaf on the day of the briefing. Before the briefing begins, take one or two long, slow, deep breaths. Breathe in and out slowly, and feel the relaxation as the fresh air goes to work.

Start with Good Posture

If you have the opportunity to do so, stand behind the lectern in advance and "get the feel of it." Plant your feet firmly on the floor and resolve to stay put unless, of course, your briefing is more informal and you plan to move about. Let your knees bend just a little, to allow the blood to circulate and to prevent the knees from locking (and knocking). If you feel that you need more blood circulation, try gently wiggling your toes. That small motion will stimulate the circulation in your feet and will be imperceptible to your audience.

Don't get a death grip on the lectern. If you clutch the sides, your white knuckles will be obvious to the audience, and when you release your grip, your hands will tremble violently. (Try it some time if you don't believe it.)

If your hands are always behind your back or your arms are folded across your chest, it will tend to restrict your breathing. That posture might even show hostility, arrogance, or smugness in your body language. Instead, let your hands rest gently atop the platform of the lectern, where you have placed your script. That way, you can follow along in the script with your fingers as you proceed through the briefing.

Stand squarely behind the lectern, your shoulders parallel to its top, your weight evenly distributed on both feet. Place your feet shoulder-width apart or wider. If either shoulder slumps forward or down, your bearing will suffer.

Avoid Distracting Gestures

It's monotonous to watch a briefer who remains absolutely motionless the entire time. Some animation is important. But when you use gestures, be sure they emphasize what you are saying. Some gestures are both meaningless and distracting, while others give away your nervousness.

Some uses or misuses of the hands call attention to your discomfort. When your hands are always in your pockets, you are displaying a casual demeanor that may not suit the briefing situation. Even worse, if you have keys or loose change in your pocket, you may find yourself playing with these items. Even though your "unseen" gesture may remain noiseless, it is remarkably distracting to the audience. If this tends to be a problem for you, remove any loose items from your pockets before the briefing.

Sometimes the very items we hope will serve us during the briefing turn out to be our worst enemies. For example, if you use a script or note cards, you may find yourself nervously thumbing the cards or shuffling the notes. Such movement might prove distracting and can be prevented—again—by simply resting your hands comfortably atop the lectern.

Another demon device in a briefer's hands is a pointer. It often becomes a plaything, twirled around like a majorette's baton, swung to and fro in the audience's face, or—in the case of those dangerous little telescoping pocket pointers—opened and closed as if the briefer were playing an accordion. If you've seen that happen during a briefing, you know that the audience becomes far more fascinated watching the gyrating pointer than listening to the content of the briefing.

Virtually anything within a briefer's reach becomes fodder for distracting gestures. Be aware of your own tendencies in that regard. When in doubt, ask a colleague to watch you give a short presentation and critique your bearing. If you believe certain distracting gestures are a part of your repertoire, ask your colleague to watch for those. Be aware, though, of the "Hawthorne effect": People being studied often modify their behavior simply because they are being studied. So you might be less inclined to have those problems because you are either consciously or subconsciously attuned to them.

Use Pointing and Purposeful Gestures

The preceding section dealt with avoiding gestures that almost certainly would distract your audience. By the same token, though, it's important to *use* some gestures to emphasize important points in your presentation, to add another dimension—body language—to the briefing, or simply to help you retain the attention of your audience.

The simple act of pointing, for example, calls attention to something. If you have a chart or graphic on the screen and want to emphasize any portion of it, point to it. Use the hand that's closest to the graphic, and use a pointer. Don't lean toward the screen when you point. Glance, point, then turn your attention back to your audience. After you've pointed, bring the pointer back toward the outside of your leg or, if you won't need it for a while, lay it down on a table or the lectern, especially if you tend to fiddle with it. Practice this maneuver ahead of time so that you can do it smoothly, without leaning or disrupting the cadence of your presentation. Better yet, ask someone to help you with the briefing by doing the pointing *for* you. But then be absolutely certain that your assistant has a copy of the script and that you rehearse all pointing together beforehand.

One pointing device becoming more common today is the laser pointer. This handy little gadget allows the briefer to stand far away from the screen and, at the touch of a button, to cast a spot of light onto the screen. In a sufficiently darkened room, that dot can effectively call the audience's attention to a town name on a map, a bullet on a slide, or an eyebrow on a gnat. But *beware*: in the trembling hands of a nervous briefer, the laser dot tends to dance wildly around the screen, pointing to nothing in particular. If you are forced to use a laser pointer and your hands are trembling, then hold the pointer with both hands when you employ it.

Some Other Gestures

Many other emphatic gestures can help you punctuate your briefing and add interest. The most common include a clenched fist to show strong feeling, a "wagging" index finger or an open hand "slicing" the air to denote caution or emphasis, and facial expressions that reflect the content of the briefing. Don't overdo it, though, especially with senior officials who might not appreciate being cautioned by a briefer.

Body language you see and use every day can serve you in a briefing as well. You might shrug your shoulders or shake your head to show uncertainty; a facial expression could convey an impression; or you might describe something geometric—a square or a circle, for example—by "sketching" it in the air.

Avoid Excessive Movement

Although some gestures and body movement help retain audience interest, excessive movement can be distracting. For most formal briefings, you should remain behind the lectern. Don't pace. Plant your weight firmly and evenly on your two feet, and move only when it is purposeful.

Look Them in the Eye

Another extremely important aspect of bearing is establishing and maintaining eye contact. It commands attention, shows you are interested in your audience, awakens their interest, and establishes rapport. Communication must be two way. Eye contact increases nonverbal feedback, and you can adjust accordingly. It also helps reduce nervousness when you speak directly to someone.

Establish eye contact before you speak. Talk directly with your audience one at a time, pausing briefly for direct eye contact. Avoid sweeping the room because you might avoid eye contact altogether or look at some more than others. Deliver one complete phrase to an area before moving on to another area.

Look directly into their eyes. It builds rapport. When you converse casually with friends or colleagues, note how the eye contact works to promote harmony within the group. The same principle applies in briefings. Avoid gazing overhead, at the wall, out the window, or down at the floor. *See* when you look. Become personally involved.

Look at your audience more than you look at your notes and visual aids. Have and reflect an earnest desire to communicate. Concentrate on the message and on your listeners' reactions.

Distractions often occur during a briefing: a latecomer arrives, a door slams, or a helicopter flies overhead. As tempting as it is to focus attention on the distraction, avoid that temptation. Doing so directs audience attention toward the distraction and away from your briefing. Continue to look them in the eye.

Cognizance: Knowledge Really *Is* Power

Two aspects of cognizance come into play in a briefing: your subject area knowledge and your environmental awareness. You must be cognizant in both areas or the briefing will suffer and you will lose credibility in the eyes of the audience.

Subject Area Knowledge: I Know More Than They Know!

Knowing the subject is rarely a problem because it's extraordinary for someone to give a briefing in a subject about which he or she has no knowledge. It does happen but usually only with professional briefers such as those who present the daily intelligence briefing to the chairman of the Joint Chiefs of Staff. These briefers cannot possibly be expected to have substantive knowledge in all the areas they brief daily. For that reason, they have analytical "backup"—area experts who are available to answer questions on the spot or are on call to respond to a query after the briefing.

When you brief a subject, be certain that you are up to date on the latest information about that subject, including any current message traffic or newspaper articles about the topic. I'll talk about this aspect later when I address preparation of the briefing.

Environmental Awareness: Where Am I?

Knowing the territory is usually easy to anticipate and plan for. It involves finding out where the briefing is going to be given and paying a visit to that location. If it's to be in a conference room where you brief regularly, no problem. But if it will be at another site with which you are unfamiliar, pay a visit if possible. If the site is remote—another city or overseas, for example— talk to someone about the facilities and get a mental image of what you're up against. Ask the right questions, some of which are suggested below.

One of the most important parts of your briefing will be your visual aids. What will be accessible to you at the site? Check out all available visual aids—PowerPoint, overhead projector, 35 mm slide projector, white boards, maps, an easel with butcher paper, or whatever you may require. Find out where to get help if a bulb burns out. (A spare bulb or projector should always be on hand.) Turn the projector on and off to be sure that you know where the buttons are; they're not all in the same place, so take nothing for granted. If you use slides, see whether the room has front or rear projection or both. Rear projection requires that you use either an assistant or a remote switch to change your slides, and some slides must be arranged differently in the tray.

Find out where the light switches are in the room and how to dim or kill the lights next to the screen. Do you need a pointer? If so, there should be one readily available at the front of the room. Is the lectern satisfactory? Does it adjust up and down for different speakers?

How are the acoustics in the room? Test them if possible to determine whether you will require a microphone. If so, be sure one is available and turned on when briefing time arrives. A lectern-mounted microphone will restrict your movement. You might prefer the lavaliere (lapel-mounted) microphone. If one is not available, you might want to bring your own; but the necessary sound system must be in place for its use.

These are all items you need to know in advance because some of today's modern conference room equipment is mind-boggling and can overwhelm the novice with its complexity. In fact, many senior people who have been briefing for years get flustered when they encounter all the "newfangled" equipment in conference rooms today.

Awareness of the briefing environment adds professionalism to a briefing. It contributes to timing, boosts the briefer's self-confidence and poise, and adds an atmosphere of calm to the conference room.

Cognizance of the subject area and the briefing environment is a key factor in a successful briefing. It's also a factor over which the briefer usually exercises a considerable degree of control, assuming that there is sufficient forewarning of the time, place, and subject of the briefing. It takes a keen eye, an ability to ask the right questions, and a sincere desire to succeed. That's all.

Summing Up, from A to C

You learned earlier that a briefing must be Accurate, Brief, and Concise. In this chapter, you've seen that some of the basics of being a briefer are also as simple as ABC: as a briefer, you need to think about personal Appearance, Bearing, and Cognizance of both the subject and the briefing environment. With these basic considerations in mind, we are ready to proceed with organizing our briefing.

12

Getting Organized to Brief

Summary

Get organized to brief by zeroing in on the subject and ensuring that you understand exactly what your topic will be and how much time you are allotted. Plan ahead by analyzing your audience and developing a milestones list. Get started by *outlining* your thoughts. Plan for an introduction, a body, and a conclusion. Write a briefing script under those three major headings, developing subordinate thoughts as you proceed.

The principles of getting organized for a briefing are the same as those for writing a paper because an intelligence briefing, unless it's done extemporaneously, starts as a written product. This chapter discusses only those aspects of organization peculiar to a briefing. For more details, review the writing portion of this book.

Most of these principles are applicable across the board to all briefing types discussed earlier: organization, mission, and functions; specialty; recurring; and nonrecurring. You probably will find the most troublesome requirement, however, to be for the nonrecurring briefing. Accordingly, that will be the one upon which I will focus, assuming that your recipient, General Payne, is a onetime, high-ranking visitor to your headquarters. He's coming to receive command briefings on the organization, mission, and functions, but he will also need a particular onetime briefing from your intelligence shop. And you've been assigned to do that one.

Finding Your Subject and the Time

The subject or theme of your briefing and the time allotted for it will most often be assigned by your superiors. The degree of latitude you have within that topic may be dependent upon such factors as your analytical experience, how many times you have briefed on that subject or a similar one, or the nature of the audience.

It's important that you clearly define the briefing topic early in the organizational stages. Your task might be vaguely stated or open-ended, and you could spend an awful lot of time working on a briefing that no one wanted to hear in the first place. If there is any doubt in your mind about the intended subject, don't be afraid to ask your superiors. If it's impractical to ask face-to-face the person who tasked you, send your proposed briefing outline up the chain for approval, time permitting.

Often, the task of defining your briefing topic is little more than an exercise in problem redefinition—a technique commonly used in intelligence analysis. Clearly define the problem in all its aspects, break it down into its component parts, and integrate it again with all facets of the problem stated clearly. Then, you may be able to choose a particular part of the topic for your briefing, or have someone make that choice for you.

I suggested earlier that you tailor the time to the briefing, not the briefing to the time. That applies especially to longer briefings (20 minutes or more), where you might wind up padding the script with superfluous material just to meet an assigned time. You usually won't have to worry about padding in a shorter briefing because the time constraint alone will tend to restrict you to the topic at hand.

Remember that times assigned to briefings are often arbitrary, and your superiors may be willing to compromise on the time to ensure a higher quality briefing. They will probably appreciate the extra time with General Payne so that they can talk about other things or go into more discussion about your topic.

But what if you determine that the time allotted to you is too short? That happens, too. You can take steps to solve the problem. Look at the full proposed agenda for the visitor and see if there is other time you might "borrow" from a friend or fellow briefer. If the schedule looks tight, and there doesn't appear to be anyone who will cede you the extra time you need, your options are limited: either "bite the bullet" and go with the assigned time, tailoring the briefing to the allotted time, or go back to the individual who assigned the times in the first place, and ask for more.

Now you have a specific subject to cover and an allotted time in which to cover it. Who could ask for anything more? Perhaps by the day of the briefing you'll be asking for an assistant or two, but right now your immediate task has been clarified with respect to the exact topic of the briefing and the time allotted to you.

Plan Ahead

The tallest skyscraper starts with a plan—a blueprint to guide the engineers, carpenters, and others step-by-step through their work. You've already read that a written intelligence product, too, starts out with its own blueprint: an outline to form the foundation of the final product. Your briefing will be a written product. (I'll talk later about using scripts.) So before you write the script, start your planning for the briefing with an outline. But first, you need to focus on your subject and a few other important considerations.

Remember that you've been assigned a *specific topic*, and you need to *focus your efforts* on that topic. So the first thing you do is take a piece of paper and write at the top of the page the proposed title for your briefing, or its major theme if it is untitled.

Keep that paper in front of you throughout the planning and preparation stages, just as a reminder to stick to the subject.

Next you have to do two things as a part of your planning and organization for the briefing: *plan your time schedule* and *analyze your audience.*

Plan Your Milestones

Just as you did with the written product earlier, you must now initiate the "backward planning sequence" that results in your milestones list. Start with the date and time of the proposed briefing, and work backward from there to the present time. Be sure to include in *bold print* or underline all those items over which you have no direct control: typing or word processing of the final script (if you're using a formal one), preparation of the graphics, and scheduled rehearsals for "intermediates"—all those in the chain of command between you and the ultimate principal recipient of your briefing. You'd better believe that they will want to hear the presentation first.

As part of your milestone planning, you can take the initiative and fill in a couple of the blanks in your schedule. If you're preparing the briefing on your own computer and building your own PowerPoint graphics, you have only yourself to work with. But occasionally you must rely upon people outside your office to help you. Alert administrative support people of the coming word-processing requirement, and let the graphics shop know that you'll be hitting them for some timely support. Try to give each of them an idea of the approximate magnitude of the final product. (You can do that by determining approximately how many pages of script there will be and how many graphics may be required. I'll give you some planning factors for that later.) Then visit or call the office(s) of your superior(s) who will need to hear the briefing in rehearsal before it goes to the distinguished visitor. You might be able to schedule a couple of them simultaneously, which would save you a step in the process.

Give yourself some leeway in scheduling the rehearsals. Unless you're really pressed for time, try to allow a full day between the last rehearsal and the final briefing, to give your supporting people the time they need to change script and graphics, and to allow for your own last-minute checks and self-rehearsal. If the briefing is to be 30 minutes long, schedule at least one full hour for each rehearsal. Use that factor of 2:1 for planning rehearsal time to final briefing time.

You will seldom have the luxury of devoting your time entirely to preparation for a briefing. Depending upon the rank and status of the proposed recipient(s), you may be given some slack on other projects, but there will always be the day-to-day business to keep up with. Check your own suspense list or calendar for the dates between "today" and the proposed briefing date. If you have outstanding papers, projects, or other briefings, include them on your milestones list as necessary evils.

Outline Your Thoughts

At the risk of beating the proverbial dead horse, I stress again that the outline is your single best tool for organizing your thoughts and structuring your briefing in a logical, clear, concise manner. If you are the top expert in your headquarters on the subject you're scheduled to present, you may need the outline even more, to help focus your thoughts and narrow the scope of what might otherwise be a broad, overstuffed presentation.

Remember that earlier piece of paper, where you wrote the subject across the top to ensure that you'd stick to it? Well, you need that piece of paper now. Build your outline right under that title. Use the principles I discussed in the prewriting portion of this book; but for this outline use three major headings:

I. Introduction
II. Body
III. Conclusion

Space those headings out, or better yet, put one of the headings at the top of three separate sheets of paper. Set aside the "introduction" page for a minute, and go to the "body." That's the part you'll outline first. Consider the main topics you want to cover in the briefing (chances are some of them have already been provided to you by your superiors), and outline those subjects, either as a topic outline or a topic sentence outline. Once you're satisfied that you've covered all the main points you wanted to, reread your outline and extract the key points. Include those in your introduction as summary points. Also plan to review those points in your conclusion.

At this point in your outline, you will have sketched out roughly the major topics you want to cover in your introduction and in the body. Now you can tentatively allot time to the segments of your briefing. Assuming that you're scheduled to give a 30-minute presentation, anticipate at least one minute for the introduction and one minute for the conclusion. Then set aside five minutes for questions and/or discussion. That leaves you with 23 minutes for the main body of your briefing. That figure will be important to your planning as you begin to write your script.

Analyze Your Audience

Even though you may know General Payne well, you always need to stop and think about his potential area of knowledge in the specific subject you'll be briefing. You don't want to waste an important visitor's time by starting your briefing with a lot of background, geography, or history if he already has a strong foundation in those subjects. If this were a newcomer or a visitor to your headquarters, and you were briefing him for the first time, you might want to start with some of those subjects to set the stage.

Let's assume that you haven't met General Payne and don't know anything about him. There are many ways you can find out about a senior official before you give that person a briefing. It's usually much easier to analyze the audience for a briefing than it is for a written product being cast out into a faceless void.

Senior officials usually have secretaries, aides-de-camp, executive officers, or all of the above. These people are hard workers whose jobs depend upon the boss's schedule and ensuring that everything goes well. The last thing any of them wants is to waste the general's time. So contact them ahead of time. Let them know the date and time you're supposed to be briefing their boss, and ask if there's anything that you should know. You'll probably find that they will tell you more than you ever dreamed you'd get, including how he likes his coffee, words and colors to avoid in the briefing, and how many times he's had a similar briefing in the last year or so. If this information isn't volunteered, it never hurts to ask.

It's a good idea, too, to ask for a biographic sketch of your intended listener. By reviewing his career history, you are able to discern whether particular aspects of your briefing may be superfluous. For example, if General Payne spent three years as a corps artillery commander, you wouldn't want to take up his time explaining the characteristics of the eight-inch howitzer.

Try to find out in advance, also, whether there will be others in the audience. Generals and other high-ranking officials often bring an entourage with them, and you need to ensure that everyone in the audience has both the security clearance and the need-to-know for your proposed briefing.

Do Your Homework

Like the written product, the briefing will also require that you do your research and analysis in advance and be sure that you gather all the facts. Remember that Accuracy—the "A" in our briefing "ABCs"—depends upon your thorough and timely research.

Gather all the data that you will need for preparation of your script: studies, assessments, estimates, message traffic, maps, and/or your own notes on the subject. Have them readily accessible before you begin to prepare your briefing script, which is the subject of our next chapter.

13

Writing the Briefing

Summary

Get started by *outlining* your thoughts. Plan an introduction, a body, and a conclusion. Write a briefing script under those three major headings, developing subordinate thoughts as you proceed. In the briefing's *introduction*, greet your audience and introduce yourself and your subject. Tell your recipient(s) how the briefing is organized and its significance to them. Give a brief introductory summary of the main points to be covered. Tell them the length of your presentation and of the question-and-answer session (if any), and the overall classification. In the *body* of your briefing, write clearly, concisely, and coherently. Design visual aids to *map* your listeners' journey, to *illustrate* specific points, to *reinforce* what you're saying, or to *dramatize* your words. Put the words and pictures together so they complement each other. In your *conclusion*, summarize again the main points you covered. Remind the audience of the classification, and ask if there are (further) questions.

Writing the Briefing Script

Many briefings, especially recurring ones that the briefer has given numerous times, do not rely on a script. But chances are that they at least started out as scripted briefings. As the briefer becomes more familiar with the subject matter, the script is consulted less frequently and, finally, not at all. The principles discussed in this chapter are general ones that should help you construct a good working script for your presentations.

An axiom says if you're going to be a good briefer, you must do three things: "Tell 'em what you're gonna tell 'em; tell 'em; and tell 'em what you told 'em." That simple tenet is right on target, for intelligence writing as well as an intelligence briefing.

Tell 'em What You're Gonna Tell 'em

The first ingredient in the formula is the briefing's introduction. When you constructed your outline for this briefing, you took the major points from the main body of your presentation and wrote them into the "introduction" portion of the outline. You'll also want to cover those points in the summary portion of your introduction.

Other points you will want to include are a greeting, self-introduction, subject of the briefing, its length and classification, its significance to the audience, and the time allotted (if any) for questions and/or discussion.

Greeting and Self-Introduction

It's the simplest thing in the world for a briefer to smile pleasantly at the audience and greet the senior person present by name; yet, many briefers act like they really don't care much for their audience and they just want to get this thing over with. (Maybe that's true for most of us, but we certainly don't want our audiences to know it!) Your listeners don't care about your life history; just give them a one-liner with your name, rank or grade, and position in the organization. If you're the desk analyst for the country you're about to brief, that statement lends *credibility* to your discussion.

Often it's a good idea to have someone else introduce you as the briefer, giving a short summary of your qualifications and maybe an offhand remark like, "Lieutenant Eeger is our command's expert on this subject, so we decided to let the brains do the talking."

Subject, Significance, and Summary of the Briefing

It's not always enough to say something like, "Today we're going to brief you on the Fizzle fighter." The briefing will be far more meaningful to your listeners if you can bring it home to them with what I term a "significance statement." Tell the audience in just a few words *why* your briefing is important to them. They must be there for *some* reason, and it helps their retention of the subject matter, and usually piques their interest, if you can answer the question, "What's it mean to *me*?" You should also, in as few words as possible, summarize the content of the briefing. That can be done by highlighting verbally the main points or by using a visual aid to convey those points. (See the sample introduction in appendix C for an example of a significance statement and a summary.)

Length, Classification, and Time Allotted for Questions

Chances are the general will know when he takes his seat that he'll be there for 30 minutes. But don't count on it. Busy people often shuffle between appointments on the arm of an aide or exec., and even though they may have a note card or reminder about what's coming, they will appreciate your reminding them. Just make a quick reference to the length of your prepared presentation.

Remind the audience, too, if your briefing is classified. It may be necessary to display a sign in advance, turn on a red light, or perform some other procedure that your command or agency requires for a classified briefing. Be sure all that is accomplished beforehand, and then remind the audience briefly during the introduction not only of the classification (confidential, secret, top secret) but also of any caveats that may apply (Orcon, SI, TK, Noforn, TGIF, or whatever).

If you have allotted 5 of your 30 minutes for questions and discussion, *tell* your audience that fact. You know, of course, that senior officials will ask questions whenever they see fit; but most of them are polite about it and try to adhere to the time allotted. If they run overtime, then, at least you have warned them.

"Free Sample" Briefing Introduction

A Brief Assignment

Read the example of a comprehensive briefing introduction in appendix C. Read it once slowly and carefully, noting all the remarks to the right and the parts of the introduction to which they apply. Then try something a little different. Go to some place where you can be alone, and *time yourself* once through, reading it aloud at a normal speaking pace and ignoring the remarks. See how long it takes you compared to this writer's time.
Do that now. I'll wait for you.

. . . .

Welcome Back

Reading at a good, steady pace for a briefing, it should have taken you from 50 to 60 seconds to read the sample introduction in the appendix, including the 15 seconds of pauses for the general to absorb what's on the screen. (It took me an average of 53 seconds in 3 readings, with a range from 52 to 54.)

Here are a couple of pointers about the script. First, you might want to type it in all uppercase letters for ease of reading. Leave a wide margin at the right or left to make your notations, just as I made notes in the right margin of the appendix. You might pen in "Slide #1 on"; "Pause 10 seconds"; or "Check time." Use only one-half to three-quarters of the page for the script. That way, when you place the script on a lectern and glance at it, your chin won't be tucked into your chest as you read the lowest lines.

In a typical intelligence paper, you generally would spell out numbers from one through nine, and use numerals for 10 and above. In a briefing script, however, use the numerals in all cases. They're easier to read and, in case there's a question, to find again. Round off big numbers. The general will never remember that there are 251,612 trained Fizzle pilots; but he will probably retain it if you say that there are more than 250,000 or that there are a quarter of a million pilots.

Something else you probably noted in our "free sample" was the use of contractions ("I'm," "we'll," and "we've"). That usage is discouraged in more formal writing but is recommended for briefings. It sounds stilted or memorized to say "*I am* Lieutenant Eeger," or "*We have* allotted 5 minutes. . . ."

Tell 'em

You've introduced yourself and your subject, made your audience aware of the briefing's importance to them, and told them about the length and classification. Now you're ready to plunge into the second part of the equation: the main body of the briefing, where you "tell 'em."

Putting the Words Together

If you've done your outline well, this part should be considerably easier for you. Use that outline just as you would for a written product: as a foundation upon which to build your words. Add the results of your accumulated research to the framework, building paragraphs onto the topic sentences. Be sure that each paragraph contains one major idea or central assertion, and *only* one. When you begin to talk about a new subject, or a different aspect of the same subject, move on to the next paragraph.

It's even more important in a briefing than in writing that you use short, precise, understandable words and sentences. Pause periodically and read aloud what you've written. If that's not feasible because of your working conditions or other considerations, try to "hear" the words in your mind as you read silently.

As you write the words, keep in mind the time allotted for the briefing. Remember that earlier we assumed this would be a

336 / Chapter 13

30-minute briefing. We allowed one minute for the introduction (and it looks like we stayed within that limit), one minute for the conclusion (stay tuned to see if we make it), and five minutes for questions and/or discussion. That left us with 23 minutes for our main body.

How do you plan the amount of writing that will fill 23 minutes of talking? In truth, that's a factor that requires individual briefing experience. I have learned, after many times behind the lectern, that it takes me approximately two and one-half minutes to read, at a steady briefing pace, a double-spaced, typewritten page of script (assuming normal margins).

The only way to determine your own speed is to try it. But don't just read one page and click off the stopwatch. It's best to have a longer script—4 to 10 pages—and strike an average. Time yourself *at least* three times, and try it at different times of the day. You may speak a little faster after your midmorning coffee break when you're fresh and chipper than at 4:30 p.m. when you're hassled after a long day's work.

Assuming that you, too, average out at about two and one-half minutes per page, the determination of the briefing's typewritten length is simply a matter of mathematics: Your 23-minute briefing should be about 9 pages long (23 divided by 2.5 = 9.2).

Putting the Pictures Together

Remember that a briefing depends upon two senses for its success: hearing *and* sight; so always keep in mind the *visual* aspects of the presentation. As you talk about a person, place, or thing, decide as you're writing whether you will use a graphic to illustrate that portion of your topic. Know your command or agency's policies in that regard: *Must* you have a picture on the screen at *all* times? How many slides per minute do you need? Is a blank or black screen acceptable at times? Know the answers to those questions before you start to plan your visuals.

If possible, don't use graphics *solely* for the purpose of having something on the screen. It's just as distracting to your audience to have a meaningless visual aid in front of them as it is to have nothing. Good visuals should *really* aid by performing one or more of the functions discussed below.

They should *map* your listeners' journey through your presentation, telling them where you've been, where you are, and where you're going. The "summary" slide in our example introduction would have served that purpose. It laid out for the audience a direction in which the briefing would go and told them what they could expect en route.

Visual aids should *illustrate* something that might otherwise be difficult to grasp. Our introductory picture of the Fizzle fighter met this criterion. Trends or events that lend themselves to portrayal by bar graphs, pie charts, or other such means are also good candidates for illustration.

Visuals almost always *reinforce* what you're saying by bringing to bear the eyes as well as the ears of your audience. Try to describe something like a fighter aircraft without using either a photograph or a drawing of it. Need I say how many words are encompassed by that one image?

Finally, a graphic can *dramatize* what you're trying to say by making a clear, concise visual statement. If, for example, you are emphasizing the rapid production rate of the Fizzle fighter, you could show a bar graph or another type of visual aid designed to highlight its production rate compared to a similar U.S. or NATO fighter.

One source of ideas for your visual aids might be news broadcasts on any of the major television networks. Even though you may hold a low opinion of the newscaster or the network's editorial biases, try to focus on the way graphics are created to support a news story. Many news items, in fact, are fully intelligible with the sound muted! That's a real compliment to the graphic artist's work. By following the same general principles you, too, can have graphics that speak for themselves. Your only limitation is your imagination.

There are many types of visual aids, and each has its own advantages and disadvantages. Be familiar with the ones available to your own organization. Learn how they work—the way to use them to your best advantage in supporting a briefing.

Ubiquitous Technology: PowerPoint and Beyond

Increasingly, commands and agencies have available state-of-the-art electronic equipment to use for briefings. "Projectors" are being replaced by computers with highly sophisticated programs for generating PowerPoint graphics and projecting them, using fade-ins, fade-outs, lap dissolves, and other techniques. Gone are the grease-pencil-and-acetate days of briefing. The array of possibilities is too vast to warrant discussion here. Suffice it to say that you must be familiar with whatever medium or media your organization might have for briefing support. That might require additional training because of the complex equipment.

If you have a chance to work with the newest technology, take advantage of the opportunity and innovate. Just as computer-generated images astound us on the movie screen, such images can often add significant impact to a presentation. Just be careful not to allow the technology to overpower your message. Sometimes the "bells and whistles" obscure the message.

Other Visual Aids

Use a map whenever you talk about a geographic location, and point out that location on the map the first time around. It need not be a wall-mounted map; usually a simple projected one will suffice, and it will probably be easier to see.

Overhead transparencies—also known as vugraphs or VGTs—are also common visual aids. They are relatively easy to prepare, and they project a larger image than most other media. Overheads are particularly suited to slides with words on them ("billboard"-type slides). They are not always suitable when you want intimate detail (such as imagery or a terrain map) because they tend to be less crisp in the detail.

One type of overhead transparency is commonly referred to as the "poor-boy" graphic. It's one of the easiest visual aids to prepare. You can use a special audiovisual pen and write directly on a piece of acetate for projection; or you can print your graphic on a plain sheet of paper (use a dark ink and a broad line like a felt-tip pen), then use certain types of copying machines to convert it to a transparency. Many maps, photographs, and other images are suitable for this process, too. In using poor boys, be sure to print neatly and legibly. Leave wide margins all around because most projectors won't accommodate a full 8½" × 11" transparency.

The 35 mm projector has advantages of projected image clarity and ease of handling. One round tray and a remote button can take you painlessly through more than 100 slides, giving you a mobility to walk away from the projector that you don't have with the overhead unless you use an assistant. But 35 mm slides take more time to prepare because of the processing involved; so you need to program extra time for them.

Other briefing media (for example, "butcher-paper" charts mounted on easels or standard-sized photographs) are more suited to smaller audiences or to particular briefing situations. The white board, for example, may suffice for a fairly large classroom but is not always satisfactory for a briefing because of the time it takes to write on it. Writing out the material in advance is an alternative, but that may result in distractions for your audience as they stare at the board instead of you. The white board may be necessary, however, if you are explaining detailed mathematical equations or other work that would not lend itself to a medium you could prepare in advance.

The choice of your presentation medium is not always yours to make. It is often dictated by what is *available* in the place where you'll be briefing. Know well ahead of time, if possible, exactly where you will be briefing and what types of projectors or other media are available.

Tell 'em What You Told 'em

The words and pictures that will constitute the main body of your briefing are the hardest ones to write and visualize. Once you've completed that portion of your briefing, review it carefully to ensure that all your proposed main points have been included in your introduction. Then include those points again in your conclusion. Don't be redundant, though, by repeating the

340 / Chapter 13

exact words you used before. Rephrase them as a means of reemphasizing the point.

Always introduce the concluding part of your briefing with some key words like, "In conclusion," or "In summary. . . ." That phrase lets your audience know you are approaching the last minute or so of your presentation, and they should pay particular attention to the points you're about to make, because those are the ones you want them to take away with them.

The briefing conclusion, like the introduction, should always contain two key elements: the summary and a reminder of the classification. In appendix D is a sample conclusion for the 30-minute presentation to General Payne on the Fizzle fighter.

Putting the Words and Pictures Together

By the time you've written the words and decided what graphics you'll need, you should find the remainder of your preparation largely a matter of following through and ensuring that others stay on track. Check your milestones list, and be sure you're still adhering to your time schedule. If it appears that you are late with any of your projected milestones, you may need to do some adjustment at this point. Be sure that everyone outside your immediate sphere of influence is notified of any slippage in the dates or times; for example, if you told your supporting graphics people that you'd have draft graphics to them by noon Wednesday, and you realize that time will slip into Thursday morning, let them know. Either tell them that you're running late with everything or deliver a portion of the graphics to them so that they can start working. They will usually prefer to get a part of the job early and begin work, rather than having the entire package "dumped" on them with a tight deadline they can't meet without considerable overtime.

If time and circumstances permit, have your draft script approved by as many of your superiors as possible. Deliver a legible copy of the script and paper copies of the proposed graphics to them, and ask that they get it back to you by a certain date and time for your rehearsal. *Be sure to keep a copy!* While the package is being reviewed, you can be doing some preliminary rehearsal. Don't change too much at this point because if your briefing comes back approved as is from the front office, you'll have to go back and have any changes approved, too.

The next step is to get the approved script to your typing or word-processing support and the graphics to the appropriate people. Instruct the typist to use a large font in preparing the script; to type it all in uppercase, leaving wide margins (specify the exact dimensions you prefer); and to use only ½ to ¾ of the page. Sit down with your graphics people and be sure that they understand exactly what you want on the visual aids. You will often think that you've done a great job building a transparency, and then one of your graphics specialists will suggest something that will make a vast improvement.

Again, keep a copy of everything so that you can be rehearsing during the final preparation stages. Give realistic due dates to your administrative support staff, but try to allow yourself enough lead time so that you'll have everything in hand with plenty of time for proofreading and double-checking.

If you have the option to work without a prepared script, and you prefer to use note cards, a few suggestions may be in order. Use 3" × 5" note cards if you intend to move about in front of your audience. They fit easily into the palm of the hand. If you plan to remain at the lectern, you may wish to use 5" × 8" cards instead. You'll need fewer of them, and there's less chance of losing your place as you "shuffle the deck." Whichever style you choose, be certain to *number* the cards in case you drop them or momentarily become disoriented. Put the number in a conspicuous place like the upper right-hand corner of each card, and use a bright color like red.

Before the final briefing time, try standing at a lectern and reading or glancing at your note cards. Be sure that the writing or printing is large enough for you to see easily. If you're not bound to a script word for word, use phrases instead of complete sentences, main points instead of verbatim transcript.

Summing Up

You've seen in this chapter that you can't write a briefing script in isolation from the supporting visual aids. The two must be produced simultaneously. The script, using clear, concise, understandable words, must flow from point to point in an orderly, logical manner. The graphics must be designed to complement and supplement every aspect of the script.

A briefing is designed for both the eyes and the ears. The senses of sight and hearing must be kept in mind throughout the process of writing the script and designing the graphics. Once these steps have been taken, and you (and your superiors) are satisfied with the final product, you're ready to go to the lectern.

14

Fine-Tuning Your Briefing: Voice, Notes, and Visuals

Summary

Important elements of a briefing can be improved—"fine-tuned" —with practice. You can have a higher quality voice and speak with greater intelligibility, variety, and emphasis, gaining a more attentive audience in the process. Techniques for fine-tuning your voice include practice, critique, and proper care. You can also improve your use of notes by proper note-taking techniques and practice in using them. Finally, your visual aids will be more meaningful and will contribute more to your presentation if you construct them properly and use them to your advantage.

Use of Voice

Like many other aspects of a briefing, your voice is something that will make a real difference in the way the material is presented and received. While you can't change your voice, you can train yourself to use it more effectively.

Characteristics of a Good Voice

You've probably watched a television newscaster or news anchor and thought what a good voice that person has. If you've

343

never thought about what goes into making a "good" voice, then consider these characteristics: A good voice has a reasonably pleasant *quality*; it is *intelligible*, making it easily understood; it employs *variety* in rate, force, and pitch; and it employs all forms of vocal variety for appropriate *emphasis*.

Quality

A high quality voice expresses a pleasantness that is hard to define but is easily recognizable. It may be difficult to change the basic quality of a voice that is by nature harsh, nasal, flat, or breathy. But practice can improve voice quality.

The quality of your voice may also vary with emotional states. Nervousness, boredom, enthusiasm, or timidity often affects voice quality. At the beginning of a briefing, you may find that your voice quivers slightly and that it is an octave higher than usual. That is normal under stress and will pass quickly after you "warm up." It might require a minute or so, but you'll find the quality of your voice restored as you proceed.

Either consciously or subconsciously, your voice can reflect your inner feelings. Defensiveness, hostility, friendliness, calmness, indifference, concern, and sincerity can all be detected in a briefer's voice. That characteristic can be to your advantage by adding interest to the presentation if you are aware of it and can keep it under control.

Improve your voice quality by relaxing the muscles in your jaw, neck, and upper torso. Try a few exercises to loosen those muscles before you go the lectern. *Use* your voice before a briefing, too. That is, if you are briefing early in the morning, don't let the first words out of your mouth that morning be your greeting to the audience. Sing along with the radio in the car. At the office, find an empty room somewhere and speak aloud for a few minutes in a normal speaking voice to warm up the vocal chords.

You'd be surprised, too, at how much your voice quality is improved by having a good attitude toward your audience. A positive attitude will be obvious in your voice. So if you positively *hate* the fact that you have to give this briefing, leave that attitude at home and go for a pleasant demeanor at the lectern.

Intelligibility

If you've ever found yourself wondering what in the world a speaker is talking about, then you know about the characteristic of intelligibility. The best speakers are those who can be easily understood. Intelligibility comes from a combination of well-articulated words and clear pronunciation.

The dictionary defines *articulation* not only in terms of enunciation but also in the sense of joining together or fusing. In that sense, you are using crisp, understandable words to join the thoughts that constitute your main points in the briefing. You are, in short, trying to be sure that your audience understands what you are saying the first time you say it. Generally, it is better to overarticulate rather than underarticulate, as long as you don't get too dramatic with it. One way to get a sense for your own articulation is to record your voice as you practice the briefing.

When a television announcer stumbles over the *pronunciation* of a word, it can be humorous. But when it happens to you during a briefing, it's no laughing matter. Some words are inherently difficult to pronounce. (I've always had trouble, for example, with "statistics.") When in doubt, consult a good dictionary. Whenever possible, simply *omit* tough words from your script, replacing them with words that are easier to pronounce.

If you need to know the correct pronunciation for a place name or a person's name, ask someone who should know—an analyst for the area in question, or someone in the person's office. You do *not* want to address a senior official and find that you have mispronounced his or her surname.

Variety

"The spice of life" can add spice to your briefings as well. By varying the rate, force, and pitch of your voice, you can express a whole range of meanings.

Vary the *rate* of your speech, either faster or slower, for emphasis. For example, you might lay out facts or stories at a lively pace, but present main ideas, more difficult points, and transitions slowly and emphatically. Combined with appropriate gestures, such variations can add a powerful dimension to your presentation.

Pause between thought units, not in the middle; and pause for emphasis as well. You'll be tempted to fill the empty space with a vocalized pause (uh, um, er, ah, okay), but those are distracting and show your audience that you are uncomfortable. So avoid that temptation by practicing. A pause is seldom as long as you think it is.

You can prepare your script in advance to show where you want variety and pauses. Use markers or highlighters to annotate the text, or simply write the word "pause" at an appropriate juncture in the script.

A *forceful* speaker tends to be dynamic and, more often, remembered. Think about speakers whose voices stand out in your memory: John F. Kennedy? Martin Luther King Jr.? Ronald Reagan? Each of them demonstrated elements of *force* in their speeches. Those elements include volume, variation, amount, manner, and stress.

In considering the volume of your speech, you'll want to talk loudly enough to be heard easily and to use an appropriate volume for the room size. There's only one way to know if you can be heard in a room, and that is to speak in that room. Keep in mind, of course, that acoustics will vary depending upon whether the room is empty or full. If you are in a large room and are not using a microphone, ask the people in the back rows whether they can hear you all right.

Vary the force in your voice for emphasis. While a lack of force will bore an audience, remember that continuous force will tire them just as readily. You neither want to sound like a "fire-and-brimstone" preacher nor a monotonous slug. Vary the amount of force, from a whisper to a louder voice. Don't shout, though. Move down as well as up, while being careful not to let your voice "trail off" as volume or force diminishes.

Consider in advance the manner in which you apply force. Let your voice peak gradually so as not to startle your audience. Apply force to stress syllables and words. Use your voice to underline or italicize words in your speech. Remember, for example, how President John F. Kennedy applied that technique in his inaugural address: "Ask *not* what your country can do for you; ask what *you* can do for your country."

The *pitch* of your voice is the property of its sound, especially the higher or lower tones. To keep the attention of your audience, vary your pitch throughout the entire normal range (high to low), but work mostly in the lower half, which conveys assurance, poise, and strength. Avoid monotonous melody or "singsong" patterns. Don't end every sentence with an upward inflection, or trail off after every sentence.

Emphasis

Emphasis is a combination of all forms of vocal variety. The more drastic the change, the more emphasis. Like force, you also want to avoid continuous emphasis because then nothing will stand out. Before the briefing, pick out the most important ideas to emphasize. Highlight them in your script and provide the proper vocal tone for emphasis.

Fine-Tuning Your Voice

You've probably heard singers as they prepare for a show, running scales or mouthing syllables. They perform these "verbal aerobics" for the same reason athletes exercise before a game or a performance: to "warm up." In the same fashion, you should "stretch" your vocal chords before a briefing. Other tips for improving your voice include practice, critique, and proper care.

Improve Your Voice by Practice

Read aloud to a friend or family member. Use difficult material like Shakespeare or William F. Buckley. Break words and sentences into units of thought. Try reading poetry, which lends itself very well to voice practice.

Improve Your Voice by Critique

Read newspaper editorials or other periodicals into a recorder, then listen and critique. Whenever you have the opportunity, give a speech for an audience—even one or two people—and ask them for feedback. Absent the critique of others, use a full-length mirror; stand before it, give your presentation, and critique yourself. Probably the best way to "see yourself as others see you" is to videotape your practice briefings, then watch the playback. You can learn a great deal by watching yourself on tape.

Improve Your Voice by Care

Use relaxation techniques to save your throat. Those warm-ups similar to the ones singers use, as I mentioned earlier, will help. Also, prior to talking, try relaxing your neck muscles, gargling with warm water, and taking deep breaths. Your voice is an indispensable asset in your briefing. Take care of it.

Use of Notes

Unless you've given a briefing scores of times, you'll need notes to remind you of the key points. If you don't use a script for your briefing, then you should be aware of proper techniques for using notes. This section deals with some tips for note use to help you fine-tune that aspect of your briefing.

Why Notes?

A more formal scripted briefing alleviates the problem of memory lapses that often happen under pressure at the podium. Many times, though, you will not want to use a script. If that is the case, *don't memorize* the briefing. Memorizing is fine for lines in a play, but if you forget a word or two in a memorized briefing, that simple act will cause you to stumble and will probably make you more flustered. Use notes instead.

Notes help you ensure the accuracy of your presentation by having important facts and figures right on hand. They also keep you on track, serving as an "outline" for you to follow. They let you adjust to your audience and change what you say just before you speak if necessary, as opposed to the more rigid script. And of course, notes jog your memory and help dispel your fear of forgetting.

Types of Notes

A *manuscript* is usually best when accuracy is a must or when you are not completely familiar with the subject matter being briefed. Use a *talking paper*, with short, cryptic phrases, as a rough outline of what you must cover. If you need only the main ideas, though, try a *key word outline*, which is planned idea by idea rather than word by word and contains key words or phrases such as purpose statement or transitions to trigger your memory.

Where to Write Notes

It's a good idea to consider what medium you'll use for note keeping. Some are easier to use than others, but for the most part it's a matter of personal preference: What are *you* most comfortable using? You might use note cards, either 3" × 5" or 5× 8". The smaller ones are easier to "palm" if you're standing in front of your audience without a lectern; but they're also easier to drop. An alternative is to use standard-sized paper, 8½" × 11". Use only ½ to ¾ of the page, and leave wide margins for notes or cues.

Some briefers like to make notes right on the frames of their vugraph transparencies (VGTs). That's generally a good idea only when you're handling your own visual aids. If you do it, use a dark felt-tip pen and be sure you'll be able to read the notes from wherever you are. You might also let your visual aids serve as your briefing notes—a sort of projected outline.

Techniques for Good Note Use

Use notes as reminders, not as crutches. When you need to refer to them, glance at the notes and resume eye contact with the audience immediately. Don't read from your notes, except for direct quotes.

Position your notes so that you don't have to bend your head to look at them. Place them on the lectern in advance, then raise the lectern, if possible, to a comfortable viewing angle. You don't want to obscure your view of any part of the audience, or the audience's view of you. If you hold the notes in your hands, raise them to a comfortable reading level as necessary. Make it as smooth a motion as possible. It sounds easy, but you should practice this maneuver, especially if you wear glasses.

Some briefers like to place their notes at different locations in the briefing room, to enhance movement. It's not a technique that I would recommend unless you're very, very comfortable with the room, the audience, and the subject matter. Imagine what can happen if you move to the wrong notes at the wrong time: "The Panaraguan Air Force has upgraded its inventory significantly, so that it now totals . . . *47 trucks?*"

Glance at your notes toward the end of a main point, then transition to the next main point looking directly at the audience. Don't wait until you have finished one idea to look at notes. That often results in some overly long pauses, loss of momentum, and occasional stammering on the part of the briefer.

Bad Habits

Overreliance on notes hinders eye contact. It limits your movement or ties you to the lectern, giving the audience the impression that you lack confidence or are not relaxed. When you hold your notes with both hands, it restricts other uses of your hands, such as gestures. It also calls attention to trembling hands.

If you hold the notes in your hands, you may find yourself playing with them or even shuffling the cards. That can be disastrous if you get the cards out of order. That is another reason to place your notes on the lectern.

Any time you're looking at your notes, you're not looking at your audience. Try to avoid looking at the notes excessively. Audience members can lose their attentiveness very quickly when they believe something else is demanding more of your attention than they are. That happens when your notes are too detailed, requiring more frequent reading or glancing.

Fine-Tuning Your Use of Notes

Use notes when you are not briefing extemporaneously or from a prepared script. Prepare your notes before practicing your briefing. Practice integrating the notes smoothly into your briefing. Rehearse handling the notes, and don't overuse them.

Use of Visual Aids

Remember that the visual dimension is half of a briefing. Good visual aids help to promote understanding of your key ideas. They increase the audience's retention. By holding the attention of the audience, they help focus the listeners' concentration on the subject. Visual aids also save valuable time and words, clarify the organization of the briefing, and emphasize transitions.

Most Words Can Be Visualized

As you begin to put together a briefing, try to visualize the words as you are writing. Some visuals will come easily: When you write about a person, an object, or a place, a picture of the person or object and a map of the place will reinforce the verbal description. Visual comparisons can also help highlight similarities and differences. Other material may be a little more difficult. But you can show facts, figures, or statistics graphically, and there's always the old standby "billboard" graphic, where you simply use words to convey your main points in bullet form.

Concepts for Using Visual Aids

You control the pace, the emphasis, and the selection of visual aids. Use them to complement your words, to add a visual dimension to an otherwise aural presentation. They should not dominate your briefing—that is, they shouldn't draw attention to themselves because of their brilliant colors or their stunning language. Develop your visual aids by selecting key elements in the briefing that need visual emphasis and reinforcement.

If you have trouble envisioning the visuals to accompany your words, seek help from someone who might be more visually oriented. Most commands and agencies have staff members who specialize in graphic arts and can provide invaluable assistance not only in constructing the graphics you have designed but also in conceptualizing new visual aids to fill gaps in your presentation.

Major Types of Visual Aids

Probably the most commonly used visual aids are PowerPoint slides, VGTs, and 35 mm slides. As computer-generated graphics programs become more readily available, commands and agencies are turning to computers for their visual aids. Other popular standbys include butcher paper on a tripod or easel and a white board. Most boards these days use the "dry marker" rather than chalk. Other visual aids are limited only by their availability to your organization and your imagination.

Preparing Slides

Keep your graphics simple. Don't use a lot of points. Usually three to six "bullets" per slide are plenty. Remember the "3" × 5" Rule": if you can type it, double-spaced, on a 3" × 5" card, it will be readable as a graphic. Use your agency or organization's specified format and production facilities when appropriate. Check to see if a standard slide template is available online.

Use a horizontal rather than vertical format, especially for billboard slides. The long axis projects easier, facilitates your handling of slides, and is more comfortable for the eye to read. Some pictures or maps, though, may be better formatted on a vertical axis. The way to determine which looks better is to project them both ways.

You might be relying upon someone else to prepare the final graphics for you. If that is the case, be sure to allow sufficient production time. Talk with your graphics support people in advance to find out how much lead time they need. Rushing the production process only increases the chances that something will go wrong.

Preparing Butcher Paper or Charts

Butcher paper charts are suitable only in a small briefing room or a conference room where you can be sure that everyone can read the words on the charts. Print neatly, in large block letters. Ensure readability from all audience viewpoints by physically moving to all corners of the room and reading the charts. Check for "bleed-through" when you use the heavy felt-tip markers. If the next page shows through, remove it or skip one page between each graphic. Tape or staple blank sheets to the previous sheet to facilitate page turning.

Using Projectors and the Screen

Positioning

Position the screen for best visibility throughout the room. You may have no choice in its placement if the screen is affixed to the wall. But even then you have the option of bringing in a portable screen and placing it elsewhere if you believe it serves your purposes better. If you are using vugraphs, place the projector where it is easiest to access and where it will allow movement. With 35 mm slides, be sure the projector is far enough away from the screen to project a full image, and use a long-cord remote slide changer. Be sure you know exactly where all the cords are, so that you don't trip over them.

Don't allow the projector to obstruct your audience's view of the screen. On occasion that simply won't be possible because of the room's configuration. In that case, place the projector where it will block the fewest possible members of the audience.

Check beforehand to determine whether you will have front or rear projection. Arrange 35 mm slides accordingly. You will have to use an assistant for rear-projected vugraphs unless there is a remote-controlled VGT "carousel" device that you can operate yourself. The vugraphs will then have to be properly loaded into the carousel ahead of time.

Techniques

When a slide comes on screen, the audience's attention turns to that slide and away from the briefer. On occasion you will need to refocus that attention to yourself, perhaps to make a point. Use a blank slide or a lens cover to "black out" the screen and focus audience attention back toward you.

Avoid "white-out" of the audience—the condition that occurs when the screen is illuminated with no slide on it. At best, it is distracting; at worst, it is uncomfortable or irritating, especially in an otherwise darkened room. Use blank slides or a lens cover to darken the screen between slides when you have nothing to show. If your slides are continuous, practice changing them so that you can smoothly remove one from the projector while replacing it with another. That procedure requires rehearsal, but it can add considerable professionalism to your presentation.

If it is appropriate to do so, you might try writing on your vugraphs extemporaneously to add or to highlight ideas. Be sure you have an instrument that will write on transparencies. And if you plan to reuse the slides, find out first if the marks will erase. Another technique is to project the slides on a white board and write on the board. But if that board is metal, you'll see a prominent glare in the middle of the slide. So be careful using that technique.

Fine-Tuning Your Use of Visual Aids

Like so many other facets of briefing, practice makes perfect in the techniques for using visual aids. Anticipate in advance the types of visual aids available to you, then whether you can handle them yourself or will need an assistant. A few pointers are listed in the following paragraphs; keep them in mind as you prepare your briefing.

Be sure that your visuals can be seen by the entire audience. Often there's only one way to find that out: project the visual and move around the room to look.

Don't stand between your visual aids and the audience. If you have good eye contact, you can tell if you're blocking the audience's view because they will be leaning one way or the other or craning their necks to see above the obstruction. If you don't have good eye contact, then your audience probably won't care that you're blocking the screen. They will be tuned out.

Talk to the audience, not to your visual aid. Just as an audience looks at a graphic when it's put on screen, there's a strong tendency for briefers to turn their attention toward the screen as well. Practice taking a quick glance at the slide—just to be sure it's projected correctly and that it's in sequence—then returning your eyes to the audience. *Never* insult your audience's attention by *reading* a visual aid to them. If there are many words, a complex diagram, or a difficult chart on the graphic, pause a few moments to let the audience read. But *don't read to them.*

Expose visual aids only while they are pertinent to what you are saying. Graphics left visible compete with the speaker unless they specifically support the point you're making. They can even confuse your audience as they begin to wonder, "What's that slide got to do with what the briefer is saying?"

Locate visual aids for best use: to your side or slightly behind you. Avoid leaning forward or across the visual aid. Don't pace back and forth to use your visual aid. Always point with the arm closest to the screen, using a pointer if necessary.

To best support your speech and hold audience attention, visual aids should be clear, simple, and readable. They should conform to agency or organization standards when appropriate. Check the spelling, punctuation, and parallel structure: if the first bullet starts with a verb, each subsequent bullet should start with a verb. Underline and use contrasting colors, or otherwise highlight key words for emphasis on more detailed visual aids.

Don't overdo your visual aids. They do add emphasis, but overemphasis is like no emphasis at all. Your organization will probably have specific guidance regarding numbers of graphics to use; but as a general guideline, I suggest you plan on *no more* than two graphics per minute of briefing time, and *no fewer* than one for every two minutes.

Always practice with your visual aids. If possible, dry run at the location and under the conditions the briefing will be given. Arrange the room to your advantage. Check the equipment positioning and operation. Know how to dim or douse the lights.

The Best Tip of All

In this chapter I've given you lots of tips for fine-tuning your voice, your use of notes, and your visual aids. There are, of course, far too many suggestions to remember. That's why I've included an "Intelligence Briefing Checklist" as appendix B to this book. It includes hints for actions to take before the briefing, on the day of the briefing, and after the presentation. My "best tip" for you would be to keep that checklist handy and to use it.

15

Doing It!

Summary

Rehearse, rehearse, rehearse. It will help you gain self-confidence, avoid word traps, time yourself, and check your script and graphics for accuracy. When the big day for the briefing finally arrives, you'll be ready to *communicate intelligence*.

Getting Up to Brief

The next time you're in your local library or favorite bookstore, look for books on public speaking. You'll probably see scores of them. Why? Do books really help people learn to speak in public? Myriad authors and publishers seem to think so. (Count me among them for writing this book.)

A book like this one might provide you timely advice and handy tips on how to avoid your own worst enemy: butterflies, sweaty palms, trembling hands, or quivering voice. But there's only one way you will ever become an accomplished briefer, and that's by facing an audience and giving them a briefing.

Rehearse First

Never give a briefing where you hear the words for the first time as you face your audience. Rehearsal is an absolute necessity in preparing for a briefing you've never given before. It helps you gain confidence, avoid word traps, and check your script and graphics.

"I Know More Than He Knows"

Say that sentence to yourself as you begin your rehearsal. *Convince* yourself that you are the command's expert on the subject, and even if there are minor points with which you are not familiar, you'll have backup analysts there to answer the questions. Find a mirror, look yourself in the eye, and tell yourself that you'll be ready.

Your superiors have entrusted you with giving this briefing, so *they* must have faith in you. Share that faith with them. Rarely will you find a briefing recipient who knows more about the subject than you do. In the unlikely event that *should* happen to you, your listener will let you know. In the meantime, you've studied the background and experience of your potential audience, and you're ready for them.

Falling into the Word Trap

The phrase "red leather, yellow leather" is easy to say. But try repeating it aloud over and over again.

So it is with many words in a briefing script. You may write a script that is pleasing to the eye and ingenious in its verbal gymnastics. But when you speak those words aloud, some of them may tumble from your mouth like a child's gibberish!

Always say the words aloud at least once before you give your briefing, even if you say them only to your most receptive audience—yourself. Speak at a normal pace, and note the words and phrases that cause you to stutter, stammer, or use a spoonerism (reversing initial letters or syllables, such as saying "Mussian rissiles" instead of "Russian missiles"). Look for groups of words that sound unpleasant together, like a series of sounds with hisses and other *s* sounds. (Read that previous sentence aloud and you'll see what I mean, especially if you're using a microphone.) Watch for individual words that you may have trouble pronouncing. Classic examples that cause many people problems include "statistics" and "misconstrued."

Wherever you find a word trap lurking in your script, strike it out. Replace it with words you can say more easily, or words that sound better when spoken aloud.

Check Your Scrpt and Graphcs for Accuracy

No matter how many times you check your own visual aids, the Graphics Gremlins will get you! It may be during the first rehearsal for your immediate supervisor, or in the final dry run before the briefing; but suddenly, someone will point to a headline and tell you there are words misspelled. (For example, look at the words "Script" and "Graphics" in the subheading above.)

Remember that I suggested you always have someone else proofread and edit your written work. The admonition applies here, too, because we're dealing with written products. That second set of eyes on your script and your visual aids will prove invaluable to your rehearsals and, of course, to the final presentation.

If you find errors in the last roundup before the final briefing, your best bet is to drop that graphic from the briefing. If there's no way to do that, have it on the screen for the minimum possible amount of time. As a last resort, if the slide is essential to your presentation and the mistake is certain to be seen, point it out to your audience and say that you realize it is in error. At least it shows that you rehearsed.

Always check your graphics in their projected form. Don't try to proofread a transparency (and certainly not a 35 mm slide!) by holding it up to a light. Look at them as your audience will see them.

The Big Day at Last

Talk to paratroopers about their experiences jumping out of airplanes. You may think of it as an act requiring nerves of steel and an iron will to accomplish. Many paratroopers, however, will tell you that by the time the first jump arrives, all the intensive training takes over and makes them act without thinking about it. The actual jump is almost an anticlimax.

I'm not trying to compare a briefing to a leap into space from an airplane; but ask someone who's done both, and they will probably tell you the briefing made them more nervous. In fact, David Wallechinsky's *Book of Lists* notes that fear of public speaking is the number 1 fear people cite (even ahead of *death*, which comes in at number seven).

The last thing remaining to be done before you go into the briefing room is to scan the day's newspapers and message traffic to be sure you're up to date on the latest information about the subject. Just look for articles or messages that relate specifically to the topic you're briefing. Sometime on the morning of the presentation, time permitting, watch *CNN Headline News* or scan the Internet. Check for anything relevant to your topic. You don't want to be caught short by the current news!

If you've done everything I've suggested up to now, *you're ready!* It remains only for you to go back through your checklist, be sure everything is in order, and give your briefing. (To make it easier for you, I've included a concise briefing checklist as appendix B to this book.) You may also want to review "The ABCs of a Good Intelligence Briefer" in chapter 11.

The final recipients of your briefing are usually a piece of cake compared to all the intermediate echelons you've gone through. And you should be prepared now to look your audience squarely in the eye. Reluctance on the part of a briefer to establish eye contact is not usually interpreted as shyness; it's more often considered a lack of confidence. By now you should have all the confidence you need to proceed. You've put a lot of work into this presentation, and the final product shows it. You're ready for that audience now. Remember that you know more than they know. You're briefing with intelligence.

Appendix A: A Usage Glossary for Intelligence Writers

a/an. Use *an* before words that begin with a vowel *sound* (an apple, an heir). "An historian" is incorrect because the *h* is sounded; but, "*an* hour." "An unique idea" is incorrect, also, because the initial sound in *unique* is that of the consonant *y*; but, "*an* unwarranted assumption."

abbreviations and acronyms. Shortened forms of words and phrases can be useful at times, such as in a newspaper ad where you pay by the word or line. Avoid the use of nonstandard abbreviations or acronyms wherever possible. When you do use one, spell it out the first time, then put the short form in parentheses; thereafter, you may use the short form: for example, Strategic Defense Initiative (SDI).

adapt/adopt. *To adapt* is to adjust oneself to a new or changed situation. *To adopt* is to choose and follow a new course of action: "East German leaders found it difficult to *adapt* to the wave of democracy sweeping Eastern Europe. The people, however, readily *adopted* democracy."

advance/advanced. *Advance* party; *advance* payment; *advanced* training program.

adverse/averse. Both words are adjectives. "Most nations had an *adverse* (unfavorable) reaction to North Korea's handling of its nuclear program. The United Nations, however, was *averse* (disinclined) to imposing sanctions."

advice/advise. *Advice*, a noun, is counsel or assistance that is given. *Advise* is a verb. "The lieutenant could not *advise* me what to do, so I took the sergeant's *advice*."

affect/effect. Both words may be verbs. To *affect* something is to have an impression on it or to change it: "Glasnost may *affect* our foreign policy." To *effect* something is to create it: "The Soviets *effected* a change in their policy with glasnost." Effect may also be a noun, meaning result or consequence: "The *effects* of glasnost remain to be seen."

afterward/afterwards. *Afterward* is preferred.

all/all of. Except when a personal pronoun is involved ("We saw all of them."), "of" is redundant. "They interviewed *all* the candidates."

all ready/already. *All ready* means everyone or everything is ready: "The troops were *all ready* for muster." *Already* means before a specified or implied time: "Private Jones was missing, and it was *already* time for muster."

all right/alright. *All right* is the correct form; *alright* is not a word.

all together/altogether. *All together* means in unison: "The analysts were *all together* in their assessment." *Altogether* means all told, in all, or completely: "The analysts were *altogether* confused about the new developments."

allude/elude/illusion. *To allude* to something is to mention it indirectly. The noun form is *allusion*. "Her *allusion* to the bastions of communism made me think of Cuba and North Korea." One gets away or escapes by *eluding*. "He *eluded* capture for 15 days before being rescued." Finally, an *illusion* is something that is not really there—a mistaken impression or belief. "Absolute certainty in intelligence estimates is an *illusion*."

along with. *Along with* does not affect the verb: "The captain, *along with* other personnel, was on deck." This rule also holds true for *as well as, in addition to, like,* and *together with*.

alot/a lot. *Alot* is not a word. There is a word *allot*, meaning "to distribute, or to assign shares or portions," but that is usually not what the writer of "alot" has in mind. Most of the time a better sentence will result by rewriting to avoid the use of "a lot"; even though grammatically correct, it is imprecise.

Incorrect: *Alot* of reservists are leaving the service early.

Correct: *A lot* of reservists are leaving the service early.

Better: Almost 60 percent of reservists are leaving the service early.

altar/alter. You are likely to find an *altar* in a place of worship, where one's attitude might be *altered* (changed).

alternate/alternative. Used as a verb, a noun, or an adjective (and pronounced differently depending upon its usage), *alternate* means to change back and forth in turn or to substitute. "They *alternate* their shift work, producing *alternate* estimates in the process." *Alternatives* are choices: "They had no *alternative* but to accept the figures given in the assessment." It is redundant to use the word "other" with alternatives; that is, do not write "We had no *other* alternative."

altitude/elevation. Use *altitude* when describing something in the air, *elevation* when referring to the ground: "The new jet fighter may attain a record *altitude*." "The *elevation* of that mountain range averages 7,000 meters."

amid/amidst. *Amidst* sounds poetic, but it is not for intelligence writing. Use *amid*.

among/amongst. You will be right at home in the United Kingdom with *amongst*, but as long as you're writing papers in the United States, the preferred form is *among*.

among/between. *Among* always implies more than two: "War reparations were distributed among the six nations." *Between* expresses the relationship of two things: "There was a dispute *between* the two countries." But *between* is also used for more than two to indicate a reciprocal relationship: "A treaty was concluded *between* the three nations."

amount/number. *Amount* refers to things judged by their weight, bulk, or sums: "The *amount* of cargo carried by the new truck is impressive." *Number* refers to things that can be counted: "The rebels lost a staggering *number* of men in August." See also **fewer/less**.

analyzation. This is an ostentatious way of saying *analysis*.

and/or. Means one or the other or both. Obviously imprecise. Avoid this form.

anymore. Always spell this as two words: *any more*.

appraise/apprise. *Appraise* means to assign a value to something. "We were unable to *appraise* the worth of the captured equipment." *Apprise* means to tell. "Our commander *apprised* us of the situation."

approximately/about/some. Never use these words when a figure is stated precisely.

Incorrect: We counted approximately 37 tanks. Some 64 divisions opposed us.

Correct: We counted approximately 40 tanks and more than 60 divisions facing us.

(Note: All estimates should be rounded. Also, do not use the words "estimated" and "approximately" [about, some] together because they both show approximations.)

assure/ensure/insure. All mean to make sure or certain. *Assure* applies to persons. It alone has the sense of setting a person's mind at rest: "I *assured* the professor of my attentiveness." *Ensure* implies making an outcome certain or making something safe: "Abundant crops *ensure* a nation against famine." *Insure* means to cover with insurance. The distinction between *ensure* and *insure* is disappearing in American English usage. While it is in transition, though, you should distinguish between the two in your formal writing. Consult a current dictionary if you have any doubt about correct usage.

as well as. See **along with**.

at present/currently/presently. These terms are overused in intelligence writing: "The situation is stable *at present*." "They *currently* have shortages of men and materiel." In almost every case the term may be omitted because the present tense of the verb—"is," "have"—already conveys that meaning.

average. An *average* can be only one figure.

Incorrect: The new Fizzle fighter *averages between* 900 and 1,000 knots.

Correct: The new Fizzle fighter *averages* 950 knots.

averse. See **adverse/averse**.

awhile/a while. *Awhile* is an adverb, analogous to expressions such as *ago*, in "a month *ago*." Use *awhile* in constructions such as "We rested *awhile*." With a preposition, use the noun form "(a) while," as in "We rested for *a while*."

because of. See **due to.**

between/among. See **among/between.**

boat/ship. A *ship* is a large vessel, capable of going to sea. A *boat* is relatively small, stays mostly in coastal or inland waters, and can be carried on a ship.

can/may. The attentive writer will use *can* for ability or power to do something, and *may* for permission to do it: "Even though our children *can* write on the walls, it is unlikely that we will say they *may* do so." Note: In intelligence writing, "can" is often used as a synonym for "has the capability to" or "is capable of," when speaking of a nation or force's capabilities: "The North Koreans *can* exercise that option at any time." The word does not, and should not, imply any *intention*. "May," on the other hand, is also used to imply a probability: "The Cubans *may* be serious about improving trade relations." To facilitate understanding, substitute "might" in the previous sentence.

capital/capitol. The *capital* is the city or the money, or an adjective meaning first or primary (capital letter, capital offense, capital punishment); the *capitol* is a building. To remember, think of the round, O-like dome of the capitOl building.

careen/career. Although these two words are often used interchangeably, they have different meanings. To *careen* is to sway from side to side: "Our ship *careened* dangerously in the heavy seas." As a noun, *career* means a profession; but as a verb it means to go at top speed, especially in a headlong or reckless manner: "The tank *careered* out of control down the hill."

center around/center about. Neither of these phrases is correct. Use *center upon* or *center on.* "U.S. foreign policy is said to *center upon* neo-Wilsonian pragmatism."

cite, site, or sight. *Cite* is a verb, meaning to quote, mention, or commend: "She *cited* the dictionary as her source." "The captain *cited* the sergeant for bravery." *Site*, as a noun, means a place: "We visited the *site* of the battle." Used as a verb, it means to locate something on a site: "They *sited* the new classroom building in Columbia, Maryland." *Sight* may be either a verb or a noun, and means the act or fact of seeing: "She *sighted* the classroom building. His *sight* was inadequate at night."

collocate. To set or place together. *Not* spelled "colocate," although some dictionaries now differ.

communication/communications. Both words may be either a noun or an adjective. *Communication* refers to the process or the act of communicating: "Skills in interpersonal *communication* are essential for intelligence professionals." *Communications* are the means of sending messages: "The *communications* satellite provides instantaneous transmission worldwide."

compare to/with. To compare one thing *to* another is to emphasize the similarity between the two: "She *compared* the Soviet tank regiment *to* a U.S. Army armored battalion." To compare one thing *with* another is to examine all aspects and qualities for similarity or dissimilarity, as in "He *compared* the regiment *with* the division."

complement/compliment. A ship's crew is its *complement*; one object or event may complete or coordinate with another. A positive comment about another person is a *compliment*. "The professor *complimented* Jones on his writing."

compose/comprise/constitute. These three words are often confused. *Comprise* means to embrace, include, or contain—the whole *comprises* the parts. Conversely, the parts *constitute* or *compose* the whole. "The home guard *comprises* ten units." "Ten units *constitute* (or compose) the home guard."

compounding words. Compounding confounds many students. Some of the most common compound words you will encounter are in the following list. Notice how they are formed: anticommunist, antiguerrilla, antiterrorist; *but*, anti-American, anti-European; counterguerrilla, counterterrorism, counterterrorist.

conduct. A vague, overused word, as in "The Iranians *conducted* an amphibious operation." Instead, try *engaged in*, *launched*, or *performed*.

continual/continuous. *Continual* means frequently repeated with only brief interruptions: "*Continual* misunderstandings highlighted the negotiations." *Continuous* means absolutely without interruption: "*Continuous* misunderstandings marred the seventh day of negotiations."

contractions. Do not use them in formal writing.

council/counsel. *Counsel* is both a noun and a verb. "You might need to secure legal *counsel* if you want to breach a contract agreement. Your lawyer will *counsel* you then on your rights." A *council* is some form of advisory committee. "Perhaps you will argue that the ruling *council* needs to word its contract more clearly."

courts-martial/court-martials. Either is acceptable, but *courts-martial* is preferred as the plural form.

crisis. Denotes a turning point, a period of abrupt and decisive change. Iraq's invasion of Kuwait was a *crisis*; frequent changes of government in an unstable political environment are not. The plural form is *crises*.

criteria/criterion. A *criterion* is a standard for judgment; the plural form is *criteria*: "One *criterion* of a well-written paper is clarity, but many other *criteria* also contribute to readability."

currently. See **at present/currently/presently.**

data/errata/media/phenomena. These are the plural forms of *datum* (rarely used), *erratum*, *medium*, and *phenomenon*, respectively. Each requires a plural verb.

dates/decades. Use commas after the day and the year when you write a complete date (month, day, year) within a sentence. "Her assessment is given in the March 11, 2008, estimate." Style and grammar guides differ on this one, however; so consult yours for guidance.

deactivate/inactivate. Both words mean to make inactive. In military usage, *deactivate* usually means rendering explosives inert. *Inactivate* is to disband or cause to go out of existence a military unit, government agency, or other organized body.

different from/than. *Different from* is the preferred term. (Even better, *differs from*.) "This rule is *different from* that one." However, if the object of the preposition is a clause, *different than* is preferred: "How *different* things appear in Washington *than* in Paris."

dilemma. A *dilemma* is a situation involving distasteful alternatives. Avoid using the term when all you are discussing is a problem. Preferred synonyms include *plight*, *predicament*, or *quandary*. Avoid the trite "horns of a dilemma."

disburse/disperse. To *disburse* is to pay out or distribute: "The pay officer *disbursed* the monthly payroll to the troops." To *disperse* is to scatter or spread something: "National Guard troops *dispersed* the crowd."

discreet/discrete. *Discreet* means showing good judgment or being able to maintain a prudent silence: "An intelligence professional must always be *discreet* in handling classified information." *Discrete* means separate, distinct: "The intelligence process has three *discrete* phases: collection, production, and dissemination."

disinterested/uninterested. *Disinterested* means impartial, unbiased: "You should have your first written draft read by a *disinterested* individual." A mediator should be *disinterested*. *Uninterested* means indifferent: "The students appeared *uninterested* in my topic for discussion."

dissent/dissension. *Dissent* can be both a noun and a verb. If you do not agree with a particular policy, you can *dissent* or "differ in opinion." Such a difference of opinion is called a *dissent* or a *dissenting* opinion. *Dissension* (note the spelling) goes beyond a difference of opinion—which can be expressed amicably— and indicates discord or quarreling.

due to/because of/owing to/on account of. Grammar textbooks and dictionaries disagree on proper usage for this term, but in most cases of standard written English, *due to* is becoming acceptable as a prepositional phrase. Technically, though, *due* is an adjective that needs a noun to modify. If *due to* comes after a form of the verb *to be*, then *due* is being used—correctly—as an adjective: "The project's failure was *due to* insufficient planning." (The adjective *due* modifies the noun *failure*.) *Because of, owing to,* and *on account of* are compound prepositions: "The project failed *because of* (or owing to, on account of) insufficient planning." Avoid beginning a sentence with *due to*.
Incorrect: *Due to* improper assembly, the temporary bridge collapsed.
Correct: *Because of* improper assembly, the temporary bridge collapsed.
Also correct: The collapse of the temporary bridge was *due to* improper assembly.

each. *Each*, used as a subject, takes a singular verb and related pronoun: "*Each* student, graduate and undergraduate, *has* his or her own style of writing."

each and every. Redundant. *Each* is enough by itself.

east/eastern. Indefinite or general terms of broad application commonly end in *-ern* and are not capitalized unless they refer to specific blocs (see the next entry): "The unit trained in the *eastern* part of the country." Terms of definite designation commonly use the short form, as in "the *east* bank of the river" or "the *east* side of town."

East/Soviet bloc. These terms are vague and may confuse your reader. Be precise in writing about former communist countries or regional alliances. The term "Eastern Europe," for example, includes the former Non-Soviet Warsaw Pact countries, the former Yugoslavia, and Albania.

economic/economics/economical. *Economic*, an adjective, pertains to the science of economics, a singular noun: "The country devalued its currency because of *economic* problems." "*Economics* is an imprecise science." *Economical* means thrifty: "Cutting 50 dollars from my food budget was an *economical* move."

effect. See **affect/effect**.

e.g./i.e. *E.g.* is the abbreviation for *exempli gratia*, meaning "for example." Do not confuse it with *i.e.* (*id est*), which means "that is." They are *not* interchangeable. It is best just to avoid the abbreviations and spell out "for example" or "that is."

either . . . or/neither . . . nor. When all elements of an *either . . . or/neither . . . nor* construction are singular or plural, the verb is singular or plural, respectively: "*Either* DIA *or* CIA *has* the information I need." "*Neither* the studies from DIA *nor* the estimates from CIA *have* the data I am seeking." When the elements differ, the verb takes the number of the nearer element: "*Either* the heavy rain *or* the elephants *are* responsible for the ground-cover loss."

electronic/electronics. The singular form is an adjective: "The Special Operations Forces have sophisticated *electronic* equipment." The plural form is a noun and takes a singular verb when it refers to the science as a whole: "*Electronics is* a complicated science." Often, in intelligence writing, the term takes a plural verb: "The *electronics* of that new aircraft *are* incredibly complex." Note: The term *"electronics"* is usually used in place of a phrase such as "the electronic components" or "the suite of electronics."

elevation. See **altitude/elevation**.

elicit/illicit. You *elicit* information, a confession, or a response of some kind by coaxing or bringing forth; the word is a verb: "The interrogator skillfully *elicited* a response from the refugee." The adjective *illicit* means illegal, unlawful: "The Department of Defense is working closely with the Drug Enforcement Administration to curb *illicit* drug trafficking."

emigrate/immigrate. People emigrate *from* a country and immigrate *to* a country. Remember: *"em-"* = "exit," and *"im-"* = *"into."*

eminent/imminent. An *eminent* person is famous or otherwise well-known in his or her field: "The faculty recognized Dr. Rongar as the *eminent* authority in intelligence analysis." *Imminent* means "about to happen," as in the *imminence* of hostilities.

enormity. Many frown on using *enormity* to indicate bigness. Use it instead to refer to "monstrous wickedness." "The enormity of Saddam Hussein's treatment of Kurds created unrest in Iraq for decades." Do not write about the *enormity* of the coalition's decision to liberate Kuwait—unless you are a member of the Iraqi army.

ensure. See **assure/ensure/insure**.

errata. See **data/errata/media/phenomena**.

et al. The Latin abbreviation for *et alii* or *et alia*, meaning "and others." Why not just say "and others"?

etc./et cetera. Another of those perfectly good Latin phrases, meaning "and so forth"; but do not use it in intelligence writing, because it signals your readers that you are leaving it up to them to complete whatever list you ended with that phrase: "The new battlefield formation is known to have tanks, armored personnel carriers, air defense artillery, *etc.*" (Might the "etc." include chemical weapons?)

eventhough. Not a word. Use *even though*.

everyday/every day. *Everyday* means ordinary: "Military maneuvers are an *everyday* occurrence in that training area." *Every day* means daily: "We observe their training *every day*."

everyone/everybody. As subjects, these words take singular verbs: "*Everyone (or Everybody) is* expected to agree on the latest intelligence assessment."

explicit/implicit. Sometimes confused with its opposite, *implicit*. An *explicit* understanding has been stated: "The United Nations warning to North Korea was *explicit*." An *implicit* understanding is perceived but has not been expressly stated: "The diplomats adjourned their session with an *implicit* understanding of the terms of reference."

explosive/explosives. Use *explosive* in specific reference to a bursting or propelling charge (high explosive). Normally the plural form is used in such expressions as "*explosives* storage."

(the) fact that. The phrase "*the fact that*" can usually be avoided with a little rewriting. The phrase "due to the fact that" can *always* be replaced by "because."

fake analysis. Avoid "phony" phrases such as the following: anything can happen; further developments are expected; it is difficult to determine; it is not possible to predict; it is too early to tell; it remains to be seen; only the future will tell; only time will tell.

farther/further. *Farther* is generally applied to physical distance: "It is *farther* from Moscow to Vladivostok than it is from Chicago to Honolulu." *Further* is used for a metaphorical distance: "His assessment could not be *further* from the truth."

fear. Fear is an extreme emotion. The word should not be applied to ordinary concern or uneasiness.
Incorrect: "We *fear* that the armed forces are having another reorganization."
Correct: Use "we believe" or "we estimate" instead.

feel. *Feel* as a synonym for *believe* or *think* is sloppy usage.

fewer/less. *Fewer* refers to numbers or units considered individually: "We have *fewer* order-of-battle analysts than the other section." *Less* refers to quantity or degree: "We published *less* material this month because of the shortage of analysts."

flounder/founder. When a ship fills with water and sinks, it *founders*. When a horse breaks down, it also *founders*. So too if an enterprise or plan totally collapses, it may be said to *founder*. Hope still remains if the verb is *flounder*, which means to struggle helplessly in embarrassment or confusion.

forego/forgo. For *precede*, use *forego*: "The key judgment of that estimate appeared to be a *foregone* conclusion." For *relinquish*, use *forgo*: "I must *forgo* attending the conference because of a shortage of travel funds."

(Note: Often sentences with *forgo*, like the previous one, can be rewritten more forcefully: "I cannot attend the conference because of a shortage of travel funds.")

foreseeable future/near term. Fuzzy clichés. Your "foreseeable future" might be someone else's "near term." Be specific.

former. See **latter/last/first/former**.

forthcoming. Means about to appear, or available when required or as promised: "The *forthcoming* estimate will address that issue." *Avoid* the usage intended to mean cooperative or outgoing because of the possibility of confusion: "The ambassador was *forthcoming*."

from . . . to. The sentence, "The exercise took place *from* 1 *to* 5 October" means that it was a four-day exercise, *not including* the final date. To include the final date, the phrase should read "from 1 *through* 5 October."

gender. See **he or she**.

he or she vs. he/she or s/he. The commotion about gender-specific nouns and pronouns is not likely to go away soon. The use of *he or she* (*him or her* and *his or her*) is one solution, but many writers find it cumbersome. The slashed constructions *he/she* and *s/he* are ugly. The least annoying option is to use plurals. Instead of writing "A student should carefully research his topic," write "Students should carefully research their topics." Note that *service members*, not just *servicemen*, died in the Iraq War.

headquarters. May take either a singular or a plural verb. "His *headquarters is* in Washington" implies only one building or organization. "Their *headquarters are* in Washington" means more than one building or organization.

historic/historical. *Historic* means important in the framework of history: "Gettysburg was a *historic* battle." *Historical* can mean the same thing but also covers other things concerned with history: "*The Killer Angels* is a *historical* novel."

hopefully. Some die-hard grammatical conservatives will argue with you over this one, but modern English-language usage is accepting *hopefully* in the sense of "it is hoped" or "I hope." Note the following usage citation from the Random House *Unabridged Dictionary*:

> Although some strongly object to its use as a sentence modifier, *hopefully* meaning "it is hoped (that)" has been in use since the 1930s and is fully standard in all varieties of speech and writing: *Hopefully*, tensions between the two nations will ease. This use of *hopefully* is parallel to that of certainly, curiously, frankly, regrettably, and other sentence modifiers.[1]

Hopefully, that will clarify the issue. Nonetheless, you should use the term sparingly in writing with intelligence, especially when you are writing estimative intelligence. Remember that you are expressing a personal hope or desire for something to happen when you say *hopefully*. That may not be your intent; for example, "*Hopefully*, the government of Panaragua will solve its problems in the long term."

however, comma. The word *however* seems to cause more problems for students than any other single word in the English language. Remember that *however* almost always requires punctuation on both sides of it. When a complete sentence (an independent clause) is on both sides of it, precede it with a period or semicolon and follow it with a comma: "I proofread my paper 13 times; *however*, the professor still found errors." If it has no complete sentence before it or after it, *however*, the word may be set off by commas on both sides. Notice that the phrase preceding "however" in the previous sentence and after it in the following sentence is not a complete sentence: "My paper was perfect, *however*, when I handed it in the 14th time."

hyphens. A few of the common uses of hyphens in your papers will be as unit modifiers and as substitutes for a printed dash.

Unit modifiers are combinations of words that stand before a noun as a single unit, modifying it as a whole rather than in part. For example, you might write, "No change is expected in the short term." But, written another way, *short term* becomes a unit modifier: "The short-term outlook is bleak." Apply the same principle to such phrases as *long-term and high-level*. In the printing process, a dash is used in certain grammatical constructions. When the occasion calls for it, use two hyphens—typed together with no space between them on either side—as we have used them in this sentence. Microsoft Word automatically converts those two hyphens to a dash.

i.e. See **e.g.**

illicit. See **elicit/illicit.**

illusion. See **allude/elude.**

immigrate. See **emigrate/immigrate.**

imminent. See **eminent/imminent.**

impending/pending. *Pending* means yet to come or awaiting settlement: "Our assessment of the situation is *pending* coordination." *Impending* adds a hint of threat or menace: "*Impending* economic sanctions promise to cause severe problems for the military dictatorship."

implicit. See **explicit/implicit.**

imply/infer. The writer or speaker *implies* when stating something indirectly: "She *implied* in her article that there might be a coup d'etat." Readers or listeners *infer* when drawing a conclusion or making a deduction based upon what they have read or heard: "I *inferred* a mistaken conclusion from his estimate."

important/importantly. When introducing a second and more worthy consideration, *more important* is preferable to *more importantly*: "The truth is evident; *more important*, it will prevail."

in/into. *In* indicates location or condition; *into* suggests movement, direction, or change of condition.

inactivate. See **deactivate/inactivate.**

in addition to. See **along with.**

incite/insight. *Incite,* a verb, means to stir up or cause to happen, often with violence suggested: "The Homeland Guard troops *incited* a riot in front of the U.S. Embassy." The noun *insight* means an act of comprehension or understanding, especially through intuition. "Her *insight* into the Iraqi culture was unique."

(to) include. Used by bureaucrats to mean *including*: "The rebels received 12 tons of arms, *to include* 130 grenade launchers." Use *including*. There is a place for "to include," as in the following: "They updated their estimate *to include* [for the purpose of including] the latest information."

incomparables. Terms such as *very unique, more fatal*, and *more equal* are misuses of words that express absolutes. That which is unique, fatal, or equal can be no more or less so. Other incomparable words include absolute, eternal, final, perfect, supreme, total, and unanimous.

infer. See **imply/infer**.

infrastructure. Bureaucratically ostentatious. Try *foundation* or *framework* instead.

in regards to. Use *in regard to* or, better yet, *regarding*: "We have not heard from her *regarding* the changes to our publication."

inside/outside (of). When *inside* is used as a preposition, the "of" is unnecessary: "*Inside* the house" and "*inside* the circle of terrorists" are acceptable usages. The same principle is true of *outside* and *all*.

insight. See **incite/insight**.

insure. See **assure/ensure/insure**.

interface. An overused term, best avoided.

irregardless. There is no such word. Use either *regardless* or *irrespective*.

it is. Avoid this pair of words, especially at the beginning of a sentence or phrase. The result will usually be better prose.
Not: "It is necessary that the L-14 fastener be redesigned."
But: "The L-14 fastener must be redesigned."
Even better (using active voice): "Widgits Inc. must redesign the L-14 fastener."

its/it's. *It's* always means "it is" or "it has." The possessive form of the pronoun *it* is *its*. You would not say *their's* or *your's*, so do not misuse the possessive form here.

(Note: It is best simply to avoid contractions in formal writing. If you do not use them in your papers, then you will never misuse *it's*.)

judgment. The preferred spelling is the one at left, *not* the chiefly British "judgement."

last/latest. *Last* denotes finality, while *latest* can mean only the most recent: "This is the *latest* of Captain Szwerdlodvski's reports; because he was shot just after he mailed it, it is also his *last*."

latter/last/first/former. *Latter* is applied only to the second of two items. A writer referring to the final one of three or more items would use *last*: "To assist you, I am sending Lieutenant Smith and Ensign Bowen, the *latter* because of his experience in riverine warfare." Similarly, *former* is applied only to the first of two items. If more than two items are listed, use the terms *first* and *last*.

lead/led. *Led* is the past tense of the verb form *to lead*: "The captain *led* his men bravely." *Lead*, when pronounced "led," is the metal.

less. See **fewer/less**.

like. See also **along with**. The word *like* is never a conjunction and should not be used to replace *as*, *as if*, or *as though*. If you can substitute the words "similar to" or "similarly to," and the sentence still makes sense, then the word you want is *like*.
Incorrect: "The new regime deals with insurgencies like the old dictatorship dealt with them."
Correct: "The new regime deals with insurgencies as the old dictatorship dealt with them."
Also correct: "The new regime deals with insurgencies similar to the old dictatorship."

like/such as. *Like* introduces a comparison with something else: "Hills in this part of the country are low and rounded *like* those near the coast." *Such as* introduces an example of the group itself: "Special operations forces *such as* Army Rangers and Navy SEALs are elite units."

likely. When *likely* is used as an adverb, it must be preceded by such qualifiers as *very*, *quite*, or *most*. Otherwise, it is incorrect, as in, "The Pakistani forces *likely* will deploy their tanks."

Likely, as an adjective expressing inclination or probability, is followed by the infinitive: "The armed forces are *likely* to have a difficult time restoring order."

locate(d). The term *locate(d)* is overused in intelligence writing, as in, "The installation is *located* 60 kilometers west of here." Often the term can be eliminated with no harm done: "The installation is 60 kilometers west of here."

logistic/logistics/logistical. *Logistic* as the adjective and *logistics* as the noun form are preferred. *Logistical* is discouraged.

loose/lose. The error with this pair of words tends to be one of careless spelling rather than improper usage. Remember that *loose* rhymes with *goose* and *lose* rhymes with *choose*. "He could *lose* his job as security chief if the guard dogs get *loose*."

material/materiel. In military usage, *materiel* means arms, ammunition, and equipment.

may. See **can/may**.

media. A plural form. See **data/errata/media/phenomena**.

methodology. If *method* or *system* is meant, use those words and avoid the term *methodology* (the study of the science of methods).

militate/mitigate. *Militate* means to have weight or effect, for or against: "The facts *militate* against his interpretation." *Mitigate* means to appease, lessen, moderate, or soften: "*Mitigating* circumstances affected her assessment."

moral/morale. *Moral* is an adjective meaning "having to do with right conduct." *Morale* is a noun meaning "degree of cheerfulness and confidence." Confusing the two can be comical: "The opposing forces had low *moral*."

more than one. Takes a singular verb: "More than one division *was* involved in the exercise."

multiple qualifiers. Avoid using more than one qualifier to describe a situation, such as "suggests . . . may," "may possibly," "could perhaps," "probably indicates," "reportedly may," and "suggests the possibility that the army might deploy its forces."

munition/munitions. The -s form is generally used: munitions storage building, munitions loading area.

myself. This word is a reflexive pronoun, often erroneously used where *I* or *me* would be correct.
Incorrect: Ambassador Myslinski and *myself* agree that the plan should go forward.
Correct: Ambassador Myslinski and *I*. . . ."
Incorrect: Any such orders must be approved by Ambassador Catlin or *myself*.
Correct: . . . Catlin or *me*.

near term. Fuzzy. See **foreseeable future/near term**.

neither . . . nor. See **either . . . or/neither . . . nor**.

none/not one. Depending on what you intend, *none* may be singular or plural. When the meaning is *not one* or *no one*, the verb is singular: "*None* of the treaties *was* ratified by the newly elected president." Sometimes, though, the meaning of the sentence is clearly plural; in these cases, *none* takes a plural verb: "*None are* so ambitious as those who desire absolute power." (In the latter case, you might also have said: "*None is* so ambitious as one who desires absolute power.")

Non-Soviet Warsaw Pact. A specific term for the six nations of the former Warsaw Treaty Organization ("Warsaw Pact"): Bulgaria, Czechoslovakia, the German Democratic Republic (East Germany), Hungary, Poland, and Romania.

north/northern. See **east/eastern**. The same principles apply.

not only/but also. These terms are called correlative conjunctions, and as such they must be followed by grammatically similar words or phrases. If *not only* is followed by a verb, then for the sake of parallelism *but also* must have a verb after it as well. For example, "The student *not only* wrote his thesis during the summer *but also* took a vacation."

number/amount. See **amount/number**.

number, the/a. When *number* is preceded by *the*, a *singular* verb is required: "*The number* of well-written theses *has* increased dramatically this year." If *number* is preceded by *a*, the verb is plural: "*A number* of students *have* failed this year because they could not write well."

numbers/numerals. Keep a few rules in mind when you use numbers: Spell out one through nine; use numerals for 10 or more: "We saw one smoker and nine nonsmokers in the designated smoking area during the break." However, if the numbers are mixed—some below nine and some above—use all numerals: "A total of 3 smokers and 472 nonsmokers used the facilities today." Always spell out a number at the beginning of a sentence, unless it becomes unwieldy; then rewrite the sentence: "Twelve thousand men died in that battle." *But*: "Total losses were 11,991." *Not*: "Eleven thousand nine hundred and ninety-one men died."

offload/unload. *Unload* is preferred.

ongoing. Try *continuing, underway*, or *in progress*, or leave it out altogether and see if your sentence still makes sense: "The *ongoing* research will prove my hypothesis." *Better*: "Research will prove my hypothesis."

only. Place *only* as close as possible to the word it modifies, to avoid ambiguity. Observe the change in meaning caused by shifting *only* in the following sentences: "*Only* I wrote the correct answer for the professor." (No one else did.) "I *only* wrote the correct answer for the professor." (I did nothing else.) "I wrote *only* the correct answer for the professor." (I wrote nothing else.) "I wrote the *only* correct answer for the professor." (No other answers were correct.) "I wrote the correct answer *only* for the professor." (Or, for the professor *only*.) (And nothing else; or, I wrote it for no one else. This one is ambiguous.) Other words requiring similar treatment include *almost, even, merely*, and *scarcely*.

operation/operations. Use the singular as a modifier: *operation* map, *operation* plan, *operation* order (in each case, presumably one specific operation pertains). But acceptable usages include *operations* center, *operations* building, *operations* research, and *operations* officer.

optimize. A word to be avoided, like many other words that end in "*-ize*."

oral/verbal. Spoken words are *oral*. Anything constructed of words, either spoken or written, is *verbal*.

outside/inside (of). See **inside/outside (of)**.

overall. As an adjective, *overall* is much overworked and vague. Consider substitutes such as *average, complete, comprehensive, total*, or *whole*.

380 / Appendix A

parameter. A word often overused in bureaucratic prose to mean boundary, limit, or outline.

parliamentarian. The word means an expert on parliamentary procedure. It does *not* mean "a member of parliament."

partially/partly. These words are not interchangeable. *Partially* carries the sense of "to a certain degree"; it means "incompletely," as in "*partially* dependent." *Partly* stresses the part in contrast to the whole; it is equivalent to "in part."

pending/impending. See **impending/pending**.

percentages. Spell out the percentage (10 percent); do not use the % sign. Always use numerals: 1 percent; 100 percent.

phenomena. A plural form. See **data/errata/media/phenomena**.

phony phrases. See **fake analysis**.

practicable/practical. *Practicable* means that which appears achievable but has not yet been tested: "A deployable Strategic Defense Initiative appears *practicable* within the next 10 years." *Practical* means known to be useful, effective, sound: "Her analysis of that situation is *practical*."

precede/proceed/procedure. Spelling seems to be a more common problem than usage with these words. Consult a dictionary if you have any doubt. Note the forms of these two:
precede: preceded, preceding.
proceed: proceeded, proceeding, *but* procedure.

precedence/precedent. *Precedence* is simply the act of preceding or coming before. In military communications parlance, the word is used to mean the priority of a message or a telephone call: routine, priority, immediate, or flash precedence. A *precedent* is an established fact or form that serves as a guide thereafter: "The general's use of flash *precedence* on his message set a *precedent* for the traffic that followed."

predominantly/predominately. *Predominantly* is preferred.

presently. See **at present/currently/presently**.

preventative/preventive. *Preventive* is preferred.

principal/principle. *Principal* is usually an adjective meaning first in authority or importance: "The *principal* architect of the reforms was Mikhail Gorbachev." As a noun it refers either to money ("Spend the interest, not the *principal*.") or to a key person ("Though each team had over 30 members, the *principals* were Dr. Henry Kissinger and Le Duc Tho.") *Principle* is always a noun, never an adjective. It means a standard of conduct, an essential element, or a general truth: "Anwar Sadat was dedicated to the *principle* of peace in the Middle East." "The *principles* of good writing are a *principal* concern at our college."

prioritize. Substitute "rank" or another synonym. See also **optimize**.

proceed/procedure. See **precede/proceed/procedure**.

purposefully/purposely. *Purposefully* indicates determination to reach a goal: "The United States proceeded *purposefully* with its policy of troop reductions." *Purposely* means intentionally: "The delegates to the arms control talks *purposely* withheld comment from the press."

qualifiers. Intelligence analysts must often use qualifiers if they are to be objective and accurate. Do not, however, habitually hide judgment behind words such as *apparently, conceivably, evidently, likely, perhaps, possibly, probably, purportedly, reportedly, seemingly, undoubtedly,* and *virtually*. Multiple qualifiers are never justified.

question (as to) whether. When *question* is followed by *whether*, many writers mistakenly insert *as to* between them. Avoid the practice. However, when a noun follows, the phrase "question of" may be used: "The troop movements raised the *question of* the enemy's intentions."

quite. An adverb with shades of meaning for different people. It is usually quite avoidable in intelligence writing.

quota. Means an allotted number, akin to rationing.

quotations. A few tips on quotations: Use them sparingly, but when you use them, use them *correctly* and cite your source appropriately. Be certain to quote material *exactly* when you have it within quotation marks. If your quoted material has an error in it—factual or mechanical—do not correct it; include it as is and put the bracketed expression [sic] immediately after it, to tell your reader that it was that way in the original. Use standard double quotation marks (". . .") for short quotations. Use single quotation marks only to show a quotation within a quotation: The dean said, "The professor told me he is 'the brightest student in the class.'" Notice that periods and commas *always* go inside the final quotation marks, whether or not they are a part of the quoted material. Other punctuation marks go *outside* the quotation marks unless they are a part of the quoted material. Quotations of four typewritten lines or more should be inset and single-spaced. It is not necessary to use quotation marks with an inset quotation; its printed style shows that it is a direct quotation.

range/vary. To *range* is to change or differ within limits: "Elevations *range* between 500 and 1,500 meters above sea level." To *vary* is to change in succession: "Temperatures *vary* from season to season."

recurrence/reoccurrence. *Recurrence* has the sense of happening repeatedly or periodically, whereas a *reoccurrence* means a second occurrence. It is redundant to say "another recurrence."

regards to. *Regards,* a noun plural, is used to convey good wishes or an expression of affection: "Give my *regards* to the family." *In regards to* is substandard; use *about, on, with regard to,* or *regarding.*

relatively. Use only when the intended comparison can be easily grasped: "He has a *relatively* heavy workload." (Relative to what? Last week? His peers?)

represent. Means to depict or symbolize, not constitute. Do not write "South African gold *represents* most of the world's output."

reticent. Means uncommunicative or reserved; it does not mean reluctant.

sanction. As a verb, *sanction* means to authorize, approve, or allow; to ratify or confirm.

saving/savings. *Savings* should *not* be used as a singular noun. We may buy a *savings* bond and keep our money in a *savings* bank; *but*: "The budget reduction would mean an annual *saving* (not savings) of $200,000."

secondly/thirdly. Don't "prettify" numbers with the *-ly* suffix. It is unnecessary for the meaning of the sentence.

sector. *Sector* is correct in economics or position warfare but should not be used in political, religious, or sociological contexts. Instead, try *sect, faction, clique, group, side,* or *party.*

sexism. See **he or she**.

she/her. It is no longer preferable to apply these pronouns to countries, although tradition still calls for their use when referring to ships. Use *it* or *its* when referring to a country. "Yugoslavia lost *its* national identity after the Cold War."

ship. See **boat/ship**.

sic. The Latin word *sic* literally means *so* or *thus*. It is handy to use when you are quoting material or citing a source and you find an error or omission in the material you are quoting. To show your reader that your source—and not you—made the error, use a bracketed [*sic*]: One humorist misquoted President George H. W. Bush's inaugural address by calling for "a thousand pints [sic] of light."

sometime/sometimes. *Sometime* is preferred.

south/southern. See **east/eastern**. The same principles apply.

Soviet bloc. See **East/Soviet bloc**.

stalemate. Chess players will tell you that a stalemate is as final as a checkmate and cannot be eased, broken, or lifted. If you have in mind an *impasse*, use that word instead.

stanch/staunch. Use *stanch* as a verb meaning to stop the flow of something: "The authorities cannot *stanch* the wave of terrorism in the United States." *Staunch*, an adjective, means loyal, faithful, or strong: "They are *staunch* supporters of more severe penalties for terrorism."

such as. See **like/such as**.

tenant/tenet. A *tenant* pays rent; a *tenet* is a principle or guiding thought. "The *Tenants'* Association believed in the *tenet* of service first, rent later."

that/which. *That* is better to introduce a restrictive clause. A restrictive clause narrows the item under consideration from what it would be if the sentence did not contain the clause: "The computer *that* is broken is in the repair shop." Presumably multiple computers are available, and the speaker is focusing on the one that is broken. In contrast, a nonrestrictive clause merely adds information about the set of items under consideration: "The computer, *which* is broken, is in the repair shop." Here the speaker does not narrow the set of items—one computer—but merely provides additional information about it. We also know from that sentence that only one computer is available. Often the "that" in a restrictive clause can be profitably eliminated, making your writing more concise: "The broken computer is in the repair shop."

their/there. *Their* is the plural possessive pronoun, and *there* is usually an adverb but also can be other parts of speech: "*Their* ship is the destroyer in the harbor, over *there*."

there are. Like its singular counterpart *it is,* this phrase usually signals a sentence in need of improvement. See also **it is.**

together with. See **along with.**

toward/towards. *Toward* is preferred.

uninterested. See **disinterested/uninterested.**

unique. If a thing is unique, there is precisely one of it, no more and no less. See also **incomparables.**

unknown. A fact is unknown only if absolutely no one knows about it. Use such terms as *unidentified, undisclosed,* or *undetermined.*

unload. See **offload/unload.**

upward/upwards. *Upward* is preferred.

usage/use. Use the shorter form in most instances, except when referring to the way in which language or its elements are used, related, or pronounced.

utilize. Try using the more direct word, *use.*

vary. See **range/vary.**

verbal. See **oral/verbal.**

very. A *very, very* overworked word. Give it a rest.

viable. *Viable* means workable and likely to survive. It has become a "vogue word" and is commonly used in the sense of workable or achievable. Adjectives such as *durable, lasting, effective,* and *practical* are more appropriate.

vogue words. Vogue words, phrases, or expressions suddenly and inexplicably crop up in speeches of bureaucrats, in comments of columnists, and in broadcasts. These expressions soon become debased by overuse and eventually become obsolete. Even though you may use them regularly in speech, avoid using such phrases as *positive feedback, think outside the box,* and *behind the power curve* in your writing.

waiver/waver. A *waiver* is an intentional relinquishment of some right or interest. To hesitate is to *waver*.

way/ways. *Way* is preferred: "He is a long *way* from home."

weapon/weapons. As an adjective, the singular form is preferable, except in *weapons* carrier, *weapons* selection, *weapons* list, or *weapons* assignment.

west/western. See **east/eastern**. The same principles apply.

which. See **that/which**.

while. Do not use *while* in the sense of *and*, or *although*, as in: "He spent his youth in Ohio, *while* his father grew up in California." It is not likely that the person in that sentence spent his or her childhood in Ohio *at the same time as* dear old Dad was growing up on the West Coast. *While* refers to time, in the sense of "at the same time as": "I will sauté the onions *while* you marinate the meat."

with. Does not have the conjunctive force of *and*. *With* is too often used to attach to a sentence an additional thought that would be better treated as an independent clause preceded by *and* or a semicolon: "English and history are his major subjects, *with* economics as his first elective," should be rewritten: "English and history are his major subjects, *and* economics is his first elective," or "English and history are his major subjects; economics is his first elective."

Note

1. *Random House Webster's Unabridged Dictionary*, 2nd ed. (New York: Random House, 2001), under the word "hopefully."

Appendix B:
Intelligence Briefing Checklist

Prebriefing

The Briefing: Subject/Time

- Clearly define your subject; be *sure* it is specifically what was requested.
- Pinpoint the exact time allotted for the briefing; if "open," recommend the time you need.
- Confirm the date, time, and place for the briefing.
- Analyze your audience; use biographies and any other information at your disposal to determine background, experience, subject area knowledge, and likes and dislikes.

The Briefing: Milestones

- Develop a milestones list, working backward from the established date and time.
- Identify "critical nodes" in milestones dependent on others' actions; for example, typing of script, preparation of graphics, and scheduling rehearsals.

The Briefing: Outline

- Draft an outline for your presentation, using three major headings: *introduction, body,* and *conclusion.*
- Outline the *body* of the briefing first.
- Extract *key points* from the body and include them in your introduction as *summary* points; also review these points in the *conclusion.*
- *Tentatively* allot time to each segment: 10 percent for introduction, 10 percent for conclusion, and remainder for body.

The Briefing Script: *Introduction*

Using your outline, prepare the introduction in draft. Know how long it takes you to read one page of double-spaced, typewritten script, and plan accordingly.

- Greeting and self-introduction.
- Briefing subject, time length, and classification.
- Significance to audience.
- Organization of briefing (major topics to be covered).
- Time allotted (if any) for questions and discussion.

The Briefing Script: *Body*

Using your outline, prepare the body in draft. Use the same time-planning factors as above.

- Keep the briefing subject in front of you. Don't stray.
- Use clear, concise, short, precise words and sentences.
- Plan your visual aids simultaneously with script development (see Visual Aids, below).
- Do research and analysis, using all available sources, to ensure accuracy.

The Briefing Script: *Conclusion*

Using your outline, prepare the conclusion in draft. Use the same time-planning factors as above.

- After a concluding phrase such as "In conclusion . . ." or "In summary . . . ," review the key points made in the main body of the briefing.
- Conclude with a statement such as, "Sir, that concludes our unclassified presentation on the situation in Iraq. Do you have any (further) questions?"

The Briefing: Preparation

- Have your draft script approved by supervisor(s) if possible.
- At least once before the final script preparation, *read the words aloud* to check for word traps, tongue twisters, assonance, or harsh-sounding words.
- In preparing the script, use a large font and all caps; wide margins; and only ½–¾ of the page.
- If you prefer, or have the option, to work from note cards, print legibly and *number* the cards.

The Visual Aids

- Know in advance what presentation media will be available to you: PowerPoint, overhead transparency, 35 mm projector, white board, butcher paper, and others.
- Use visual aids to clarify, illustrate, reinforce, or dramatize the words you'll be saying.
- Ask graphic artists or supporting visual aids shop for assistance early in briefing development—not only in preparation of graphics but also in creative ideas for visual aids.
- Draft your "paper copies" clearly and legibly.
- Get your supervisor's approval before final preparation of the graphics.

- Allow sufficient time for visual aid preparation and for proofing and correcting them.
- Proofread visual aids in their projected form.

The Facility

- Check out the briefing site in advance, especially if it is unfamiliar to you.
- Know the location and operation of all visual aids, light switches, and temperature controls.
- Determine the availability of a lectern, pointer, and sufficient chairs for the anticipated audience.
- Try to conduct at least one rehearsal of your briefing at the site where it will be given.
- Know where to get help if Murphy's Law is in force (and it will be!) on the day you brief.

The Briefing Day

The Briefer

- Read the morning newspaper and/or listen to a headline newscast, and read anything in the morning message traffic or e-mail relevant to your briefing topic.
- Review these checklists.
- Check your appearance in a mirror immediately before the briefing.
- Be friendly to your audience.
- As the briefing begins, establish eye contact with your audience. Maintain it throughout.
- Stand firmly and confidently behind the lectern or, if you will be "mobile," confine your movements to a minimum.

The Briefing

- Gain your audience's attention early, and try to maintain it.

- Proceed logically, in a well-organized manner, through the body of your briefing.
- Give accurate, full exposition to all your ideas.
- Don't ad lib unless you have timely information that must be mentioned; use separate notes for that information or have a backup analyst explain it in more detail.
- Ask your backup analyst or someone else in the room to make notes of any questions asked or comments made. Don't try to do that yourself.
- Transition smoothly between your main points.
- Use notes or script, but don't read extensively with your head down. Keep your eye contact.

Questions, Answers, and Discussions

- When your listener asks a question, be sure of your answer before you respond definitively.
- Use backup analyst(s) for subject areas that are not your specialty.
- If the answer is unknown, don't use a trite phrase like, "I don't know, Ma'am, but I'll find out." Give your questioner a reasonable expectation of an answer by saying something like this: "Ma'am, we don't have that information at hand, but we'll find it immediately after this briefing, and we'll respond to your secretary later today [or tomorrow morning]."
- If something in your briefing precipitates a discussion among the senior members of your audience, pause and wait for them to signal you that they are ready to proceed.

Postbriefing

- Always follow up promptly on questions you've promised to answer. Provide an information copy of the response to your supervisor.

- Store your briefing script and visual aids in a readily accessible place. You may need them again soon, especially if the briefing was well received.
- Write a memorandum for record (only for yourself, so it can be handwritten) on the briefing circumstances: date, time, location, principal recipient(s), how received, key questions asked, and responses given. That memo will come in handy for future iterations of the briefing, if any.

Appendix C: A "Free Sample" Briefing Introduction

Good morning, General Payne.

I'm Lieutenant Eeger, the Libyan air order-of-battle analyst here at the 33rd Widowmaker Wing.

←*Greeting. Lieutenant Eeger is smiling and friendly.*
←*Self-introduction includes credibility statement.*

This morning's 30-minute briefing is on the new SU-44/Fizzle fighter, which you see pictured on the screen. (pause 5 seconds)

←*Scheduled time for the presentation.*
←*Briefing subject.*
←*Just one technique that might be used for effect.*

We consider this new fighter of exceptional importance to our mission because of its look-down/shoot-down capability and the likelihood of accelerated production rates in the years to come.

←*Significance statement.*

These are the main points I'll cover in today's

←*Summary/organization of the briefing.*

393

briefing. (summary slide on, pause 10 seconds)

The briefing is unclassified. ←*Classification, including any caveats.*

I've allotted 5 of our total 30 minutes for questions and discussion. Please feel free to ask questions at any time during the briefing. ←*Time allotted for questions and/or discussion.*

Appendix D:
A Sample Briefing Conclusion

General Payne, ladies and
    gentlemen, that concludes   ←*"Cue" for conclusion.*
    my unclassified presentation ←*Classification reminder.*
    on the new Fizzle fighter.
    These are the key points I've
    covered this morning.   ←*Summary.*
    (pause, let audience read). ←*10–30 seconds. Watch their*
    Sir, subject to your (further)   *eyes.*
    questions or discussion, that
    concludes my briefing.

Appendix E:
Briefing Evaluation Form

In this appendix is a form that can be used to evaluate a briefing. I developed the form after a number of years at a degree-granting U.S. Government college, where I routinely critiqued student presentations. The evaluation is based on a number of forms I have used over the years, adapted from similar ones used by the military services, most of which are longer. I find this form particularly useful because everything one needs to critique someone's briefing is on one side of one page.

You will see lines at the top where the evaluator may enter his or her name and the name of the briefer being evaluated. Note that the form is divided into five "sections." The three main parts of a briefing are there (introduction, body, and conclusion), each assigned a number of points. The introduction, for example, is allotted 16 points and has 8 gradable items; so each item is worth 2 points. As evaluators listen to the briefing, they need only circle or check off each item to score it. There is also a section to evaluate the briefer. The scores are for classroom use and may be ignored if you are simply using the form as a training device or to assist you in critiquing a colleague. Total points should be added only at the end of the briefing to avoid distraction during the presentation. There is room in the right margin and at the bottom of the form ("Comments") for the evaluator to make notations about *specific items* of the briefing that are particularly well done or that require corrective action. That kind of feedback is far more valuable to a briefer than the point grade.

Note the "Timing" block at the bottom of the page. I teach students in my classes that they must be sensitive to time requirements in their briefings, and I *insist* that they adhere to a strict allotted time. As their briefing begins, I check the time and note it in the "Start Time" box on the lower left. As the briefing concludes, I note the "Stop Time" and enter it in the designated box. The rest is mathematics. I deduct points for overtime at the rate of one point for every 30 seconds overtime or portion thereof. So if a briefing is allotted five minutes, and the student takes a total of seven minutes, I deduct four points for overtime. Of course, if you have a stop watch, the timing is much simpler.

In addition to my own critique of student briefings, I require students to use this form to evaluate fellow students' presentations. I believe there is great value in having someone listen to a briefing with evaluation in mind. It is no longer a passive receiving mode for the student: he or she must actively participate in the evaluation process. We learn briefing, as I have said several times in this book, by briefing. But there is much to learn as well by watching someone else brief. This form might help with that experience.

Briefer's Name _____   Evaluator's Name _____

INTRODUCTION (16 points)

Did the briefing introduction include all necessary elements, clearly recognizable as such?   (Circle)

Greeting	Self-Introduction	Subject	Significance	
Length	Classification	Summary	Q&A Time	Points:

BODY (35 points)

Main Points	Poor	Fair	Good	Excellent	Outstanding
Organization	Poor	Fair	Good	Excellent	Outstanding
Transitions	Poor	Fair	Good	Excellent	Outstanding
Use of Notes	Poor	Fair	Good	Excellent	Outstanding
Visual Aids					
Appearance	Poor	Fair	Good	Excellent	Outstanding
Use	Poor	Fair	Good	Excellent	Outstanding
Support	Poor	Fair	Good	Excellent	Outstanding	Points:

B R I E F E R (40 points)

Eye Contact	Poor	Fair	Good	Excellent	Outstanding
Body Movement	Poor	Fair	Good	Excellent	Outstanding
Gestures	Poor	Fair	Good	Excellent	Outstanding
Voice Quality	Poor	Fair	Good	Excellent	Outstanding
Word Use	Poor	Fair	Good	Excellent	Outstanding
Clarity	Poor	Fair	Good	Excellent	Outstanding
Confidence	Poor	Fair	Good	Excellent	Outstanding
Knowledge	Poor	Fair	Good	Excellent	Outstanding

Points: _____

C O N C L U S I O N (9 points)

Did the conclusion contain all necessary elements, clearly recognizable as such? (Circle)

Cue	Summary	Classification	Points:

T I M I N G

Stop Time:	Overtime (Deduct Points)	Minus Points:
Minus *Start Time*		
= Time Length:	10 9 8 7 6 5 4 3 2 1	

Comments:		Total Points:

Annotated Bibliography

Dictionaries and Thesauruses

Note to the user: Many of the works cited here are available in other editions, including paperbacks, CDs, and even online. Some publication dates are old, but the books have endured as classics in their field. You should also be aware that the name "Webster's" in the title of a dictionary is not a guarantee of quality because the name is not copyrighted.

American Heritage College Dictionary. 4th ed., with CD-ROM. Boston: Houghton Mifflin, 2004. Outstanding usage notes for our dynamic language. Good synonym lists. Extensive biographic and geographic entries at the end. Thumb indexed.

American Heritage Dictionary of the English Language. 4th ed. Boston: Houghton Mifflin, 2000. Also available as a CD. Easy-to-read typeface. My favorite dictionary.

Bartlett's Roget's Thesaurus. Boston: Little, Brown, 1996. Easy to use. Thumb indexed. Organized by concept, not alphabetically. Some users find that difficult.

Fowler, H. W. *A Dictionary of Modern English Usage.* 3rd rev. ed. by R. W. Burchfield. Oxford, U.K.: Oxford University Press, 2004. A classic reference source, but use caution because this is the Queen's English. You'll see things like "colour" and "defence." Still a good reference for usages.

Merriam Webster's Collegiate Dictionary. 11th ed. Springfield, Mass.: Merriam-Webster, 2003. Easy-to-read print style. Gives the date of a word's earliest recorded use. Excellent "Handbook of Style" at the end, as well as abbreviations, biographies, and geographic names. A standard.

Merriam-Webster's Collegiate Thesaurus. Springfield, Mass.: Merriam-Webster, 1995. Another standard, with the reliable "Merriam" name.

Random House Webster's Unabridged Dictionary. 2nd ed. New York: Random House, 2001. A relative newcomer to the market but getting good reviews.

Rodale, J. I., ed. *The Synonym Finder.* New York: Warner Books, 1986. The best thesaurus this writer has ever used. Aging but indispensable.

Roget's International Thesaurus. Edited by Robert L. Chapman. 5th ed. New York: Harper College, 1993. A standard. Highly recommended.

Shaw, Harry. *Dictionary of Problem Words and Expressions.* Rev. ed. New York: McGraw-Hill, 1987. An "old master" looks at perennial problems. Quick reference for the bugaboos.

Webster's Dictionary of English Usage. Springfield, Mass.: Merriam-Webster, 1994. Detailed descriptions of many problem words, although some are merely descriptive, leaving the reader to wonder what really *is* the correct usage.

Books on Writing Style, Grammar, Composition, and Research

Associated Press Stylebook. Edited by Norm Goldstein. New York: Perseus Books Group, 2007. An excellent reference that shows how professional journalists do it.

Babbie, Earl R. *The Practice of Social Research.* 11th ed. Belmont, Calif.: Wadsworth, 2006. Good text for the research process, from an established master in the field.

———. *The Basics of Social Research.* Belmont, Calif.: Wadsworth, 2007.

Baker, Sheridan. *The Practical Stylist, with Readings and Handbook.* 8th ed. New York: Addison-Wesley Education Publishers,1998. One of the best. Packed with innovative exercises that make even the apathetic writer take up pen.

Barzun, Jacques, and Henry F. Graff. *The Modern Researcher.* 6th ed. Belmont, Calif.: Wadsworth, 2003. A best-seller, especially in the social sciences.

Bernstein, Theodore M. *The Careful Writer: A Modern Guide to English Usage.* 2nd ed. New York: Free Press, 1995.

Campbell, William G., Stephen V. Ballou, and Carol Slade. *Form and Style.* 8th ed. Boston: Houghton Mifflin, 1990. Spiral binding for easy handling. Good format for scholarly research and writing.

Chicago Manual of Style. 15th ed. Chicago: University of Chicago Press, 2003. Classic reference for scholars and publishers. Newest edition has more on documentation styles.

Crews, Frederick. *The Random House Handbook.* 6th ed. New York: McGraw-Hill, 1991. Not only addresses problems of grammar and usage but also focuses on how to develop writing topics. Provides well-designed charts and exercises.

Crews, Frederick, and Sandra Schor. *The Borzoi Handbook for Writers.* 3rd ed. New York: McGraw-Hill, 1993. Thorough guide to all aspects of writing—prewriting through final proofreading. Ask for the *Borzoi Practice Book for Writers* that complements the text.

Dornan, Edward A., and Charles W. Dawe. *The Brief English Handbook.* 3rd ed. New York: Scott Foresman, 1997. Contains a section on punctuation with exercises that tell interesting stories. Spiral binding for easy handling.

Elbow, Peter. *Writing without Teachers.* 2nd ed. London: Oxford University Press, 1998. Great self-help text.

———. *Writing with Power: Techniques for Mastering the Writing Process.* 2nd ed. New York: Oxford University Press, 1998. A powerful treatment of the writing process, especially prewriting.

Flesch, Rudolf. *The Classic Guide to Better Writing.* 50th anniv. ed. New York: Collins, 1996. An enduring standard in the field, from the developer of the Flesch-Kincaid Reading Index.

Flesch, Rudolf, and A. H. Lass. *A New Guide to Better Writing.* New York: Warner Books, 1989.

Flynn, James, and Joseph Glaser. *Writer's Handbook.* New York: Prentice Hall College Division, 1984. Excellent format and index make quick reference a snap.

Hacker, Diana. *A Writer's Reference.* 5th ed. Boston: Bedford Books of St. Martin's Press, 2003. Spiral binding and tabular format make this book one of the most user-friendly writing references.

———. *Rules for Writers.* 5th ed. Boston: Bedford Books of St. Martin's Press, 2005.

Hennessy, Michael. *The Borzoi Practice Book for Writers.* 3rd ed. New York: McGraw-Hill College, 1992. This handbook goes with *The Borzoi Handbook for Writers* and features exercises on every stage of the writing process.

Hodges, John C. *Hodges' Harbrace Handbook.* 13th ed. New York: Harcourt Brace Jovanovich, 1999. Well-organized combination of endpapers, index, and standout red colors throughout the book makes this a classic in quick and easy grammar and usage reference. Small, easy-to-handle format. Widely used in colleges and universities.

Johnson, Edward D. *The Handbook of Good English.* Rev. ed. New York: Facts on File, 1991. Easy-to-use, comprehensive grammar reference. Highly recommended.

Kaye, Sanford. *Writing under Pressure: The Quick Writing Process.* New York: Oxford University Press, 1990. Chapter 10, "Examwriting," is a *must* for students.

Lewis, Norman. *Word Power Made Easy.* New York: Pocket Books, 1995. Comprehensive quizzes and achievement tests help you measure progress. Well organized.

Lunsford, Andrea, and Robert Connors. *The New St. Martin's Handbook*. 2nd ed. Boston: Bedford Books, 1999. My personal favorite for ease of use and comprehensiveness of content. Especially useful section on argumentative writing.

Markman, Roberta H., Peter T. Markman, and Marie L. Waddell. *10 Steps in Writing the Research Paper*. 5th ed. New York: Barron's Educational Series, 1994.

McIntosh, William A. *Guide to Effective Military Writing*. 3rd ed. Harrisburg, Pa.: Stackpole Books, 2003. Should be on the bookshelf of every "military writer."

Nelson, Victoria. *On Writer's Block: A New Approach to Creativity*. Boston: Houghton Mifflin, 1993. This book works. Use it, and you'll break the writer's block.

———. *Writer's Block and How to Use It*. Cincinnati, Ohio: Writer's Digest Books, 1985.

New York Times Manual of Style and Usage. Edited by Allan M. Siegal and William G. Connolly. Rev. and expanded ed. New York: Three Rivers Press, 2002.

Ogden, Evelyn Hunt. *Completing Your Doctoral Dissertation or Master's Thesis in Two Semesters or Less*. 2nd ed. Lanham, Md.: Scarecrow Education, 1997. A handy guide for graduate students.

Pinckert, Robert C. *Pinckert's Practical Grammar*. Cincinnati, Ohio: Writer's Digest Books, 1991. The book's jacket says, "A Lively, Unintimidating Guide to Usage, Punctuation, and Style." It is.

Shaw, Harry. *Errors in English and Ways to Correct Them*. 4th ed. New York: Harper Torch, 1996.

———. *Punctuate It Right!* 2nd ed. New York: Harper Torch, 1996.

———. *Spell It Right!* 4th ed. New York: Collins, 1994. This and the other two Shaw books cited are exceptionally valuable references that are timeless.

Shertzer, Margaret. *The Elements of Grammar*. Boston: Longman, 1996. In the classic manner of Strunk and White's *The Elements of Style* (see below), this book is helpful for problems with grammar.

Skillin, Marjorie E., and Robert M. Gay. *Words into Type*. 3rd ed. Englewood Cliffs, N.J.: Prentice Hall, 1974.

Strunk, William, Jr., and E. B. White. *The Elements of Style*. 4th ed. New York: Allyn & Bacon, 1999. No writer can be without this classic little guide. Its 128 pages are packed with the enduring power of the English language.

Success with Words. 4th ed. New York: Peterson's, 2004. You'd never believe that a book about "modern American usage" could be so readable. But this one is.

Troyka, Lynn Quitman. *Simon and Schuster Handbook for Writers*. 6th ed. Englewood Cliffs, N.J.: Prentice Hall, 2003. A good source for clear explanations.

Tufte, Edward. *Envisioning Information*. Cheshire, Conn.: Graphics Press, 1990. This book and the other two by Tufte cited here are particularly useful to a writer who seeks to display information graphically. Helpful for writer and reader alike.

——. *Visual and Statistical Thinking: Displays of Evidence for Decision Making.* Cheshire, Conn.: Graphics Press, 1997. Intelligence writers and briefers are called upon regularly to display evidence to convince decision makers. This book tells you how to do it.

——. *The Visual Display of Quantitative Information.* 2nd ed. Cheshire, Conn.: Graphics Press, 2001.

Turabian, Kate L., et al. *A Manual for Writers of Research Papers, Theses, and Dissertations.* 7th ed. Chicago: University of Chicago Press, 2007. An indispensable guide for serious scholarly writing, especially at the undergraduate level.

U.S. Government Printing Office. *United States Government Printing Office Style Manual.* Washington, D.C.: Government Printing Office, 2003. A must for writers in the government. Often called simply the "GPO Style Manual." Excellent chapters on abbreviations, capitalization, compounding, and punctuation.

Briefing-Related Sources

Ailes, Roger, with Jon Kraushar. *You Are the Message: Secrets of the Master Communicators.* Homewood, Ill.: Dow-Jones–Irwin, 1988. Ailes is well positioned to offer advice, having consulted for some of the best—including former president Ronald Reagan.

Anderson, James B. *Speaking to Groups: Eyeball to Eyeball.* Vienna, Va.: Wyndmoor Press, 1995. A reader-friendly offering on the subject.

Aslett, Don. *Is There a Speech Inside You?* Cincinnati, Ohio: Writer's Digest Books, 1989. If there *is* a speech inside you, Aslett can bring it out.

Barrack, Martin K. *How We Communicate: The Most Vital Skill.* Macomb, Ill.: Glenbridge Publishing, 1988. A true "how-to" book that goes to the heart of communication skills.

Boylan, Bob. *What's Your Point? The Proven Method for Making Powerful, Winning Presentations.* New York: Warner Books, 1988. A good little primer on getting that bottom line up front.

Brilliant, Ashleigh. *I May Not Be Totally Perfect, but Parts of Me Are Excellent, and Other Brilliant Thoughts.* Santa Barbara, Calif.: Woodbridge Press, 1979. This book is one of a collection of Ashleigh Brilliant's seventeen-word-or-less "Pot Shots." The pithy sayings alone make the books memorable, but the accompanying illustrations and text add to the utility of the book.

Carnegie, Dale. *How to Develop Self-Confidence and Influence People by Public Speaking.* New York: Pocket Books, 1956. An enduring classic by a master in the field. Any book by Carnegie will help you with your communication skills.

——. *The Quick and Easy Way to Effective Speaking.* New York: Pocket Books, 1977.

Copeland, Lewis, and Lawrence W. Lamm, eds. *The World's Greatest Speeches.* 3rd enlarged ed. New York: Dover Publications, 1973. Reading the words of dynamic speakers can often help us in our own public speaking.

Flesch, Rudolf. *How to Write, Speak, and Think More Effectively.* New York: Signet, 1960. Another classic from the originator of the Flesch-Kinkaid Reading Index.

Frank, Milo. *How to Get Your Point Across in 30 Seconds—or Less.* New York: Simon and Schuster, 1986. If you have trouble being concise in writing or a briefing, this is the book for you. Written primarily for use by advertisers, it can be extremely helpful in considering brevity and clarity in your own presentations.

Hoff, Ron. *Do Not Go Naked into Your Next Presentation: Nifty Little Nuggets to Quiet the Nerves and Please the Crowd.* Kansas City, Mo.: Andrews and McMeel, 1997. A humorous approach to overcoming flop sweat and stage jitters.

———. *I Can See You Naked: A New Revised Edition of the National Bestseller on Making Fearless Presentations.* Kansas City, Mo.: Andrews and McMeel, 1993. Lots of useful advice and, like Hoff's other works cited here, very readable.

———. *Say It in Six: How to Say Exactly What You Mean in Six Minutes or Less.* Kansas City, Mo.: Andrews and McMeel, 1996. As the title suggests, this book focuses on conciseness in speaking—trimming the fat. Includes great exercises and worksheets. Highly recommended.

Lend Me Your Ears: Great Speeches in History. Selected and introduced by William Safire. New York: W. W. Norton, 1992. More speeches from the masters, for your practice.

Martel, Myles. *The Persuasive Edge: The Executive's Guide to Speaking and Presenting.* Rev. ed. New York: Fawcett Columbine, 1989.

McMahon, Ed. *The Art of Public Speaking.* New York: Ballantine Books, 1986. Johnny Carson's long-time sidekick and announcer is himself a master of public speaking, offering some timeless hints in this book.

Prochnow, Herbert V., and Herbert V. Prochnow Jr. *The Public Speaker's Treasure Chest.* 4th rev. and enlarged ed. New York: Harper & Row, 1986. Useful in finding material to "frame" your presentation.

Sarnoff, Dorothy. *Speech Can Change Your Life.* New York: Doubleday, 1970. This timeless work offers some convincing evidence that will help you in all your public speaking.

———. *Never Be Nervous Again.* New York: Ballantine Books, 1997. Nothing really new here, but some of her tried and true techniques are worth reviewing.

Schloff, Laurie, and Marcia Yudkin. *Smart Speaking: Sixty-Second Strategies for More Than 100 Speaking Problems and Fears.* New York: Penguin Books USA, 1992. A series of short articles that deal with specific problem areas. Very helpful after you have identified where you *need* help.

Spinrad, Leonard, and Thelma Spinrad. *Complete Speaker's Almanac*. New York: Prentice Hall Trade, 1988. Helpful in identifying material to set a briefing in context.

Wallechinsky, David, and Amy Wallace. *The People's Almanac Presents the Book of Lists*. Toronto: Little, Brown, 1993.

Wohlmuth, Ed. *The Overnight Guide to Public Speaking: The Ed Wohlmuth Method*. Philadelphia, Pa.: Running Press, 1983. Not really "overnight" but helpful nonetheless.

Words of Martin Luther King, Jr. Selected by Coretta Scott King. New York: Newmarket Press, 1987. Inspiring words from the late Reverend King offer some moving speeches to practice your own pitch, force, and emphasis.

Other Sources Used or Consulted for This Book

Asimov, Janet, and Isaac Asimov. *How to Enjoy Writing: A Book of Aid and Comfort*. New York: Walker and Company, 1987. If this book doesn't help you get started, nothing will. Enjoyable reading that shows you how to "cope."

Barkas, J. L. *How to Write Like a Professional*. New York: Arco Publishing, 1985. Takes you step-by-step from breaking writer's block through getting published.

Bates, Jefferson D. *Writing with Precision: How to Write So That You Cannot Possibly Be Misunderstood*. 6th ed. Washington, D.C.: Acropolis Books, 1993. A readable combination of a "guidebook" with seven axioms to help you write more precisely and a "handbook" of usage. Added bonus of helpful examples and a thorough bibliography.

Bax, Frans. Handout material from "Workshop on Reviewing Analytical Papers." Held at the Joint Military Intelligence College, Washington, D.C., on March 27, 1989. Sponsored by the Central Intelligence Agency Office of Training and Education, Intelligence Training Division.

Boiarsky, Carolyn. "Writing a Thesis Statement: A Right-Brain Activity." In *Activities to Promote Critical Thinking*, edited by Jeff Golub, 11–18. Urbana, Ill.: NCTE, 1986.

Claiborne, Robert. *Our Marvelous Native Tongue*. New York: Times Books, 1983. Marvelous it is indeed. Great reading about the life and times of our English language.

Cousins, Norman. "The Communication Collapse." *Time*, December 17, 1990, 114.

Delton, Judy. *The 29 Most Common Writing Mistakes and How to Avoid Them*. Cincinnati, Ohio: Writer's Digest Books, 1986. One of the series "Writer's Basic Bookshelf." Excellent reference to some of the most common errors writers make, from procrastination through publication.

Department of Defense. Joint Chiefs of Staff. Joint Pub 1-02 (formerly JCS Pub 1). *Department of Defense Dictionary of Military and Associated Terms.* Washington, D.C.: Government Printing Office, December 1, 1989.

———. Joint Pub 2-0. *Joint Doctrine for Intelligence Support to Operations.* Washington, D.C.: Government Printing Office, October 12, 1993.

Diederich, Paul B. "In Praise of Praise." In *A Guide for Evaluating Student Composition,* edited by Sister M. Judine, I.H.M., 38–40. Urbana, Ill.: National Council of Teachers of English, 1965.

Editorial Eye: Focusing on Publications Standards and Practices. Alexandria, Va.: Editorial Experts. Assorted issues.

Faulkner, William. *Absalom, Absalom.* New York: Random House, 1936.

Garner, Diane L., and Diane H. Smith. *The Complete Guide to Citing Government Information Resources: A Manual for Writers and Librarians.* Bethesda, Md.: Congressional Information Service, 1993.

Gere, Ann Ruggles. *Writing and Learning.* 2nd ed. New York: Macmillan, 1988. Geared toward a liberal arts writing audience, this composition book might offer the most help to intelligence professionals in chapters 6 through 9, dealing with supporting assertions, analyzing information, explaining causes and effects, and arguing proposals. Well written and easy reading.

Goodman, Allan E. "Reforming U.S. Intelligence." *Foreign Policy* 67 (Summer 1987): 132+.

Hall, Donald, and Sven P. Birkerts. *Writing Well.* 8th ed. New York: Harper College, 1993. Lively and particularly good on getting started, diction, and different patterns for structuring papers.

Haring-Smith, Tori. Paper on collaborative learning, and various workshop exercises. Presented at the Winter Workshop of the Conference on College Composition and Communication. Clearwater, Fla., January 1987.

Hitler, Adolf. *Mein Kampf.* Marburg-Lahn, Germany: Blindenstudienanstalt, 1933.

Howell, Deborah. "A Dilemma within Quotation Marks." *Washington Post,* August 19, 2007, B6.

Huntington, Samuel. "Coping with the Lippman Gap." *Foreign Affairs* 66, no. 3 (1988): 453–77.

Kilpatrick, James J. *The Writer's Art.* Kansas City: Andreus, McMeel, & Parker, 1984. In the witty style of his daily newspaper column, this nationally syndicated columnist helps you think about writing in an enjoyable way.

Lanham, Richard A. *Revising Prose.* New York: Macmillan, 1984. Provides a concise (126 pages in all) and sharply pointed look at some of the worst writing pitfalls.

Larson, Richard. "Training New Teachers of Composition in the Writing of Comments on Themes." *College Composition and Composition* 17 (1966): 152–55.

Layne, Christopher. "Atlanticism without NATO." *Foreign Policy* 67 (Summer 1987): 24+.

Lewis, C. Day. *The Poetic Image*. London: Oxford University Press, 1948.

Licklider, Patricia. *Building a College Vocabulary*. Boston: Little, Brown, 1981. Offers new words in the context of sentences or longer prose passages and encourages the learning of new words through combining contextual clues with word-part clues.

McCrimmon, James M. *Writing with a Purpose*. Short ed. Boston: Houghton Mifflin, 1980. Relates writing concerns and problems to contemporary life. Full of thorough explanations, examples, and useful exercises.

Meyer, Herbert E. *How to Analyze Information: A Step-by-Step Guide to Life's Most Vital Skill*. www.howtoanalyzeinformation.com (August 23, 2007). A new—and free—website by a writer and scholar in the field (see next entry). Takes you through the entire process: figuring out where you are, determining what you need, collecting it, and turning it into something useful. Indispensable to anyone in the intelligence profession or aspiring to it.

Meyer, Herbert E., and Jill E. Meyer. *How to Write: Communicating Ideas and Information*. New ed. Washington, D.C.: Storm King Press, 1993. An easy, step-by-step guide to writing that follows the scheme of teaching intelligence writing. The Meyers combine a wealth of experience in teaching and in government service—she a teacher of English and writing, he a businessman, journalist, publisher, and former vice chairman of the National Intelligence Council. Highly recommended.

Middleman, Louis I. *In Short: A Concise Guide to Good Writing*. New York: St. Martin's Press, 1981. This 108-page guide is a complement to a more comprehensive rhetoric book.

Murray, Donald. "The Listening Eye: Reflections on the Writing Conference." *College English* 41 (1979): 13–18.

———. *Writing for Your Readers*. Chester, Conn.: Globe Pequot, 1983. Although written in a journalistic perspective, this readable little book has many tips on invigorating your writing and making it more palatable to the person who counts the most: your reader.

National Council of Teachers of English. "Doublespeak and the Invasion of Panama." *Quarterly Review of Doublespeak* 16, no. 3 (April 1990): 1.

Nelson, Brad, Captain, U.S. Army. *Prospects for a U.S. Drug Cartel: A Comparative Study of the Medellin Cocaine Cartel and U.S. Drug-Trafficking Gangs*. Unclassified master's thesis. Washington, D.C.: Defense Intelligence College, 1990.

O'Reilly, Timothy P., Captain, U.S. Marine Corps. *The Irish Republican Movement: Historical Basis for American Support*. Unclassified master's thesis. Washington, D.C.: Defense Intelligence College, 1987.

Petersen, Martin. "Managing/Teaching New Analysts." *Studies in Intelligence*. Unclassified ed. (Fall 1986).

Price, Jonathan. *Thirty Days to More Powerful Writing*. New York: Fawcett, 1984. A "self-help" format with plenty of guidance to take you through some well-paced exercises.

Safire, William. *Fumblerules: A Lighthearted Guide to Grammar and Good Usage.* New York: Doubleday, 1990. "A writer must not shift your point of view," warns Safire in this book that offers the reader—believe it or not—some fun, served up with (fumble)rules of grammar.

———. *On Language.* New York: Avon, 1980. A compilation of some of Safire's best nationally syndicated columns. This and subsequent Safire books in the series are all enjoyable and informative reading about our language.

Schwarzkopf, H. Norman, General. Testimony before the Senate Armed Services Committee. June 12, 1991. Quoted in Frederick J. Kroesen, General, "Intelligence: Now a Two-Way Street?" *Army* (September 1994): 7–9.

Seitz, Michael, Lieutenant, U.S. Navy. "The 600-Ship Navy: National Strategy or Personal Mission?" Unclassified seminar paper. Washington, D.C.: Defense Intelligence College, February 1990.

Stanley, Linda C., David Shimkin, and Allen H. Lanner. *Ways to Writing: Purpose, Task, Process.* 3rd ed. New York: Macmillan, 1991. Well-organized textbook format; style handbook included.

Trimble, John R. *Writing with Style: Conversations on the Art of Writing.* Upper Saddle River, N.J.: Prentice Hall, 1975. This book talks *to* the reader but never *down to* or *above* the reader, and it addresses the common problems every writer faces.

Ulam, Adam. *Stalin: The Man and His Era.* New York: Viking, 1973.

Vert, Richard F. *Frunze's Mixed System of Organization: A Model for the Future?* Unclassified master's thesis. Washington, D.C.: Defense Intelligence College, 1989.

Wallechinsky, David, and Irving Wallace. *The People's Almanac #2.* New York: Bantam Books, 1978.

Write Better, Speak Better. Pleasantville, N.Y.: Reader's Digest, 1977. Everything you ever wanted to know about writing and briefing, addressed in readable articles.

Zinsser, William. *On Writing Well, 30th Anniversary Edition: The Classic Guide to Writing Nonfiction.* New York: Collins, 2006. Critics call it "the natural companion of Strunk and White's *The Elements of Style*." A classic in readable prose on how to write nonfiction.

Indexes

Index to Part One:
Writing with Intelligence, Including Appendix A

draft, first. *See* first draft
drafting, 149
due to, 368

each, as subject, 369
each and every, 369
east/eastern, 369
East/Soviet bloc, 369
economic/economics/economical, 369
economy of words, 41
editing. *See* revision
effect/affect, 369
e.g., 369
either/or hypothesis, 168
either/or . . . neither/nor, 369
electronic/electronics, 369
elevation/altitude, 363
elicit/illicit, 370
ellipses in quoted material, 64
elude/allude, 362
emigrate/immigrate, 370
eminent/imminent, 370
emotion, appeals to, 169
encyclopedia. *See* reference works
end, in intelligence publication, 10
enormity, 370
ensure/assure/insure, 364
errata (plural), 370
estimative intelligence, 8, 238
et al., 370
etc., et cetera, 370
evaluating intelligence, 11, 23;
    exercises, 23; exercise answers,
    25
evaluative intelligence, 6
eventhough, 370
everyday/every day, 371
everyone/everybody, 371
exclamation points, 64
executive summary. *See* key
    judgments

exercises, supplemental, 271; *See
    also* subject headings
explanatory intelligence, 6, 238
explicit/implicit, 371
explosive/explosives, 371

fact that, 371
fake analysis, 371
fallacies, 168
farther/further, 371
fear, 371
feel, 371
fewer/less, 371
finished intelligence, evaluating, 11,
    23
first draft, 141
flounder/founder, 372
focus, in writing, 136, 162
forego/forgo, 372
foreseeable future/near term, 372
form and format, 5, 115
format of intelligence publications, 8
former. *See* latter
forthcoming, 372
founder. *See* flounder
freewriting, 119, 137
from . . . to, 372
front section of a publication, 12
further. *See* farther

gender. *See* he or she
generalizations, hasty, 168
goals, realistic, in writing, 150
grammar-checkers, 214
graphic material, 18
groups, writing. *See* peer writing
    groups

he or she, 372
headings and subheadings, 171
headquarters, 372

Index to Part Two:
Briefing with Intelligence, Including Appendixes B–E

About the Author

James S. ("Jim") Major spent more than 40 years in intelligence, serving in both a military and civilian capacity, in assignments at the tactical, operational, strategic, and national levels.

Major was commissioned from army ROTC in 1963. After airborne and ranger training at Fort Benning, Georgia, he served as an infantry officer in West Germany. In 1966 he transferred to military intelligence (MI) branch and went to Fort Holabird, Maryland, for basic MI training. Following a one-year advisory tour in Pleiku, Vietnam, he returned to Fort Holabird for advanced intelligence training. There he entered Foreign Area Officer training, specializing in Indonesia and spent a year in Bandung, West Java, at the Indonesian Army Command and General Staff College. Returning to Ohio University, he earned a master's degree in international affairs, specializing in Indonesia and Southwest Asia. He then served three years with the Defense Intelligence Agency (DIA) at Arlington Hall Station, Virginia.

In 1975, "Major Major" moved to Fort Gordon, Georgia, where he established and commanded the first Special Security Detachment at the U.S. Army Signal School. Promoted to lieutenant colonel in 1978, he served in Germany as a plans officer and later a division chief on the V (U.S.) Corps staff. In 1980 he was reassigned to DIA at the Pentagon, where he was first the intelligence support coordinator for the North Atlantic Treaty

Organization (NATO), then the executive officer to John T. Hughes, the senior civilian in DIA. In 1982 he transferred to Tampa, Florida, where he served as DIA's first liaison officer to the U.S. Central Command and the U.S. Readiness Command. He returned to Washington in September 1985 and joined the faculty of the Joint Military Intelligence College (JMIC). He retired from the army in November 1988 and, as a government civilian, created the Writing Center at the JMIC.

Major has previously written 15 books, all published by the U.S. Government. Those include the textbooks *Writing with Intelligence, Briefing with Intelligence, Wordshops,* and *Communicating Intelligence,* as well as the JMIC style manual (*Style: Usage, Composition, and Form*) and two editions of a book on footnotes and bibliographies entitled *Citation.* Major has also published articles and anecdotes in regional and national publications, including the *Washington Times, Quarterly Review of Doublespeak,* the *Writing Lab Newsletter, SpellBinder,* and *Army* magazine. In 1994 he received the JMIC award for Excellence in Teaching, presented to the Outstanding Faculty Member of the Year. In 1997, he was awarded the National Intelligence Medal of Achievement.

Major's military awards include the Legion of Merit, Defense Meritorious Service Medal with two Oak Leaf Clusters, Bronze Star Medal, Cross of Gallantry with Palm, Presidential Unit Citation, Airborne Wings, and Ranger Tab. Jim and his wife Joan live in Arlington, Virginia, with their miniature Australian shepherds Amber and Glory.